Career Coach

An Insider's Guide

PRAISE FOR *CAREER COACHING*

"I'm very impressed with the quality of the work you've done. Fantastic job! I would be glad to recommend people to attend your training program for career coaching. This book represents the exact kind of solid work we need in this field. Here's to raising the bar!"

—STEPHEN FAIRLEY, AUTHOR,
GETTING STARTED IN PERSONAL AND EXECUTIVE COACHING

"If you could buy only one coaching book, this practical gem should be it. One of those rare books that beckons coaches to read it not just cover to cover but over and over."

—AUTHOR RICHARD LIEDER

"Marcia Bench is a voice of discipline, reason, and, above all else, integrity. Read this book if you are seeking the right questions to ask yourself and others!"

—SCOTT BLANCHARD, EXECUTIVE VICE PRESIDENT, CLIENT SOLUTIONS,
THE KEN BLANCHARD COMPANIES

"The definitive book on how to build, develop, and manage a profitable career coaching business. Whether new to the business or a veteran, you'll find this book useful and vital."

—WENDY S. ENELOW, EXECUTIVE RESUME WRITER, CAREER PROFESSIONAL

"A 'must read' for anyone wanting to help another person be a valuable contributor in the world of work. If you are a recruiter, a manager, a leader of teams, or someone who loves to help people, you will find this book both an inspiration and a powerful resource."

—CYNDER NIEMELA, EXECUTIVE AND TEAM COACH, HIGH IMPACT TEAMING; COAUTHOR OF LEADING HIGH IMPACT TEAMS

"One of the best books I have read. It's based soundly on behavioral theory, yet full of timely information relevant to job search logistics. A rare combination!"

—SHANNON JORDAN, DIRECTOR, CAREER DEVELOPMENT, UNIVERSITY OF CALIFORNIA, SAN DIEGO EXTENSION

"A relevant and heartfelt roadmap to guide career coaches and their clients in transforming their careers into those that evoke passion, fulfillment, and a sense of purpose."

—THOMAS CRANE, PRESIDENT, CRANE CONSULTING AND AUTHOR, THE HEART OF COACHING

"Should be on the 'must read' list for all career counselors, trainers, therapists, job search advisers—the experienced and new entrants. Life coaches who are discovering their training was inadequate for helping clients with career issues would in particular benefit from this book."

—PAUL STEVENS, FOUNDER, THE CENTRE FOR WORKLIFE COUNSELING (SYDNEY, AUSTRALIA)

Career Coaching:
An Insider's Guide
Second Edition

Marcia Bench

Career Coaching: An Insider's Guide – Second Edition

Published by High Flight Press, a division of Career Coach Institute, LLC, 2008

This publication is designed to provide accurate and authoritative information in regard to the subject matter covered. It is sold with the understanding that the publisher is not engaged in rendering professional services. If legal, accounting, medical, psychological, or any other expert assistance is required, the services of a competent professional person should be sought. Author and publisher specifically disclaim any liability for the reader's use of any forms or advice provided in this book. It is not warranted as fit for any specific use or purpose, but is intended to give general information that is as current as possible as of the date of publication.

Library of Congress Cataloging-in-Publication Data:

Bench, Marcia

Career Coaching: An Insider's Guide – Second Edition

/ Marcia Bench

ISBN 978-0-9817005-0-2; 10-digit: 0-9817005-0-0

1. Career 2. Entrepreneurship 3. Business

Printed in the United States of America

TABLE OF CONTENTS

Part Four: Job Search Mechanics

Part Five: The Career Coach's Toolbox

TABLE OF FIGURES

ACKNOWLEDGMENTS

This book—including the content drawn from class sessions—could not have been written without the support and assistance of many people over the past several years.

I must also acknowledge all of the students in the Career Coach Institute program (www.careercoachinstitute.com) —past, present and future! Thanks as well to my personal career coaching clients, for the richness you have brought to my life—and to your classmates and clients—just for being willing to follow your own calling and assist others in following theirs.

Finally, to my husband, Jay, and the many people who have supported me through-out my career. It's a joy to share my work and life with you!

My heartfelt desire is that each of us can identify and pursue the work that has such meaning and passion for us that as we wake up in the morning, that we can't wait to get started doing those things that express our Authentic Vocation™!

—Marcia Bench

INTRODUCTION

If you're thinking about becoming a career coach—whether working for yourself or coaching within your organization—then this book is written for you. Its contents were developed with several purposes in mind:

1. **To articulate definitions and standards for career coaching.** While the field of career guidance has a history spanning over 100 years, the field of coaching is less than twenty years old. And combining career guidance and coaching into career coaching has only been done in the past decade or so at most. As founder and director of the world's premier career coach training organization, Career Coach Institute, I want to share with you the definitions, standards, and models we teach our students—drawn from those of the International Coach Federation—with the hope that these will become the recognized standard in the career coaching community.

2. **To debunk the myths and misunderstandings about career coaching.** In my interaction with both coaches and client representatives worldwide, it is clear that very different concepts of the qualifications for career coaching exist. For example, in Australia and much of Europe, it is commonly thought that a career coach should have a psychology degree and/or background in order to coach. In the U.S., this is not the understanding. Career counselors provide in-person, one-hour sessions; most career coaches work by phone in half-hour increments – or more recently, even shorter than that! In chapter 1 we describe these and other differences to create greater clarity for our clients and ourselves.

3. **To help more people enjoy their work.** Over the past two decades I have worked in the career development industry, one statistic has not changed: at least 61 percent of Americans are less than completely satisfied with their work.[1]

This book contributes to changing that fact in two ways: first, people entering the field of career coaching experience the satisfaction that comes from this work; and second, as more career coaches work with clients to help them discover their Authentic Vocation™, their clients choose work that is congruent with who they are, increasing their satisfaction as well.

The book forms the basis for the curriculum we teach at Career Coach Institute (www.careercoachinstitute.com), which I founded in 2001 as the first virtual career coach training program in the world. It outlines the key principles career coaches need to know to work effectively with clients.

Part 1 introduces the field of career coaching and its history, and clarifies how career coaching differs from related fields. The ethics of coaching are also addressed.

In part 2, all eight factors of the Authentic Vocation™ model of career design are explained in detail, together with coaching tips and resources to use with clients.

In part 3, we shift gears and explore the QuantumShift!™ model of coaching which we use to draw forth the factors of our clients' Authentic Vocation and help them move quickly to the work that is most satisfying for them. QuantumShift! also enables clients to overcome obstacles that may be standing in the way of their ideal work, whether they involve the circumstances of their life or their belief system or identity. All of the coaching competencies of coaches certified by the International Coach Federation (www.coachfederation.org) are touched on in this part, culminating with a chapter discussing advanced coaching skills.

Part 4 provides the best current thinking on all aspects of "Job Search Mechanics," from how to customize job search techniques for various client needs to resume design, interviewing techniques, personal branding, and negotiation of the ideal compensation package.

The conclusion addresses coach self-care and the traits of masterful coaching.

The Career Coach's Toolbox contains thirty coaching tools including forms, worksheets, checklists and other instruments. You are free to use any of these with your individual clients if they help you to implement the concepts and principles outlined in the book. If you wish to use them in a classroom setting, we ask that you contact us directly at coach@careercoachinstitute.com to describe the type of use so that we can determine whether any use fee should be assessed.

The Career Coach's Toolbox is followed by three appendices: frequently asked questions about career coaching, a list of the ICF coaching core competencies, and guidelines for those implementing a career development program within their company.

We hope that if you find value in the concepts in this book, you will use them to facilitate transformation and new discoveries in your clients. And if you would like to experience the power of exploring them in the context of a learning community, you may wish to consider enrolling in one of the career coach training programs offered by Career Coach Institute.

We share this material in book form to demonstrate our core commitment to operating from an abundance mentality. If you use any of the content of this book in written materials—whether on the Internet, in a magazine or journal, or in the classroom—we simply ask that you respect our copyright and give credit where credit is due.

Happy coaching!

PART ONE

=====

THE PRACTICE OF CAREER COACHING

1

Getting Started in Career Coaching: What It Is and Is Not

"WORKING WITH PEOPLE IS DIFFICULT, BUT NOT IMPOSSIBLE."
—*Peter Drucker*

Emerging from the roots of career development established by Frank Parsons in the early 1900s, career coaching is the newest methodology available to help people achieve job and career satisfaction. Whether it is used to help people find greater fulfillment at work, to make job or career changes, or to retire, both individuals and organizations increasingly see a need for career coaching. Consider these recent developments:

- The average worker today holds nearly ten jobs before age 36 and from ten to fourteen (or more) careers in his/her lifetime[2] ~~5 to~~ X

- The number of those working in business services, virtual/computer businesses, and microbusiness is increasing so quickly that they now constitute the largest sector of the US labor market[3]—and a significant number of them are coaches

- Coaching has been rated one of the top ten home-based businesses to start[4]

- Hundreds of thousands of employees have been laid off by corporations of all sizes in virtually every industry due to consolidation and downsizing

- Ethics and values have taken center stage as companies such as Enron, WorldCom, Arthur Andersen, and others have had systemic breaches of ethics revealed, resulting in stricter standards for reporting in all major corporations

- Recent world events have caused many people to question their priorities and to commit to a life with greater meaning

How do people make sense of this changing climate? Today, they often seek a career coach. One of my clients, Debbie, had been employed by a world leader in the wireless telecommunication industry for eight years, beginning at the onset of the information technology boom. She worked her way up from sales representative to senior account manager and had direct contact with both new and existing corporate clients for the company's products. Then, in a reorganization of her department, she was relegated to sales administration—a back-office position, which significantly decreased Debbie's job satisfaction. What she had enjoyed most was having direct contact with the clients and "making deals." Meanwhile, Debbie's employer had made a generous stock option program available to its employees, and her options had been steadily increasing in number and projected value. This created a dilemma for Debbie: should she stay at the company for the financial benefits or should she seek other employment to regain a sense of satisfaction?

During her personal time, Debbie began exploring other positions, both within her organization and at other companies. A newly formed software company expressed interest in hiring her, and ultimately offered her a position as vice president at an increased salary. What made the position even more appealing was that the prospective employer wanted her to work from home, allowing her to spend more time with her two young children. However, Debbie's stock options from her current employer were expected to be worth $250,000 within two years. If she left the company, she would lose them all.

It was at this point that Debbie came to me for career coaching. She sought my assistance to help her make this difficult career decision and to facilitate her transition to this new job—or to further job searching, depending on which choice she made.

Through career coaching, she was able to more objectively see the conflicting values involved in the situation and the implications of the various possibilities. We discussed how she could fully take advantage of the opportunities presented. After some reflection, she decided to take the new position.

Debbie has thoroughly enjoyed her newfound independence and increased family time, and she feels challenged by her new duties. Though it would have been hard to predict, the stock options formerly valued at a quarter of a million dollars are now nearly worthless anyway: the I.T. industry's collapse caused the company's stock to plummet to a fraction of its former value. The emotional toll from staying in the unfulfilling job would only have been compounded by the loss of her stock option nest egg. Debbie is exceedingly glad she followed her passion and sought greater satisfaction elsewhere.

balance, quality of life, contributing legacy

Debbie is just one example of how career coaching can benefit individuals facing transition, and it can also benefit companies. In response to both economic and other kinds of shifts, organizations often retain career coaches to help employees become more productive. Consider some of the results:

- The approximate annual worldwide revenue produced by coaching is $1.5 billion (USD).[5]
- Companies in which employees become "engaged"—that is, become fully involved in and matched well with their work—experience a rise in sales, customer loyalty, and profits[6]
- Companies that offer training alone experience a 22.4 percent increase in productivity, but when combined with coaching it rises to 88 percent[7]
- Coaching provided to executives with major corporations provides a return on investment of at least 5.7 times the cost of the coaching[8]

The Coaching Industry

As an industry, coaching is relatively young, having begun in 1989 by the late Thomas Leonard. Leonard also founded Coach University (the first coach training organization) in 1992; the International Coach Federation (ICF) in 1994; and

Coachville in 2001, and is credited with first applying the term and concept of coaching outside the athletic context. The ICF has thousands of members worldwide. Its membership, conference attendance, and programs are steadily growing. In addition to serving as a membership organization for coaches, it also offers a referral service to help clients find coaches meeting their stated criteria, accredits coach training organizations, and sets ethical standards for the industry.

With the growth of coaching, coach training has also blossomed. There are now hundreds of coach training organizations in existence, with a wide range of specialties. (For current list, see Peer Resources, http://www.peer.ca/coaching.html.) Only since 2001 has coaching been applied to career guidance. Since coaches are not required to register with any association or body to begin practice, it is difficult to determine exactly how many coaches are currently in practice. However, the ICF and others estimate that that there are well over thirty thousand in practice, either part-time or full-time. [9]

The coaching profession is projected to continue its rapid growth for the foreseeable future. As the workplace evolves and corporations yield to new ways of doing business, career coaching will play a key role. And as individuals seek more "high touch" to compensate for the "high tech," as John Naisbitt and Patricia Aburdene describe in their book *Megatrends 2000*,[10] career coaching can be one of the channels for a personal touch, to help workers cope with an unsettled workplace.

Specialties in Coaching

Although coaching is still a relatively young profession, most successful coaches find they need to specialize. Specializing allows the coach to claim a niche in the marketplace and to establish a discrete set of issues on which to focus and develop competence. Career Coach Institute, LLC (www.careercoachinstitute.com), of which I am founder and director, was the first virtual coach training organization to focus on the career coaching niche.

Among the many other specialties that coaches may choose are the following:

- Accountants' coaching
- Addiction coaching
- Attraction coaching
- Book coaching
- Communication coaching
- Computer coaching
- Corporate coaching
- Creativity coaching
- Entrepreneur coaching
- Executive coaching
- Financial coaching
- Fitness coaching
- Human resource coaching
- Image coaching
- Lawyers' coaching
- Life coaching
- Life purpose coaching
- Marketing coaching
- Networking coaching
- Nutrition coaching
- Organization coaching
- Parenting coaching
- Performance coaching
- Personal coaching
- Relationship coaching
- Retirement coaching
- Sakes coaching
- Speakers' coaching
- Spiritual coaching
- Success coaching
- Team coaching
- Therapists' coaching
- Transition coaching
- Web coaching
- Wellness coaching
- Writers' coaching

Even within the specialty field of career coaching, our students and graduates are creating many subspecialties, including:

- Career coaching for women
- Executive career coaching
- Industry-specific career coaching (e.g., information technology, banking, sales, law, etc.)
- Internal career coaching (i.e., coaching within an organization to develop and implement a career development initiative company-wide, of which coaching is one component)
- International career coaching (i.e., working with ex patriots to transition in or out of the country in their work)
- Interview coaching

- Pre-retirement coaching
- Spiritual career coaching
- Transition coaching (e.g., for clients moving from corporate position to entrepreneur, or from one job or situation to the next)

For training in specific career coaching specialties – including entrepreneur coaching, retirement coaching, executive career coaching and more – see www.career-coachinstitute.com.

Definitions of Coaching

So what is this thing called coaching anyway? And how does it differ from counseling, mentoring, and other related specialties? Simply stated, coaching is a series of interactions between coach and client that includes questioning, observation, feedback, and other techniques through which the coach helps the client explore the issues the client wishes to resolve, clarify, or understand, and together they develop actionable outcomes for the client to implement or work on between sessions. The ultimate result is that clients achieve—and even exceed—their stated goals.

While there are many definitions of coaching, the most universally accepted is that of the International Coach Federation:

The ICF Philosophy of Coaching

The International Coach Federation (ICF) adheres to a form of coaching that honors the client as the expert in his/her life and work and believes that every client is creative, resourceful, and whole.

Standing on this foundation, the coach's responsibility is to:
- Discover, clarify, and align with what the client
- wants to achieve;
- Encourage client self-discovery;
- Elicit client-generated solutions and strategies;

- Hold the client responsible and accountable.

ICF Definition of Coaching

Professional coaching is an ongoing professional relationship that helps people produce extraordinary results in their lives, careers, businesses or organizations. Through the process of coaching, clients deepen their learning, improve their performance, and enhance their quality of life. In each meeting, the client chooses the focus of conversation, while the coach listens and contributes observations and questions. This interaction creates clarity and moves the client into action. Coaching accelerates the client's progress by providing greater focus and awareness of choice. Coaching concentrates on where clients are now and what they are willing to do to get where they want to be in the future. ICF member coaches and ICF credentialed coaches recognize that results are a matter of the client's intentions, choices and actions, supported by the coach's efforts and application of the coaching process.

—International Coach Federation, www.coachfederation.org
(Reprinted with permission)

CCI Definition of Career Coaching

focus on work-related issues not advisor a researcher

At Career Coach Institute, we carry many of the same elements into career coaching, but further elaborate on the application of coaching to job- and work-related issues. With this in mind, we define coaching as follows:

Career coaching is an interactive process of exploring work-related issues—leading to effective action—in which the coach acts as both a catalyst and facilitator of individual and, in turn, organizational development and transformation.

Career coaches connect people with their passion, purpose, values, and other critical aspects of their ideal work. They equip their clients with career management skills that can be used in future transitions in addition to enhancing their current work. They also facilitate their clients' process of developing and implementing a job search or business start-up plan to activate their Authentic Vocation™. The desired outcomes of career coaching include enhanced client self-awareness, clarity about their life purpose and goals, increased ability to be effective in today's changing workplace, and to manage their own career, and overall betterment of the client's quality of life.

That definition includes several critical elements worth reviewing:

1. **Interactive.** Unlike the related roles of consulting and speaking, coaching is characterized by its interactivity. Coaches and clients have what are referred to as "focused interactions" in which the coach asks clients probing questions about their goals and challenges and how they wish to be assisted in moving forward. Clients, in turn, respond by simultaneously noticing—and learning from—their own statements and insights.

2. **Work-related issues.** These may include the exploration of both clients' overall career direction and their job search techniques, such as resume writing and review, interview practice, negotiation assistance, and the like. Internal as well as external coaches may also assist with enhancing work satisfaction, career development planning, and similar issues. Planning clients' work in retirement, helping them get their first job after college, and assisting them with a business start-up, also constitute "work-related issues."

3. **Catalyst.** As a catalyst, a coach precipitates the process of learning at three levels: behavior, beliefs, and identity. In coaching, as in chemistry, the catalyst usually does not change during the process, but rather stimulates a change in the nature of the other elements present (i.e., clients and their behavior, outlook, and even the people with whom they interact).

4. **Facilitator.** As a facilitator, the coach remains objective and avoids getting caught up in clients' issues, while skillfully moving them toward their goals. In addition, since each of us has what in coaching are referred to as "blind spots"— resulting from severe disappointments, traumas, childhood messages, negative

role models, or other pivotal experiences—it is difficult for us to see life as it is. An effective coach explores these blind spots, uncovers clients' strengths, and thereby furthers the process of transformation as clients move through those hindrances and fully embrace their true self.

5. **Individual and, in turn, organizational development and transformation.** An organization is composed of individuals. As each person is transformed by enhancing his or her work enjoyment, the organization is often transformed too.

6. **Ideal work.** Most career coaching clients are not content to find "just another job." Rather, they seek to find work that is truly fulfilling, that allows them to make the contribution they believe they were put on earth to make (assuming this is the client's goal, of course). This emphasis on "ideal" work, rather than "suitable" or "acceptable" work, sets career coaches apart. Employment agencies, many career counselors, and the purveyors of skills-based assessments often overlook life purpose and deeper motivators in suggesting possible career moves to clients. Since most workers will change careers many times during their lifetime—some during midlife when priorities are shifting—the focus on *ideal* work can make the critical difference in quality of work and life for the career coach's clients.

7. **Equip clients with career management skills.** There is an anonymous adage that says "Give a man a fish; you have fed him for today. Teach a man to fish; and you have fed him for a lifetime." Similarly, coaching aims to teach clients to self-coach and to learn skills they can use again when other job/career transitions occur, instead of just telling them which job is right for them now, as a career advisor may do. That is the key reason why the best coaches are known for asking the right questions, not giving the right answers.

8. **Authentic Vocation.** In part 2 we investigate in depth this eight-factor model as a preferred approach to career design.

Distinguishing Career Coaching from Other Roles

In each of the following sections, we will compare and contrast coaching with similar functions. Fig. 1 summarizes the similarities and differences.

Figure 1: Comparing Coaching with Other Roles

Factor	Career Coach	Career Counselor	Consultant	Manager as Coach
Focus	Questions	Q&A	Answers	Q&A
Agenda	Client's	Shared	Consultant's	Company's
Conflict of Interest	No	No	No	Yes
Orientation	Process, what's possible, results	Process, next logical step	Results, solving problems	Results
Education	Coach training	Master's degree preferred	Varies	Varies
Voluntary?	Yes	Usually	Sometimes	No
Time perspective	Present, future	Past, present	Present, Future	Present, near future
Use of Assessments	Yes, as appropriate	Yes, standardized	Sometimes	360 most common
Time to results	Quickly!	Slower than coaching	Sometimes never!	Varies
Ownership of results	Client	Counselor	Consultant	Manager and employee

Career Coaching vs. Career Counseling

Though the lines are often blurred between career coaching and career counseling, some distinctions can be made. Coaching is generally more results oriented, less structured, and more guided by clients' agenda than is career counseling. In addition, in at least forty-seven of the U.S. states, career counselors are required to have a master's degree, whereas coaches do not have to meet any specific educational requirements. Counselors work in hourly increments, usually face-to-face, but career coaches generally work in half-hour increments (and more recently, in shorter "laser" sessions) and coach by phone and email. Less frequently, career coaching is done in person.

Career coaches may continue working with clients as they execute their job search; many career counselors stop when the client knows what his or her next job will be. Coaching closes the gap between clients' current situation and their desired state and holds them accountable for their ongoing progress. Career counselors may get more in-depth training in the use of psychological assessments, and will frequently use a battery of such assessments at the outset of the counseling relationship. While career coaches may be trained in and/or use some assessment tools, they do so only as clients' presented needs require.

Coaching vs. Consulting

The simplest way to distinguish coaching from consulting is this: coaching focuses on asking the right questions, while consulting focuses on providing the right answers. Coaching and consulting can overlap, but they are not synonymous. Consultants are subject matter experts in a specific topic area and are paid to provide advice, do analyses, write reports, and make recommendations within that subject area. Consultants typically have business experience and/or education in a client's business or in the discipline about which they are consulting (marketing, operations efficiency, etc.). Coaches, on the other hand, need not have had experience in the client's business at all. The primary experience they need is training and practice in coaching using an articulated model that leads to clients obtaining their desired results.

Coaching vs. Therapy

Coaching and therapy are discrete professions with discrete skill sets. Therapy focuses on exploring the origins of current emotional and/or psychological problems, with the goal of diagnosing and resolving the problem. They often draw on the past and try to help the client better understand it to resolve current issues. Coaching, in contrast, begins in the present and focuses on moving clients forward to get more of what they want in the future, with the goal of leveraging the perfection that lies within them and applying it to current situations. It is action oriented and results focused. Another distinction is that therapy often seeks to remedy pathology, whereas coaching focuses on developing possibilities, leveraging clients' strengths, and helping clients achieve their goals. Coaching is not a substitute for therapy and, in fact, can be used together with therapy when the client's situation warrants it -- for example, when a client is clinically depressed or suffers from some other mental illness.[11]

Coaching vs. Mentoring

Mentoring is a related skill to coaching that nevertheless can be distinguished in several ways. Great Circle Learning, a Florid-based training and consulting firm defines *mentoring* as

> a method of teaching and learning that can occur among all types of individuals across all kinds of knowledge bases and settings. In the workplace, mentoring normally consists of teaching, giving feedback, coaching on the job, counseling through change, and structuring ongoing contact over a designated time period.[12]

As shown in Fig. 2, mentoring—which usually involves passing information or knowledge from the mentor to the mentee—is somewhat more directive than coaching. However, because the ultimate goal is to help mentees act independently, the mentor may use coaching techniques and questions to help mentees think for themselves about the skills or situations at issue.

Coaching vs. Managing with a Coaching Approach

Thomas Crane, in his book *The Heart of Coaching,* defines *transformational coaching for managers,* which he defines as

> ...a comprehensive communication process in which the coach provides performance feedback to the coachee [employee]. Topics include broad, work-related dimensions of performance (personal, interpersonal, or technical) that affect the coachee's ability and willingness to contribute to meaningful personal and organizational goals.[13]

It is increasingly accepted that coaching has a place in the manager's toolkit. However, one critical difference between an independent coach and a manager-as-coach within an organization is that the manager (or a coach within the human resources umbrella) has a built-in conflict of interest in coaching the employee. Since the manager/coach is often also responsible for reviewing employees' performance, making decisions about salary increases and promotions, and disciplining employees, it is difficult (perhaps impossible) for employees to be completely candid with the manager/coach. In most cases they will preserve their job security over making personal disclosures! Ideally, the effective leader will use a coaching leadership style when appropriate and will have several of the other five leadership styles available for other situations.[14] He or she will then contract out the coaching function to independent and objective outside coaches. (For guidelines on properly integrating career coaching into a company, see Appendix 3.) Another important factor in making these distinctions is whether the primary focus lies with the professional (of whatever discipline) or the client. See Fig. 2.

Figure 2: Where is the Focus—on the Professional or the Client?

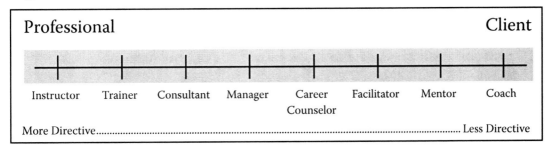

Is Career Coaching Right for You?

So how do you know whether career coaching is a field you should consider? The most successful career transitions are carefully thought out, after weighing the risks of the decision. Students in the Career Coach Institute program come from a wide variety of backgrounds. Following are some representative examples of people who have completed the CCI career coach training and become Professional Certified Career Coaches™.

- Meg had started her own resume-writing service after a thirteen-year career in private and nonprofit employment industry positions. She found herself giving away substantial amounts of advice and time to clients who wanted her to write their resumes but didn't know what jobs they were targeting. She wanted to be generous but since she couldn't build a business with unbillable hours, she was looking for a way to help clients and be paid for it.

- Jeff was a therapist who had worked both within corporations and with individuals on career issues (as well as other issues from a therapeutic standpoint), and had completed another coach training program prior to CCI. However, that program did not specialize in career coaching, and he wanted to hone his expertise to get faster, more lasting results with clients. In addition, he wanted to do work that had a more positive focus than much of his therapy, which dealt mainly with pathologies.

- Peg had transitioned from corporate communications to a position in organizational development at a pharmaceutical firm. A highly achievement-oriented woman in her late fifties, Peg wanted both to expand her coaching skills within her company and to learn a specialty that she could use independently in retirement.

- Gina had been a successful independent recruiter for over ten years and was particularly successful when the U.S. economy was strong. When a recession began, her business fell off and she began to seek other ways to leverage her substantial experience in both business and in the careers field. Like Meg, she found herself giving a lot of advice and time away to candidates (even though her actual client was the company seeking to hire them). She wanted to find a way to get paid to coach the recruiting candidates.

Dozens of other examples could be cited to illustrate the diversity of backgrounds of backgrounds of people entering the field of career coaching. (For additional real-life experiences of students and graduates I have trained, visit www.careercoachinstitute.com.) Whether you have no experience or an advanced degree and twenty-five years of professional experience, independent career coaching may be right for you if you possess the traits needed for success— the "entrepreneurial personality". The self-assessment in fig. 3 will help you decide.

Even if your score does not indicate a good match with independent career coaching, working inside an organization as a career coach to the company's employees may be very suitable for you.

What the Client Wants

In addition to these entrepreneurial traits, you need to possess skills and assets clients seek. We have surveyed dozens of individuals over the past several years to

Figure 3: Is Independent Career Coaching Right For You?

Question	Yes	No
Is it important to you to accomplish something meaningful with your life?		
Are you passionate about helping others?		
Do you usually set and achieve your goals?		
Do you enjoy working independently?		
Can you think strategically?		
Are you self-directed?		
Do you like to be in control of your working environment?		
Do you take full responsibility for your successes *and* failures?		
Are you in excellent physical, mental and emotional health?		
Do you have the drive and energy to create a successful business?		
Do you have a basic knowledge of career transition or career development or job search? (If not, CCI's Career Coach Training can help!)		
Do you long for work that makes you so engrossed in it that time passes unnoticed?		
Do you consider "failures" as opportunities to learn and grow?		
Can you hold to your ideas and goals even when others disagree with or discourage you?		
Are you willing to take moderate risks to achieve your goals?		
Can you afford to lose the money you invest in your business?		
When the need arises, are you willing to do a task that may not interest you?		
Can you establish the appropriate amount of interaction with people to balance working largely on the phone and internet?		
Do you usually stick with a project until it is completed?		
Can you ignore the distractions inherent in working at home?		

To take this quiz online and get immediate results, visit www.careercoachinstitute.com

Scoring:
17-20 "yes" Career coaching is for you!

14-16 "yes" You may be suited to career coaching

10-13 "yes" Work within a team or organization may be a better fit than self-employment

5-9 "yes"   Carefully examine your choice to be sure career coaching is what you want to do!

0-4 "yes"   Independent career coaching is probably *not* your best career choice find out what they would look for as important traits, from the client's perspective, in a career coach. Here are a few:

- Listens well
- Possesses current knowledge regarding industries and the job market
- Can motivate, provide support, and instill confidence
- Holds a credential/ has credibility
- Asks great probing questions
- Has a customized approach to different learning styles, age groups, and other client characteristics; has good soft skills
- Can reduce search time
- Is skilled in helping discover personal talents and gifts
- Listens well
- Has firsthand experience in the workplace
- Stays open, uses intuition
- Is facilitative rather than directive
- Demonstrates workable job search strategies
- Is responsive and confident
- Is a "big thinker" – can envision great possibilities for him/herself and for the client, and models big thinking in his/her life

Finally, you need to learn certain business skills such as bookkeeping, strategic planning, marketing, public relations, budgeting, and the like.

While several coaching studies indicate that less than 10 percent of new coaches overall achieve a $100,000 income after two years in practice, those with specialized knowledge (such as career coaching), a targeted market, and a sound business plan and vision can achieve this goal more quickly. Our book, *Career Infopreneur's Success Roadmap* (High Flight Press 2007) discussed the new infopreneur approach to business building. The "nuts and bolts" of launching a coaching practice and effectively marketing it are outlined in detail in the author's "Practice-Building for Coaches Series" of books and other marketing resources available at www.careercoachinstitute.com, including *Launch Your Practice, Discover Your Niche,* and *Fill Your Practice.*

KEY COACHING CONCEPTS

1. Career coaching is a growth field because of the number of career and job changes typical workers make today during their lifetime, the revolution in how corporations are doing business worldwide, and the increasing public awareness of the need for, and value of, coaching.
2. The field of coaching began in 1989, and its application to career as a specialty began in 2001.
3. A working definition of career coaching is "an interactive process of exploring work-related issues—leading to effective action—in which the coach acts as both a catalyst and facilitator of individual and, in turn, organizational development and transformation."
4. Career coaching can be distinguished from other related fields such as mentoring, therapy, consulting, career counseling, and manager-coaching based on the focus of the work, who sets the agenda, the nature of the process itself, the education required, the time perspective, use of assessments, and who owns the results.
5. Being a career coach requires specific personality traits and business skills.

2

Ethical Considerations in Coaching

"ETHICS STAYS IN THE PREFACES OF THE AVERAGE BUSINESS SCIENCE BOOK."

—*Peter Drucker*

Most of the so-called helping professions such as counseling, ministry, and social work are governed by a set of ethical standards. Coaching is no exception. And with the allegations of serious ethical breaches in corporate America by such icons as WorldCom, Enron, Arthur Andersen, even Martha Stewart, ethics and integrity have received a keener focus than at any time in recent history.

For you as a coach, adhering to a set of ethical standards adds credibility to what can be an otherwise intangible service for clients or prospects to understand. This is particularly true if you share with clients those standards to which you hold yourself—and by which you expect them to abide—during the coaching relationship.

The ICF Standards of Ethical Conduct

The model set of ethical standards in coaching is that articulated by the International Coach Federation. Compliance is required of ICF members; it is optional—though strongly recommended—for non-ICF member coaches.

Current standards (as of March 2008) are as follows:

Professional Conduct At Large

As a coach:

1) I will conduct myself in a manner that reflects positively upon the coaching profession, and I will refrain from engaging in conduct or making statements that may negatively impact the public's understanding or acceptance of coaching as a profession.

2) I will not knowingly make any public statements that are untrue or misleading, or make false claims in any written documents relating to the coaching profession.

3) I will respect different approaches to coaching. I will honor the efforts and contributions of others and not misrepresent them as my own.

4) I will be aware of any issues that may potentially lead to the misuse of my influence by recognizing the nature of coaching and the way in which it may affect the lives of others.

5) I will at all times strive to recognize personal issues that may impair, conflict or interfere with my coaching performance or my professional relationships. Whenever the facts and circumstances necessitate, I will promptly seek professional assistance and determine the action to be taken, including whether it is appropriate to suspend or terminate my coaching relationship(s).

6) As a trainer or supervisor of current and potential coaches, I will conduct myself in accordance with the ICF Code of Ethics in all training and supervisory situations.

7) I will conduct and report research with competence, honesty and within recognized scientific standards. My research will be carried out with the necessary approval or consent from those involved, and with an approach that will reasonably protect participants from any potential harm. All research efforts will be performed in a manner that complies with the laws of the country in which the research is conducted.

8) I will accurately create, maintain, store and dispose of any records of work done in relation to the practice of coaching in a way that promotes confidentiality and complies with any applicable laws.

9) I will use ICF member contact information (e-mail addresses, telephone numbers, etc.) only in the manner and to the extent authorized by the ICF.

Professional Conduct With Clients

10) I will be responsible for setting clear, appropriate, and culturally sensitive boundaries that govern any physical contact that I may have with my clients.

11) I will not become sexually involved with any of my clients.

12) I will construct clear agreements with my clients, and will honor all agreements made in the context of professional coaching relationships.

13) I will ensure that, prior to or at the initial session, my coaching client understands the nature of coaching, the bounds of confidentiality, financial arrangements and other terms of the coaching agreement.

14) I will accurately identify my qualifications, expertise and experience as a coach.

15) I will not intentionally mislead or make false claims about what my client will receive from the coaching process or from me as their coach.

16) I will not give my clients or prospective clients information or advice I know or believe to be misleading.

17) I will not knowingly exploit any aspect of the coach-client relationship for my personal, professional or monetary advantage or benefit.

18) I will respect the client's right to terminate coaching at any point during the process. I will be alert to indications that the client is no longer benefiting from our coaching relationship.

19) If I believe the client would be better served by another coach, or by another resource, I will encourage the client to make a change.

20) I will suggest that my clients seek the services of other professionals when deemed appropriate or necessary.

21) I will take all reasonable steps to notify the appropriate authorities in the event a client discloses an intention to endanger self or others.

Confidentiality/Privacy

22) I will respect the confidentiality of my client's information, except as otherwise authorized by my client, or as required by law.

23) I will obtain agreement from my clients before releasing their names as clients or references, or any other client identifying information.

24) I will obtain agreement from the person being coached before releasing information to another person compensating me.

Conflicts of Interest

25) I will seek to avoid conflicts between my interests and the interests of my clients.

26) Whenever any actual conflict of interest or the potential for a conflict of interest arises, I will openly disclose it and fully discuss with my client how to deal with it in whatever way best serves my client.

27) I will disclose to my client all anticipated compensation from third parties that I may receive for referrals of that client.

28) I will only barter for services, goods or other nonmonetary remuneration when it will not impair the coaching relationship.

Source: International Coach Federation. Reprinted with permission. See www.coachfederation.org for updates.

Case Studies

Let's see how these ethical standards apply in two common coaching situations.

Example 1

You are coaching two different clients, Nancy and Joe, who happen to know each other because Nancy has a contract at the company where Joe works. During your call this week, Joe happens to share some company-insider information with you about Nancy that could cause her to lose the contract if she doesn't act immediately. Nancy doesn't seem to be aware of this information, but she has shared with you that she is concerned about how the contract has been going. Neither Joe nor Nancy knows that you coach the other.

What standards are at issue here? What should you do? (Note to reader: try to analyze this situation yourself before you look at the answers below.)

The ICF ethical standards at issue here are 22, 23, 25 and 26. Absent client authorization, you must respect confidentiality of clients' information, which includes their identity and the fact that you are coaching them. If you are to disclose to either Joe or Nancy the fact that you are working with the other, you must get the other's permission to do so. Standards 22 and 23 prohibit giving anyone client information known to be confidential. Based on these standards standard, the company-insider information in the example may not be disclosed to Nancy. There is also a potential conflict of interest here between your relationship with Joe and your relationship with Nancy. Standard 25 requires that you try to avoid such a conflict, and standard 26 dictates that such a conflict must be disclosed. Best course of action: do not disclose the information and consider withdrawing from one of the coaching relationships on the basis of conflict of interest.

Example 2

In his first conversation with a new client, Jill, Mark made the following statements in response to Jill's question regarding what she could expect from the coaching session. "If you coach with me," Mark said, "I guarantee that you will find a job you absolutely love, making more money than you have ever made. Just last week I helped Mary Jones get a job with Quantel Computers making $85,000. With my twenty-five years of experience in all aspects of career coaching, you can't go wrong with me."

How many of the ethical standards were violated here? Which ones? (Note to reader: try to analyze this situation yourself before you look at the answers below.)

Mark violated ethical standards 1, 2, 14, 16, 22 and 23. He misrepresented what he could deliver as a career coach. Guaranteeing that a client will find a job is outside the scope of ethical representation. Capping this off by pointing to his years of experience (implying that he could help anyone with any issue) was a clear misrepresentation. And by stating with whom he worked previously (Mary Jones) and who she went to work for and at what salary, he inappropriately disclosed client information.

Critical Thinking Pathway

It can be difficult to know when an ethical issue is present, and once recognized, to describe how to resolve it. Following is a helpful process provided by the ICF known as the Critical Thinking Pathway.

> "How will I know if I've crossed the line from doing the right thing to participating in an unethical activity?" "What will I do if I feel I have crossed that line or that my client has?"

To answer these and other difficult questions that can arise regarding the ethical standards, the Critical Thinking Pathway can help. The Critical Thinking Pathway can be summarized as an eight-step process:

1. State the central moral dilemma as clearly and briefly as you can. Remember there are two sides to a dilemma.

2. Describe the two sides as completely and clearly as you can.

3. Gather facts pertinent to each side of the dilemma. Move toward discovery of a resolution.

4. Identify your bias(es) in the matter. This can assist in determining whether or not you are truly objective about the situation, and where you are not so that you may be more open in your thinking about it.

5. Bring in new or alternative views of the dilemma. This may be a sort of brainstorming process that considers every idea—from the silly to the sublime, to the logical to the dramatic.

6. Begin to weigh the various alternatives identified.

7. Bring in experts, if needed.

8. Preview the consequences of each possible decision on the matter.

At this point you may have a resolution and you may also very well have a dilemma of your own: "Should I go public with this matter?" That is not necessarily an easy question, depending on the situation, and going public requires that you consider all stakeholders in this matter, including yourself and your family. Preview those consequences. Once you have made a choice, then make your decision.

When working with a client, the coach can introduce the technique of working through a dilemma using the Critical Thinking Pathway. It is the client's task to work through the issues. Most of us are brought up in this culture to know "the right thing to do" and simply go about our lives making ethical decisions without undue stress. When a major ethics dilemma is before us, that is when we welcome a way to resolve it.

Source: The author acknowledges Christine M. Martin, MCC of the ICF Ethics and Standards Committee. *Coaching World* (ICF newsletter), 2002. Reprinted with permission of the International Coach Federation. The ICF has also developed an Ethical Conduct Review (ECR) process to provide a forum for public complaints about alleged unethical conduct. See www.coachfederation.org for details.

NOTE: In any situations in which a coach questions whether a client is coachable, or should be referred to a mental health professional, the coach should consult the ICF publication "Top 10 Indicators to Refer to a Mental Health Professional" by Lynne F. Meinke at http://tinyurl.com/24h88o.

KEY COACHING CONCEPTS

1. Coaches are encouraged, but not required (unless they are ICF members), to comply with the ethical standards promulgated by the ICF.
2. Stating clearly to clients the ethical standards to which you, and they, must comply adds credibility to your coaching practice.
3. The Critical Thinking Pathway is a process by which to navigate the difficult ethical dilemmas that can arise in coaching.

PART TWO

THE AUTHENTIC VOCATION™ MODEL OF CAREER DESIGN

3

Overview of Authentic Vocation: Blending Passion & Pocketbook in an Ideal Job

"THE SECRET OF SUCCESS IS MAKING YOUR VOCATION YOUR VACATION."
—*Mark Twain*

From the time we enter school we are asked, "What are you going to be when you grow up?" Notice that the question is not, "What will you *do*?" but, "What will you *be*?" The question itself suggests that we integrate a part of ourselves in what we do. Certainly, this notion can be taken too far if we overidentify with our occupation, for we are each far more than what we do for a living. But the typical person spends over 100,000 hours working during his or her lifetime. And more than 60 percent of people do not enjoy their work. The Authentic Vocation model asks, "Why not enjoy the time you spend working and feel like you are contributing your unique gifts in the process?"

It is common to dread going to work on Monday (or perhaps any other day) and to bring less than our full self to work (since our other gifts may not be valued or appreciated if we share them). We begin chanting "TGIF" (thank God it's Friday) as we walk into work for "casual" day at the end of the workweek. Then we cram all our shopping, errands, household tasks, and a quick movie or concert into the busy weekend and begin the process all over again. Somewhere in this routine, many people find that their true self has been left behind. They wonder where they gave up their dreams, their values, and their excitement about their work. What would it take to do something meaningful with their life?

One of my clients, Sally, hired me during a career and life crossroads. She was living apart from her estranged husband, Don, but still owned a share in their hotel located in a tourist town. As CFO, Sally went back every two to four weeks to the hotel and the town where she and Don had lived together to do the bookkeeping for the business and deal with any outstanding business issues. Sally had an MBA emphasizing finance and had worked for over fifteen years as CFO of the hotel, later dabbling in a stockbrokering, but she decided that it didn't really suit her. Her creativity had been stifled for years, mainly because the role she had in the family business required only her "hard" business skills.

Simultaneously with the work we did in exploring Authentic Vocation, Sally was also working with a therapist and reading books on assertiveness. As she learned to stand up for herself (of which she did little during her marriage) and claim what she wanted, her career exploration also blossomed. What Sally wanted was work that would blend the various parts of herself into work that was fun and meaningful. That, in short, is what Authentic Vocation is all about. We'll return to Sally's story later in this chapter.

What Authentic Vocation Is

Kahlil Gibran, in his book *The Prophet,* says that "when you work you fulfil a part of earth's furthest dream, assigned to you when that dream was born, And in keeping yourself with labour you are in truth loving life, And to love life through labour is to be intimate with life's inmost secret." The fulfillment through work Gibran describes is a far cry from the experience of the typical worker today. Instead of viewing it as "life's inmost secret," most people find themselves complaining about that so-and-so boss, how much they have to do, and how they do not have enough free time. In a recent survey of over one thousand employees, 54 percent felt overworked at least sometimes, and 55 percent felt overwhelmed by how much work they had to do.[15]

We find an entirely different attitude among people who see their work as the expression of their Authentic Vocation. They may find it hard to break away from their work because they are having so much fun. They view the challenging people in their life as catalysts for their learning and growth. Sound impossible? It's not!

One way to explain Authentic Vocation is to define the terms, elements, and principles involved; another is to observe and listen to people who are working in what they consider to be their Authentic Vocation. We will do both. *Authentic*, as used here, means real, genuine, or aligned with one's essential self; *vocation* designates a calling, a profession to which one is particularly suited, or a life's work. In other words, work that meets this standard emanates from people's authentic self and allows them to be who they truly are while doing what they most love and feel passionate about, and provides the most meaning.

Authentic Vocation includes eight factors, each of which will be explored in detail in upcoming chapters:

1. **Life purpose.** What is the core theme or message of your life?
2. **Values.** What matters most to you?
3. **Motivators and interests.** What motivates you to do something well?
4. **Knowledge, skills and abilities.** What do you know a significant amount about? What natural talents or strengths do you have, and what other marketable skills have you developed that you enjoy using? What education have you received?
5. **Work and other experience.** What kinds of work experience have you had? What about volunteer or avocational experience?
6. **Job/career targets.** What kinds of jobs or careers do you want to pursue next?

7. **Work environment.** What is the ideal setting and company culture for you?
8. **Business reality.** Are the options you have selected financially viable? Do you have a realistic view of the job search process and probabilities?

Three principles form the foundation of Authentic Vocation:

1. Every person has a central life purpose that, if realized through his or her work as it develops and changes over time, generates optimum work fulfillment.
2. It is possible for all people to find or create work that expresses their life purpose, utilizes their skills, meets a need in the world, and is financially viable.
3. To achieve this ideal, each person's purpose, values, motivators, interests, skills, experience, job goals and desired work environment must be determined and then filtered through business reality.

While living up to these principles may sound like a tall order, I suggest that the experience is available to everyone, and that no matter what your clients' situation, they can move closer to their Authentic Vocation. Whether janitors or CEOs, new graduates or professionals near retirement, as individuals or as members of a team, there is something special for them to do. If they have not found it yet, the factors in Authentic Vocation, coupled with skilled coaching and creative intuition, can open the doors to fulfillment. Identifying a common purpose can also enhance satisfaction within the work group or company. Consider the following example from Charles Garfield's book *Peak Performers.*

> A senior vice-president of an aerospace company in Southern California piqued my curiosity one afternoon as we talked about a series of workshops I had just conducted for his managers and technical people. Developing a sense or mission makes sense at the middle and higher levels of a company, he said. But he suggested that there must be levels at which peak performance is just impossible because people have so little control of their circumstances.

"For instance," he said, "there's a group here that puzzles me. They maintain the pipes in our thermodynamics plant, checking temperatures and pressures. The situation makes me nervous. On the one hand, the work is mechanical and repetitive; essentially it's plumbing, and it seems impossible to me that anybody would find it even interesting, much less an occasion for peak performance. But here is the surprise: this group's attendance record is terrific; they have the lowest turnover in the entire company; their motivation is obviously high; their productivity and performance are excellent. How come?'"

I went to visit the department. Sam Harrison, the foreman, gave me a tour. At one point I asked why all his people wore green surgical smocks. "Oh, you noticed," Harrison said. "I got them from my son. He's a cardiovascular surgeon, and he got them so I could give them to the gang." "Ah," I said, "you wear them for comfort."

"'No, no!" Harrison said. "It's because we are surgeons. Just like my son. He takes care of pipes in the body—you're worried about a heart attack, my son works on your arteries. We take care of pipes in this plant. It isn't going to have any breakdowns as long as we're working on its arteries. We take care of these pipes the way a doctor takes care of your heart."

Sure enough, the stencils on their locker doors said "Dr.," and Sam used the title— with a grin—as he introduced his colleagues. Their statement of their mission— "take care of these pipes the way a doctor takes care of your heart"—matched its importance. The way they spoke to one another, the mixed humor and pride with which they used surgery as their metaphor, helped them to share the special value that their work had for them."[16]

Authentic Vocation coaching brings that special sense of purpose to each of our clients' work and adds the often missing dimensions of meaning and fulfillment.

It's More Than Doing What You Love

In the early 1980s, the implied work contract in the U.S. began to change. Other countries are experiencing this shift now. From a work ethic based on hard work rewarded by lifetime employment with a pension and gold watch at retirement (the "Puritan" or "entitlement" work ethic), we began to move toward a workplace based on free agency—that is, working hard at whatever offers the greatest fulfillment, changing employers as needed, and thereby contributing more to the workplace and society (the "fulfillment" or "mutual benefit" work ethic). Books sprung up encouraging people to "do what you love, the money will follow" and "follow your bliss." Too many times, however, people identified what they loved but the money did not follow. This is almost worse than never pursuing one's passion at all, because job seekers become disillusioned and cautious; they doubt whether they will ever be able to merge their passion with their pocketbook.

Authentic Vocation suggests that the deep sense of fulfillment many people seek — especially in midcareer — will not occur unless they find work that unites who they are with what they do. Other authors have described this experience in various ways.

The renowned psychologist Abraham Maslow observed "peak experiences" among self-actualized people, characterized by seemingly effortless achievement, time passing unnoticed, and often resulting in outstanding outcomes.[17] More recently, Mihaly Csikszentmihalyi in his book *Flow: The Psychology of Optimal Experience,* as well as in subsequent books on the "flow" experience, describes a similar phenomenon:

> "Flow" is the way people describe their state of mind when consciousness is harmoniously ordered, and they want to pursue whatever they are doing for its own sake. In reviewing some of the activities that consistently produce flow—such as sports, games, art, and hobbies—it becomes easier to understand what makes people happy.[18]

We can also find a parallel between pursuing an Authentic Vocation and the "engagement factor," what the Gallup organization, in its study "Taking Feedback to the Bottom Line," found to be the critical connection between job satisfaction and bottom-line performance.[19] When we help our clients discover and implement their

Authentic Vocation, we are not only helping them feel more fulfilled; we are also contributing to the productivity and performance of the companies for which they work.

Fitting the Authentic Vocation Process to Client Needs

Most current models of career development—including many software programs designed to help people discover the best job for them—begin by looking at what clients are good at and what they have done before: their skills, education, and work experience. While these elements have a place in crafting a next job or career for some clients, for many others it overlooks the very insights they are seeking: "What kinds of work will leverage my skills, generate adequate income *and* be deeply fulfilling?"

What makes the Authentic Vocation model so workable is that it is scalable: it allows the coach to meet clients where they are. For new graduates or clients seeking a new job within their existing industry or occupational area, it may be quite appropriate to begin in the middle of the model with skills, experience, and desired job/career area. If they decide they also want to factor in enhanced satisfaction, the first three factors of Authentic Vocation (life purpose, values, and motivators/interests) can be explored as well. This two-phased approach may also be advisable for those who have been laid off without notice and need to find a new job immediately but who are interested in creating an Authentic Vocation once the financial pressure is relieved.

For other clients without such pressures but who desire enhanced meaning in their work, all eight factors of Authentic Vocation will be relevant and should normally be explored in the order presented. Fig. 4 illustrates the Authentic Vocation Model of Career Design. These eight factors will be discussed in detail in the following chapters.

Many of our clients are, like Sally (from the beginning of this chapter), at a crossroads where they do not know what to do next. They may have been in one occupation or industry for twenty years or more, or they may have become bored or

Figure 4: Authentic Vocation Model of Career Design

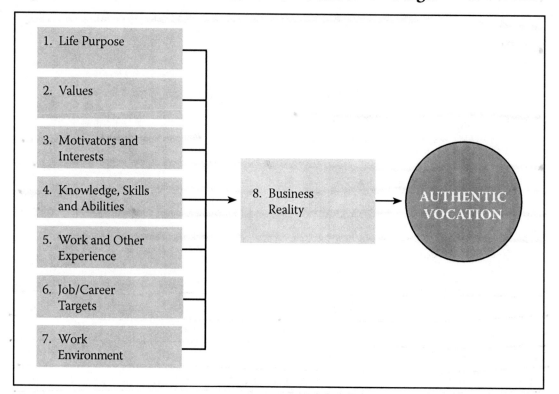

dissatisfied with what used to challenge them. And often, they have exhausted the resources and techniques that worked for them last time they were in transition—or maybe this is the first time they've considered a change. Most people never take courses called "Change Management 101" or "Career Design 101" in school. They are not offered! For clients at such a juncture, the Authentic Vocation approach is ideal. It goes beyond the data that a skills assessment or interest inventory can generate. For these clients, such instruments often fail to reveal anything they did not already know about themselves.

What It Is Like to Work from Authentic Vocation

There truly is nothing like finding and beginning to implement one's Authentic Vocation. Most clients report that their energy skyrockets, their satisfaction increases, and they have the deeply fulfilling sense that what they do matters—they're making a difference in their segment of the world.

Here are a few representative statements from people who are pursuing their Authentic Vocation:

> "It moves me. It gets me up in the morning excited to go to work. And it fulfills my need to connect deeply with people's lives—to add real value."
> —Richard Lieder, *The Power of Purpose*

> "By saying yes to our calls, we align ourselves with the natural forces instead of pitting ourselves against them."
> —Gregg LeVoy, *Callings*

> "When you are fulfilling your life's purpose, you are completely absorbed in your activities. You do not notice the passage of time; the activity completely occupies you."
> —Marcia Bench, *When 9 to 5 Isn't Enough*

And from one of our graduates and Master Certified Career Coaches™:

> "I've discovered something I never had before—a life direction that is purposeful, energizing, and absolutely right."
> —Janine Moon, MA, MCCC

To return to Sally's story, we worked together for about eight months. Sally had a different job idea nearly each week of our coaching. I reassured her that at this stage considering many different possibilities was normal; eventually she would settle on one option that was right for her. By about the seventh month, that is what happened. It occurred to Sally that if she combined her training in finance with her family-owned business experience and also offered communications skills training, she could form a niche consulting firm serving family-owned businesses. She has launched that practice, feeling a great sense of satisfaction and knowing that she can share the benefit of her experience and learning with other family-owned businesses.

KEY COACHING CONCEPTS

1. Authentic Vocation combines parts of one's self with a vocation, or calling, resulting in work that is meaningful and inspires passion. Authentic Vocation includes eight factors:
   - Life purpose
   - Values
   - Motivators and interests
   - Knowledge, skills, and abilities
   - Work and other experience
   - Desired job/career targets
   - Work environment
   - Business reality

2. Three principles form the foundation of Authentic Vocation:
   - Every person has a central life purpose that, if realized through his or her work as it develops and changes over time, generates optimum work fulfillment.
   - It is possible for all people to find or create work that expresses their life purpose, utilizes their skills, meets a need in the world, and is financially viable.
   - To achieve this ideal, each person's purpose, values, motivators, interests, skills, experience, job goals and desired work environment must be determined and then filtered through business reality.

3. The Authentic Vocation model is scalable so that it can be tailored to the needs of any client, whether first-time job seeker, seasoned worker close to retirement, or midlife career changer.

4

Authentic Vocation™ Factor 1: Life Purpose

"PURPOSE IS THE CONSCIOUS CHOICE OF WHAT, WHERE, AND HOW TO MAKE A POSITIVE CONTRIBUTION TO OUR WORLD. IT IS THE THEME, QUALITY, OR PASSION WE CHOOSE TO CENTER OUR LIVES AROUND."
—*Richard Lieder,* The Power of Purpose

Perhaps the signature trait of the Authentic Vocation model is that it begins with life purpose. I have been advocating the importance of life purpose in career decisions since the mid-1980s, but it was not until the advent of coaching as a profession that life purpose assumed the central role it deserves in career and life planning.

Authentic Vocation is based on the premise that every person has a central life purpose that, if fulfilled through one's work as it develops and changes over time, generates optimum work fulfillment. Notice first that it does not say some special people have a life purpose and others do not, but that *every* person has a central life purpose. It may take a while to discover it—I myself spent eighteen years exploring the issue before I could clearly articulate mine—but it is there.

Secondly, notice the outcome: *optimum work fulfillment.* Your clients may express their lack of fulfillment in many different ways, as shown in the following examples:

"I'm doing well at my job—I'm even considered an outstanding performer—but I feel like something is missing. I'm just not happy."

"I've been doing the same kind of work for twenty years now and feel bored with it, but I don't know what else I could do."

"I just kind of 'fell into' the jobs I have had, being in the right place at the right time. I've never consciously designed or chosen my work."

By discovering and beginning to fulfill their life purpose, our clients will finally feel the fulfillment that has eluded them.

Definitions of Life Purpose

What is encompassed by the term *life purpose?* First, in a broad sense, we all have a shared overall purpose, in that we are here to discover as much of our true self as we can and to express that through our life to the greatest possible extent. We do this through all the experiences we have, the people we relate to, the jobs we choose, and the teachers, coaches, and mentors whose message rings true for us.

But that is not our primary emphasis here. Each of us also has a specific life purpose. It is a calling, a mission, or an overall theme for our life that transcends our daily activities. It is the quality we are here on earth to develop, the type of service we are here to render, the way we can enhance or improve some segment of the planet. It is much broader than one job or career; it pervades our entire life.

In fact, most of us will have at least ten different careers in our life. Our purpose is not found in a career area or a job description. Rather, we use our career (as well as other aspects of our life) to accomplish our overall purpose. For example, one man's life purpose was to promote peace. He did so by working as a mediator and by consciously pursuing peaceful relationships. Another woman discovered her life purpose was to nurture the earth. She learned all she could about conservation, worked for the park bureau, and soon was in demand as a teacher for other nature guides and conservationists.

If your clients do not feel they have experienced the level of success they know they are capable of, or have felt that something was missing from their life, you may want to share with them a very important principle: *people will tend to experience success and fulfillment in their life to the extent that they are clear about their life purpose, and expressing it in each aspect of their life.*

Qualities of Life Purpose

Fulfilling one's life purpose is fun, joyful, and playful. When we are carrying out our life purpose, we find that the time goes by unnoticed. Hours pass by in pure bliss, complete happiness. As a central theme for our life, our life purpose also helps us decide whether to accept a particular job, whether to volunteer for a particular cause, and which kinds of relationships, professional and personal, will best contribute to fulfilling our purpose.

Discovering one's life purpose can have a tremendous impact within an organization. If employees choose to work at a specific job and for a specific company because it fulfills and expresses their life purpose, they will be more engaged, motivated, and productive.

Why It Is Important

When one's life purpose is discovered and expressed, it provides a reason for being, a sense of "coming home," a quality one brings to everyday life, and the motivation for one's activities. Not only is life incomplete without it; there is something missing in the world if each of us does not contribute the gifts we have.

> "This is the true joy in life, the being used for a purpose recognized by yourself as a mighty one; the being thoroughly worn out before you are thrown on the scrap heap; the being a force of Nature instead of a feverish selfish little clod

of ailments and grievances complaining that the world will not devote itself to making you happy."
—George Bernard Shaw

"The gifts of each of us and the value of serving others provide our mission in life."
—Richard Bolles, *What Color Is Your Parachute?*

In the affluent society of the Western world, it may seem that life purpose would be unimportant. However, research tells us otherwise:

"Sixty college students who had attempted suicide were recently surveyed, and 85 percent of them said the reason was that 'life seemed meaningless.' Ninety-three percent of them lacked a sense of purpose in their lives despite socially active lives, academic achievements, and supportive families.

"This happens in the midst of affluent societies and in the midst of welfare states! For too long we have been dreaming a dream from which we are now waking up: the dream that if you just improve the socio-economic status of people, everything will be OK, people will become happy. The truth is that as the struggle for survival has subsided, the question has emerged: survival for what? Ever more people today have the means to live, but no meaning to live for."
—Viktor Frankl, *Man's Search for Meaning*

Clues to Life Purpose

Included in fig. 5 are ten questions that serve as clues designed to help clients discover their own individual life purpose. They ask clients to look at their life and work from several different perspectives, as though examining a precious stone—or diamond in the rough—from many angles. Then, with a coach's guidance, they uncover the themes that emerge and, ultimately, formulate a statement of their life purpose.

(See "Authentic Vocation Worksheet 1" in the Career Coach's Toolbox on p. 315 for use with individual clients for this purpose.)

Figure 5: 10 Clues to Discovering Your Life's Purpose

1	WHAT DO YOU LOVE TO DO, WHETHER IN YOUR SPARE TIME OR AT WORK?
2	WHAT PARTS OF YOUR PRESENT JOB OR LIFE ACTIVITIES DO YOU THOROUGHLY ENJOY?
3	WHAT DO YOU NATURALLY DO WELL?
4	WHAT ARE YOUR TEN GREATEST SUCCESSES TO DATE (IN YOUR EYES)?
5	IS THERE A CAUSE ABOUT WHICH YOU FEEL PASSIONATE?
6	WHAT ARE THE TEN MOST IMPORTANT LESSONS YOU HAVE LEARNED IN YOUR LIFE?
7	ARE THERE SOME ISSUES OR PERCEIVED PROBLEMS THAT HAVE OCCURRED OVER AND OVER AGAIN?
8	WHAT DO YOU DAYDREAM ABOUT DOING?
9	IMAGINE YOU ARE WRITING YOUR EPITAPH. WHAT THINGS DO YOU WANT TO BE REMEMBERED FOR AT THE END OF YOUR LIFE?
10	WHAT WOULD YOU DO IF YOU KNEW YOU COULD NOT FAIL?

Following are other processes that may assist clients in discovering their life purpose.

Listen to your intuition. Key aspects of our life purpose often emerge through our intuition. We may experience it as an audible voice, a physical sensation, an urge to call someone, to buy a particular book, or to attend an event we might not otherwise attend. When we follow it, the meaning behind the sensation eventually becomes clear. (If clients are not accustomed to listening to their intuition, sources such as Laura Day's *Practical Intuition* may be helpful.[20])

Decide that you matter, and that you can have clarity about your purpose.
> "A sense of purpose is rarely handed to us. We get it by deciding to have it. We get it by deciding that, yes, I matter. A sense of purpose comes from within, and only we know if we have it."
> —Richard Lieder, *The Power of Purpose*

No matter how much you, the coach, believe that your clients can have clarity about their life purpose, they will not uncover it until they too believe it is possible. Perhaps they are facing a particular obstacle (see below), or maybe their self-esteem is so low that they need coaching to raise it before they can meaningfully participate in exploring their life purpose. You can use the QuantumShift! coaching techniques discussed in Part 3 to encourage them to make this key decision: "I matter! I can have clarity about my life purpose."

Discover solitude and meditation. It is only through becoming quiet that we can hear the answers to the questions life is asking us at critical junctures such as career crossroads. Otherwise, the busyness of our daily life crowds out the still, small voice that is trying to be heard. One simple yet powerful exercise is to ask clients to dedicate fifteen minutes each morning to just sitting quietly, looking at something beautiful (e.g., scenery outside the window), and concentrating on just being there. This is not the time to solve problems or to dwell on what isn't working. Rather, it is a time just to be, to develop a sense of comfort with oneself—the self that is behind the "doer," that "more of us" that exists apart from our professional or family roles. For a specific meditation that facilitates discovery of your purpose, see the "Symbol Meditation" in the Career Coach's Toolbox (p. 319).

Obstacles to Discovering Life Purpose

If discovering our life purpose were easy, everyone would have already done it. Even the ten clues to life purpose will not result in instant awareness for every client. It is important to be patient with the process and allow it to unfold. On the other hand, clients are often anxious to gain clarity so that the rest of the Authentic Vocation factors can fall into place. One thing that I have discovered is that where it used to take weeks to guide clients to their life purpose, by adding to the process the QuantumShift!™ coaching techniques you will learn about in Part 3, many clients can articulate their purpose statement within a couple of coaching sessions.

Keep in mind that there are at least four common obstacles clients may encounter when trying to clarify their life purpose:

1. **Overlooking the value of an interest, skill, or passion, taking it for granted and assuming that everyone has it.** Certainly, we all have natural strengths and gifts. And we often tend to overlook the very things that people have always told us we are good at doing, or that have always been our role or duty when our family or close friends plan an activity. Overcoming this obstacle requires the objective feedback of a third party (e.g., a career coach) to help clients see their specialness.

2. **Insisting that one's life purpose is completely unique and different from everyone else's.** Many of the activities and goals represented by a purpose statement are far too large for one person to accomplish, outside of his or her own individual circle of influence. So for more than one person to be committed to that purpose or a similar one will simply accelerate the transformation process in the world—or whatever role in which the client wishes to work.

3. **Feeling the pressures of just needing to make a living.** This is a common trap, with everyone so busy these days. The pressures of an unexpected layoff may require that the life purpose exploration be deferred temporarily. The coach can help clients evaluate whether the financial issues are so pressing as to require immediate attention. If so, the coach may want to help clients obtain a transitional position that will pay the bills—but not require 100 percent of their time—so that they can then explore their life purpose. Most people will not be fulfilled and satisfied in their work until it becomes an expression of their life purpose (see Fig. 6).

4. **Thinking that only "special" people have a life purpose, and they are not special people.** The truth is, everyone has a purpose—not just writers, artists, musicians, or religious leaders (or insert the category of your choice). Discovering it inevitably increases work and/or life satisfaction. However, some people do not feel the longing to explore it until later in life; others begin early.

Examples of Purpose Statements

The life purpose statement itself—if it is to be useful as the central theme of one's life—should be articulated in a specific format, divided into two parts: (1) the *essence,* which is relatively unchanged over one's life, and (2) the *expression,* which changes as life circumstances change. Following are some samples of the essence portion, the hardest for most people to articulate, of several life purpose statements:

- To promote corporate integrity through...
- To increase the harmony and love in the world through...
- To be a positive influence on women and children through...
- To help working mothers achieve the balance they desire through...
- To help people communicate with themselves and others as honestly and courageously as possible through...
- To promote win-win conflict resolution and increase world peace through...
- To find my own path and help others find their path through...
- To provide environments where self-healing can occur through...
- To help people discover their purpose and express their calling while they are still alive through...

As we mature, we may refine the way we state the essence portion, but the fundamental theme can be traced from cradle to grave. It is expressed through childhood relationships, college education, early careers, starting a family, releasing our children to move out on their own, retirement, and beyond. These latter circumstances are the changing expression portion that evolves along with us.

A sample life purpose statement including both parts might read:

> My life purpose is to increase the harmony and love in the world through working as a child and family therapist using a harmonious communication approach, pursuing peace in all of my personal and professional relationships, volunteering with Peace on the Planet Foundation, and teaching my children to seek harmony instead of discord.

Note that the life purpose addresses much more than just work. From the life purpose statement, we may then formulate a business mission statement if we are beginning our own enterprise, or a work mission statement if we are working for a company. These mission statements need to be congruent with the overall life purpose statement.

Implementing Life Purpose

Even as clients begin to explore the other elements of their Authentic Vocation, they can begin to live a more purpose-centered life by implementing their life purpose, as they understand it. Here are several easy ways to do this:

1. **Do activities related to your life purpose first thing in the morning.** This will allow you to do what is important to you before other distractions have a chance to pull you off course.

2. **Whenever you have a decision to make, ask which option takes you closer to your life purpose.** Usually, one of your options will be more joyful than the others – often the one that leads to the fulfillment of your life purpose. Each small step builds on the last, and soon you are living the life of your dreams!

3. **Be willing to change.** To fulfill your life purpose, you must be willing to change anything that does not take you there. If you are harboring resistance, fear, or old programming, merely stating a willingness to change it will propel you in the direction you want to go. You may not know the precise steps to take, but your willingness will lead you to take the right action. A helpful statement to repeat is, "I am willing to change whatever is necessary to have/be the thing I want."

4. **Think of your life purpose as an organizing principle for your life** (see Fig. 6). If we imagine our life purpose as the hub of a wheel, we can continue our efforts to implement it by moving out through the other rings of the wheel. Next, we examine our roles: which of them serve our purpose and which do not? Can we, either gradually or immediately, eliminate the roles that no longer serve our newfound purpose? Then we consider our long-term goals and life vision. What do we want to have accomplished in three years? Five years? Over our lifetime?

Setting long-term goals that facilitate the expression of our purpose ensures that we will feel fulfilled, not just satisfied that we accomplished another goal, because our purpose is being realized.

Figure 6: Life Purpose as an Organizing Principle

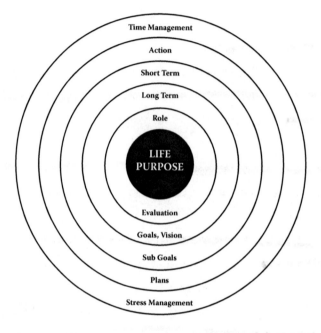

Source: Marcia Perkins-Reed (Marcia Bench), *Thriving in Transition* (New York: Simon and Schuster, 1996). Reprinted with permission.

For the goals that we wish to accomplish within the next year or so, we then set short-term subgoals—the goals within the goals we want to achieve—then the specific actions we will take to achieve those. And finally, we use principles of time and stress management to execute the daily steps toward our goals. Thus our life purpose becomes an organizing principle for the rest of our life and the basis for a career and life plan. Using this process with your clients will help ensure that their life purpose is not just a passive statement, but a theme that is actively integrated into their daily life.

Now let us return to Sally, our client from chapter 3, as an example of how this process can work.

Example

- **Life purpose statement:** To help people communicate better and leave a legacy through consulting with family-owned businesses, conscious relationships with my partner and children, volunteering at nonprofit organizations, and building my self-esteem through assertiveness training, physical fitness, and investing toward my retirement.

- **Role evaluation:** Current roles include CFO for hotel business, budding entrepreneur (family business consultant), friend, investor, docent at local museum, spiritual seeker, yoga practitioner, lover; desire to phase out of CFO role and expand entrepreneur role with other roles staying collectively at 25 percent of total.

- **Long-term goal:** To become an internationally known speaker in the field of family business.

- **Short-term subgoals:**
- Improve speaking skills
- Become visible within local and, eventually, national hotel and family business associations
- Learn how to price and promote speaking services
- **Action plans:**
- Join Toastmasters to improve speaking skills
- Present proposal to speak at regional hotel association conference
- Join National Speakers Association and network with other established professional speakers about pricing and promotion
- **Time/stress management:** Drawing from assortment of scheduling, organization, relaxation, and other skills, manage time and stress appropriately to execute plan and achieve goals

Key Coaching Concepts

1. A life purpose can be defined simply as a calling, a mission, or an overall theme for our life that transcends our daily activities.

2. One premise of Authentic Vocation is that "every person has a central life purpose that, if fulfilled through one's work as it develops and changes over time, generates optimum work fulfillment."

3. Clients can use the "10 clues" to help discover their life purpose.

4. Common obstacles to discovering one's life purpose include (a) overlooking its value, (b) insisting that it be unique, (c) feeling the pressure to "make a living," and (d) thinking that only "special" people have a purpose.

5. A life purpose statement has two parts: *essence*, which is relatively unchanged throughout one's life, and *expression*, which reflects the current circumstances through which the purpose is expressed and will change over time.

6. Life purpose can be implemented through consistent focus and through seeing it as an organizing principle for the goals and plans people have for each part of their life—including but not limited to their work.

5

Authentic Vocation™ Factor 2: Values at Work

"IF I SAY [PEOPLE ARE] PULLED BY VALUES, WHAT IS IMPLICITLY REFERRED TO IS THE FACT THAT THERE IS ALWAYS FREEDOM INVOLVED: THE FREEDOM OF [PEOPLE] TO MAKE THEIR CHOICE BETWEEN ACCEPTING OR REJECTING AN OFFER, I.E., TO FULFILL A MEANINGFUL POTENTIALITY OR ELSE TO FORFEIT IT."
—*Viktor E. Frankl,* Man's Search for Meaning

If anyone was ever in a position to speak to the importance of being pulled by values, it is Viktor Frankl, a Nazi concentration camp survivor who later wrote about his horrific experiences in *Man's Search for Meaning.*[21] Frankl can be a beacon of hope for workers who experience value conflicts in their work every day. Perhaps the narrowness of a job description limits their creativity and self-expression. Or, an overly controlling boss's micromanagement squelches their sense of autonomy or independence. Or, in a more extreme case, employees may be asked to approve deliberate misstatements of revenues, expenses, or profits to shareholders.

As widespread practices like these come to light through heightened scrutiny and government investigations, we can hope that fewer such incidents will occur in the future. But the value businesses place on money often far outweighs the value they place on employee morale, congruence between company mission and daily operations, measures to prevent constant "firefighting" (i.e., dealing with the "crisis of the day"), and open communication with staff. Conflicts between individual values and the company values (not the stated values, but rather the actual values as they are practiced each day) can create significant stress in the individual worker.

Types of Values

What are values? They are simply the things that, to us, are intrinsically valuable or desirable. They form the basis for our choices about what we will and will not do. Therefore, they are important to our career decisions and to our Authentic Vocation.

Each of us has developed a unique system of values that determines how we feel about our work and the contribution it makes to the society. We make similar value choices regarding family and lifestyle. If we choose to pursue a career or an organization with requirements or culture that are at odds with our values, we will not be happy with the choice. Most people who pursue work that is congruent with their values feel satisfied and successful in their careers. Relating our values to our work decisions and choices helps us determine our reasons for wanting to work, the characteristics of occupations that are appealing to us, and our career goals.

Values at work can be categorized in several different ways, such as the four-part model shown in fig. 7.

Figure 7: Types of Values

Intrinsic	Extrinsic
Intrinsic value of the work activities themselves, or how the work benefits society (e.g., socially responsible, automates communication)	External conditions of a job or occupation (e.g., physical setting, salary, or career growth opportunities)
Cultural	Operational
Pertaining to the purpose, character, and overall direction of one's career development (e.g., responsibility, autonomy)	Cultural values expressed in day-to-day operations (e.g., flexibility, employee orientation)

Three Major Value Systems

Psychologist David McClelland has isolated three fundamental values—achievement, affiliation, and power. Each of us favors one over the other two as an intrinsic need in our work.

- **Achievement**. Meeting or exceeding a standard of excellence and/or improving one's own performance. People who value achievement will often perform better over time, even in the absence of specific demands to do better, because they enjoy mastering challenging tasks. McClelland found that placing a high value on achievement is critical for anyone desiring to be successful as an entrepreneur.

- **Affiliation**. Establishing, maintaining, and avoiding disruption of close, friendly relationships with people. People who value affiliation will, on their own initiative, seek out people to spend time with because they enjoy their company.

- **Power**. Having an influence or making an impact on others. People who value power desire to have an impact. They focus on being perceived as strong, effective, and influential.

Identifying a Client's Work-Related Values

There are two primary approaches to value identification in the career context. One is to ask clients to list, without prompting or suggestion, their most important values. The other is to provide a list of common work values and have clients rank them in order of importance. Authentic Vocation Worksheet 2, "Values," in the Career Coach's Toolbox (p. 321) combines both of these approaches. First, it asks clients why they work and what they want to derive from the work. Then, it gives them a list of over twenty values to rank in importance, from which they are to narrow down to their top five. Once clients have identified their top five values, the coach ascertains what makes them important and how clients would like to see each value expressed in their next position and perhaps other life areas.

Identifying one's values is an important part of a successful career plan. Other tools available for further values clarification include:

- A personal values questionnaire available from the Hay Group (<u>www.
haygroup.com</u>);[22] this questionnaire helps determine for clients the relative importance of the three values identified by David McClelland: power, achievement, and authority

- A values assessment offered by the University of Waterloo, Cooperative Education and Career Services, Ontario (see "Your Values" in the Career Coach's Toolbox, p. 324)

- A values card sort available through <u>www.careertrainer.com</u>

One of my colleagues witnessed an immediate benefit of clarifying values. Her client, Vicki, was terrified of interviews and often gave untrue answers just to say something in response to the questions asked. However, during an interview for an outside sales position with a major telecommunications firm, the interviewer asked her what her top four values were. She immediately realized that she had an honest answer to the question because of her Authentic Vocation work! She stated that one of her top values was "freedom," and when asked why by the sales manager, she said, "because I was raised in South Africa where some people are not free—I'm glad I am!"

The interviewer congratulated her for being so prepared and told her that most sales candidates do not have an answer for that question. He also said that having an answer was an indicator of success and that she was the kind of person he wanted on his team. She was hired!

KEY COACHING CONCEPTS

1. Values are simply the things that, to you, are intrinsically valuable or desirable. They form the basis for your choices about what you will and will not do.
2. Values can be categorized as intrinsic vs. extrinsic, cultural vs. operational.
3. David McClelland identified three primary values— achievement, affiliation, and power—on which individuals place varying amounts of weight.
4. Identifying one's values is an important part of a successful career plan.

6

Authentic Vocation™ *Factor 3: Motivators and Interests*

"LORD, GRANT THAT I MAY ALWAYS DESIRE MORE THAN I CAN ACCOMPLISH."
—*Michelangelo*

Think back for a moment to the subject you liked least in school. If you're like most of us, you did only enough homework to get a passing grade in the class, were bored during class sessions, and could not wait for it to be over, right? Many people today have a similar attitude toward their job. This is the opposite of the kind of motivation we want our clients to experience when they are aligned with their Authentic Vocation.

Recently, the Gallup organization did a fascinating research project to determine what highly successful companies were doing that resulted in their employees being so highly motivated. They discovered that when certain key factors were present, "engagement" had occurred and productivity (as well as other business measures) increased. The research involved 200,000 employees across thirty-six companies in diverse industries.[23]

In Authentic Vocation factor 3, we explore what motivates and interests clients.

What Motivation Is

To be motivated is to feel inspired and excited, and to look forward to doing something. Each of us is motivated by different factors at work, including both the type of work and the environment in which we perform it. We will not perform at our best unless those motivating factors are present.

While many clients know the types of tasks they want to perform, they are often unaware of what really motivates them. Motives are often unconscious, and as such become a driving force that must be fulfilled. They may appear as needs, wants, or concerns and usually include a desire to reach a certain kind of goal.

For example, when Ashley volunteered for a new project—initiating a joint venture with another firm on a proposal—she may have had many motives. She may have wished to obtain recognition, to step up her responsibilities, to position herself for promotion, to explore positions with the other company, to facilitate cooperation among the companies, and so on. Regardless of her motive, her behavior would look the same externally. Therefore, uncovering motives requires that the client perform a self-assessment.

Several decades ago, psychologist Frederick Herzberg and his colleagues researched how rewards affect employee motivation. He found that increasing salary or providing an annual Christmas turkey may seem to improve motivation temporarily, but in the long run, these are merely "hygiene factors" that become expected as part of a job.[24] Only their absence will be noticed. To better motivate employees, employers must adjust the motivating factors and do such things as provide cross-training, increasing the challenge of the job, or otherwise making a substantive change, not just a monetary one.

Differentiating Values and Motivators

Psychologist David McClelland points out that values often influence our choices about where to invest our energies, while motives—what motivates us—reflect how much pleasure we get out of certain activities.[25] Values are conscious, whereas motives are unconscious (and motivators are expressions of the unconscious motives). Fig. 8 details some of the key differences.

Figure 8: Values and Motives

Values	Motives
• Choose areas of importance	• Natural Drives
• Conscious	• Unconscious
• Help an individual make decsions	• Predict types of behavior a person will gravitate toward over time
• Adaptive—developed from experience throughout one's life	• Basic—influenced by early emotional experiences and perhaps is genetic
• Less difficult to change	• More difficult to change

Source: PVQ Profile & Interpretive Notes—TRG/HayMcBer. Reprinted with permission.

In some coaching engagements you will be seeking to discover a client's motivators to determine his or her best career fit; in others you may be working to change a motive in order to instigate a behavior change. Fig. 9 illustrates the respective factors that are involved as we explore our clients' issues. Like the 90 percent of an iceberg that is not visible, life purpose, values, motives, self-image, and social roles are beneath the surface. Only skills and knowledge are clearly visible to the rest of the world.

To help clients identify their motivators, as they relate to work, you can use Authentic Vocation Worksheet 3 "Motivators and Interests" in the Career Coach's Toolbox p. 326.

Changing and Increasing Motivation: Five Basic Steps

useful for any habit or sabotaging behavior

Whether clients are seeking to access more of their known motivation regarding their work situation or to change the motivation behind a troublesome behavior, the following five steps will result in a change in both motivation and behavior.

Figure 9: The Iceberg Metaphor

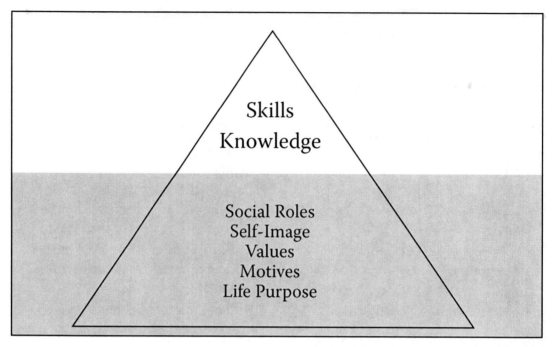

1. **Do a self-assessment.** Clients must first become aware of how naturally, or habitually, they perceive and think about the people and situations they encounter. That is, they must thoroughly understand their present motivation and its consequences. Once they understand it, they can then seek to leverage it in their work. For example, Sue was feeling frustrated with her work as a customer service representative for a software company. Her self-assessment included noticing, throughout the day, which aspects of her job upset her most. She realized that the central issue was her lack of control over the situations she would encounter with customers—especially their emotional state—and not knowing whether she could successfully resolve their problems.

2. **Define the desired state.** Clients should next fully describe the ideal situation that would allow them to feel motivated, one toward which they would want to move. Sue has several choices here, though she may not realize it. She can explore changing jobs, either within her company (e.g., to another department) or to another

company. If she does not know what other jobs would suit her, she could work with a career coach to find out. A second choice would be to change her attitude and approach to her existing job. Instead of insisting on controlling each day's activities and exchanges, she could learn to find motivation in being challenged and delighted by each day's varied experiences. This may change the way she has viewed herself in the past, and in fact may affect other experiences in her life, too.

3. **Set goals and take action to achieve them.** After setting goals, clients need to begin solving problems, planning and acting in ways consistent with their new perspective on people and situations. If Sue chose to seek a new job, for example, her goals would include identifying her job targets, updating her resume, reactivating her network of contacts, and planning and implementing a job search.

4. **Repeat new motivation/behavior.** For a new habit, idea, or motivation to be fully integrated at the subconscious level, it must be consciously repeated for at least twenty-one consecutive days. If it is replacing a deep, long-standing belief, it will take longer! In the case of seeking a new job, a powerful repetition technique is to write out a description of the desired work situation each night before going to bed. That allows the subconscious to work on the idea throughout the night and enhances the results obtained from job search activities. It should include more than the facts of the desired situation; it should also describe the excitement and other emotions—so that they are palpable!—to be most powerful.

5. **Find interpersonal and situational support.** As change begins to take shape, clients need to situate themselves among people who will give them feedback and stimulation and generally support their new way of thinking and behaving. These situational supports may include a coach, a weekly "success team" in which to celebrate victories and provide support during disappointments, or a support group organized around a common situation (e.g., people in job transition, new business owners, etc.). Sue might also participate in a job seekers' networking group to support her job change efforts. These sorts of activities work

together to create a positive feedback loop, which can continually reinforce the motivation clients such as Sue are trying to implement.

Relationship of Motives and Interests

Often, but not always, when we have a high level of interest in something, we are also highly motivated to do it. Therefore, as we evaluate this factor of Authentic Vocation, we can complete an interest inventory to identify which functional areas within an organization that may be more motivating to clients than others. Of course, just because clients have a high level of interest in something does not mean that they have any skill (transferable or otherwise) or experience in it. All Authentic Vocation elements must be considered together as we work with clients. The results of an interest inventory can affirm clients' current career focus or suggest new areas for exploration.

One interest assessment we recommend is the *Strong Interest Inventory*® instrument, which is available from CPP at www.cpp.com. Its Career Transition Report evaluates the individual's interest level in ten functional work areas of an organization. Each functional work area has a set of associated tasks to help clients gauge their interest in it. The report also includes an action plan that advises clients how to effectively apply their results from the report as well as activities they can do to ease their transition and identify satisfying career options.

Another way to assess interests is to use the Self-Directed Search Assessment (http://www.self-directed-search.com/index.html) developed by career theorist and former Case Western Reserve professor John Holland. Holland's model assumes that since vocational interests are one aspect of personality, a description of a person's vocational interests is also a description of his or her personality. Personality traits are identified by indicating preferences for school subjects, recreational activities, work, and hobbies. Following are the six types of interests evaluated by the Self-Directed Search, followed by their preferences and what they lack:

1. **Realistic.** Enjoys activities involving systematic manipulation of machinery, tools, or animals; lacks social skills.

2. **Investigative.** Enjoys activities using analytical, inquisitive, methodical, and precisionist characteristics; lacks leadership skills.

3. **Artistic.** Enjoys activities using expressive, nonconforming, original, introspective characteristics; lacks clerical skills.

4. **Social.** Enjoys working with and helping others; lacks systematic, mechanical, or scientific ability.

5. **Enterprising.** Enjoys manipulating others to attain organizational goals or economic gain, and avoids symbolic/systematic activities; lacks scientific ability.

6. **Conventional.** Enjoys manipulating data in systematic way, filing records, and reproducing materials; lacks artistic ability.

Using one or more of these motivation and interest assessments or worksheets will help clients clarify Authentic Vocation Factor 3.

KEY COACHING CONCEPTS

1. To be motivated is to feel inspired and excited, and to look forward to doing something.
2. Values are different from motives in several aspects: (a) values are conscious and motives are unconscious; (b) values are adaptive and motives are basic; and (c) values are easier to change than motives.
3. Five steps for increasing motivation include
   - Doing a self-assessment
   - Defining the desired state
   - Setting goals and taking steps to achieve them
   - Repeating the new motivation/behavior with emotion
   - Finding interpersonal and situational support
4. People are often motivated by those activities in which they have a high level of interest. Administering an interest inventory at this stage can help determine motivated interests.

7

Authentic Vocation™ Factor 4: Knowledge, Skills and Abilities

"THE MAN WE CALL A SPECIALIST TODAY WAS FORMERLY CALLED A
MAN WITH A ONE-TRACK MIND."
—*Endre Balogh*

Many current career development models begin by evaluating clients' areas of knowledge, skills and abilities—the philosophy being, apparently, that if one does work one is good at, one will find satisfaction. The problem is that by midcareer most coaching clients have already followed that track to the end and come up wanting. They have reached a point where achieving fulfillment is more important than proving competency. Generation "X" workers often begin here.

In Authentic Vocation Factor 4, we help clients inventory their knowledge (formal education and beyond), skills (work-related competencies) and abilities (inherent talents or strengths).

Skills are differentiated from experience (which is discussed in chapter 8) in that skills are specific competencies required to do a job, whereas experience refers to the types of work one has actually done.

Skills fall into three categories:

- **Technical, "hard," or job-specific skills,** which often require special training or education or are learned on-the-job, such as programming a computer or creating a spreadsheet

- **Nontechnical, "soft," or adaptive skills,** are the people skills needed to interact with others such as being a team player, building rapport, and the like, which pertain to one's work style

- **Transferable skills,** which are learned in one context or industry but can be transferred to be applied in many different work settings, such as leadership and decision making

Abilities may include job skills, but what distinguishes them is that they are innate, natural talents. They are akin to "strengths" as defined by Marcus Buckingham and colleagues in *Now Discover Your Strengths* and the *Strengthsfinder 2.0* assessment (available at www.strengthsfinder.com).

The role of clients' knowledge, skills and abilities in Authentic Vocation will vary somewhat depending on the reason they are seeking a job change. If they simply wish to take on more responsibility or broaden their expertise in an industry or job in which they already have experience, these assets will be of high importance. Clients' marketability depends on their ability to demonstrate their key assets, as they relate to the job requirements, to a prospective employer.

If, on the other hand, the client is making a midlife career change (or would like to be) and is dissatisfied or unfulfilled with his or her occupation, technical and non-technical skills *per se* are of less importance. However, transferable skills are critical, as are the first three factors of Authentic Vocation. And distinguishing the client's natural abilities may also be key in finding fulfilling work, for in these strengths lie the greatest leverage.

Believing that employers tend to focus mainly on the bottom line, many people underestimate the importance of soft skills in their job search. But soft skills such as developing and managing effective working relationships have become increasingly important. As Daniel Goleman states in *Working with Emotional Intelligence,* "four in ten [workers] are not able to work cooperatively with fellow employees, and just 19 percent of those applying for entry-level jobs have enough self-discipline in their work habits. More and more employers are complaining about the lack of social skills in new hires."[26] As many as 67 percent of the abilities deemed essential for effective performance, according to Goleman's review of 181 competence models, are emotional competencies (self-confidence, trustworthiness, initiative, optimism, conflict management, communication, and the like), not a high IQ or expertise.[27]

In a 1996 national survey of what employers seek in new workers, specific technical skills are less important than more intangible skills. The three most highly sought-after skills in new hires are oral communication, interpersonal abilities, and team-work abilities, all so-called soft skills.[28] Thus both soft and hard skills have a place in presenting the client on paper and in person as well as in determining job choice. Fig. 10 contains some examples of each.

Figure 10: Hard and Soft Skills

Soft/Intangible/Nontechnical Skills	Hard/Tangible/Technical Skills
• Team player	• Performance appraisal
• Good communicator	• Budget development/oversight
• Honest	• Marketing plan development
• Good time manager	• Advertising
• Adaptable	• Cold-calling
• Detail-oriented	• Web site design
• Build rapport easily	• Inventory control
• Reliable	• Staff supervision
• Flexible	• Process engineering
• Fair	• Recruiting
• Hard-working	• Welding

As clients identify their skills and abilities, it is important that you assure them that both hard and soft skills have a role in job targeting and job search. Hard, or tangible, skills predict what jobs or functions the client can perform. When clients are also good at a particular skill and enjoy it, it becomes a motivated skill and will be important to their Authentic Vocation. Often the soft assets are more important in predicting the company culture clients will work best in, their ability to get along with others, and their ability to manage effectively.

KSA Assessment Techniques and Tools

Following are the five approaches to assessing clients' knowledge, skills and abilities ("KSA's"):

1. **Checklists.** On Authentic Vocation Worksheet 4 in the Career Coach's Toolbox (p. 328), clients list their areas of knowledge and check off the skills which they have done personally, managed in others, trained others to use, or in which they have received education. Coach and client can then talk about the themes they notice and what they mean for the client's job targeting and search.

2. **Open list.** A second approach is to have clients list, without prompting, the skills they believe they have. A template is provided in "Open List Approach to Skills" in the Career Coach's Toolbox (p. 343).

3. **Card sorts.** To identify the skills that the person is both good at and likes to use, sorting a deck of cards with various skills typed on them into a two-dimension grid can narrow the field of so-called "motivated skills." Perhaps the best known of these is Richard Knowdell's Motivated Skills Card Sort (see http://tinyurl.com/28akl2).

4. **Work Experience Stories.** Another approach is to have job seekers write Work Experience Stories about their accomplishments in their career (discussed in chapter 8). Then they can circle key words from them and log them into a matrix listing key skills (much like those listed in Authentic Vocation Worksheet 4). This process gives them a better idea of which skills they have most experience

applying in the workplace. For another example of a skills assessment that draws on Work Experience Stories that is simple and user-friendly, see http://www.cdm.uwaterloo.ca/Step1_4.asp. This university-generated tool uses clusters based on the Holland codes (see chapter 6).

5. **Software and Internet-based programs.** There are many skills assessment software programs, many of which oversimplify the categories of skills needed in today's marketplace. The better ones will compare job seekers' skills with lists of skills required for certain jobs. A free skills assessment is the Motivational Appraisal of Personal Potential (MAPP) tool available at www.assessment.com. One of the best we have found is Careerway (www.careerway.com), which not only explores skills but compares the user's interests, motivators, and daily activities to those required in each of the hundreds of job types currently listed in the O*Net database (more on this in chapter 9). *O*Net online*

We provide you with several tools for evaluating knowledge, skills and abilities so that you can tailor your approach to your clients' professional level, learning style, and goals. For example, clients in the early stages of their career or in creative fields may find the checklist in Authentic Vocation Worksheet 4 intimidating, but they would be able to list their skills based on their resume or accomplishments.

The Importance of Education

One common measure of knowledge used by recruiters is formal education. Too often, clients dismiss a job or career interest because a college degree appears to be required. We have coached many clients who successfully obtained a job that seemed to require a degree – but who circumvented that requirement through creative job search. We will return to this topic in later chapters.

At this stage, clients should be encouraged to catalog their knowledge from all sources. Formal schooling, hobbies, training/seminars, recreational reading, and life experiences may each have contributed to clients' current knowledge bank.

KEY COACHING CONCEPTS:

1. Skills fall into three categories: technical, nontechnical, and transferable.
2. As many as 67 percent of the abilities deemed essential for effective performance require emotional competencies, or "soft" skills.
3. There are at least five approaches to assessing knowledge, skills and abilities: checklists, open lists, card sorts, work experience stories, and software and Internet-based programs.
4. While education and knowledge gained through other means are important to the career design process, clients should not reject a job possibility simply because it traditionally requires a particular degree.

8

Authentic Vocation™ Factor 5: Work and Other Experience

"LIFE IS A SERIES OF EXPERIENCES, EACH ONE OF WHICH MAKES US BIGGER, EVEN THOUGH SOMETIMES IT IS HARD TO REALIZE THIS."
—*Henry Ford*

Authentic Vocation Factor 5 asks clients to list their work history—and, if applicable, other volunteer or school-related experience—from which they can draw in their next career move. How clients approach this exercise can tell us several things.

First, industries in which clients have worked may reveal important elements of their personality and style, since certain industries often attract certain personalities. For example, those who are well organized, detail-oriented and enjoy numbers may be drawn to accounting or finance. Clients' lack of satisfaction can often be traced to their being mismatched to their industry. For a person who has worked in data processing or finance for years and is unhappy, perhaps they are ready to investigate a more creative direction.

Second, clients' work experience and their rate of progression in responsibility (or lack thereof) may indicate their level of motivation and drive. If they have rapidly progressed through the ranks to ever-increasing levels of responsibility, a high level of drive, as well as achievement motivation, is evident. On the other hand, clients who have unhappily spent a long time in a job or industry for financial or other reasons may have less drive, or may simply not have known what else to do. If they have been fired frequently, are they more suited to entrepreneurship than corporate work?

And third, a log of work experience can be a launching point for some key coaching questions to determine whether clients wish to remain in the industry they are in currently, return to an industry (or role) held previously, or do something entirely new. If it is the latter, what aspects of their current industry do they enjoy and which would they like to continue to experience? What about their current industry or role is particularly unappealing? Would they consider another position in that industry along with some other choices? These questions can clarify for clients and for you, the coach, what jobs and industries are among those to be considered in their next step. For the coach, knowing how wide the field of possibilities extends in the client's mind is extremely helpful as well.

Experience: Limiting Factor or Source of Possibilities?

Many people have great difficulty seeing how they can transfer their current skills and previous work experience from one industry to another. As career coaches, we can help clients expand their sometimes "myopic" perspective on the possibilities their skills and experience hold.

One way to do this is to think of clients' experiences as a set of building blocks from which a number of shapes could be created. We can help clients experiment with their building blocks to help them clarify what they want. We can notice where they become excited and where their voice indicates a lack of passion. We can also use our own work experience and familiarity, at whatever level, with various industries to suggest other areas where clients' skills and experiences may be transferred. (Note: we do not want to go as far as giving advice to clients, for that is outside the scope of coaching. But providing suggestions or ideas for them to consider along with other possibilities – especially in the form of a coaching question – is appropriate at this stage.) We'll explore this idea more in the next chapter.

A challenge is presented by clients who are returning to the workplace after an extended absence, whether due to raising children, an illness in the family, or a sabbatical or other leave. In these cases the coach must creatively explore clients' activities. Did they volunteer at a nonprofit, work on a United Way fundraiser, coordinate an event for their church, or coach their child's athletic team? All of these experiences can also be relevant as clients seek to decide what types of jobs to target next.

Work Experience Stories

To market oneself effectively in the twenty-first-century workplace—characterized as it is by increasing competition—candidates must demonstrate to an interviewer or hiring manager as tangibly as possible their ability to do the job. In addition, many clients need to become more aware of what they actually contribute through their work. This alone has created epiphanies among many of my clients: when they realized the many contributions they had made, their self-esteem, which may have been battered due to a layoff or other factors, increased dramatically.

One of the best ways to do this is to develop Work Experience Stories that demonstrate particular skills being applied within a workplace context. Work Experience Stories have three components:

- **Context**—the challenge or circumstance encountered when the project began, or the problem that was solved
- **Action** taken to complete the project or solve the problem
- **Result** obtained, quantified whenever possible

Example

> **Context.** "When I was promoted to sales and marketing director for region 5, we were the lowest-performing region of the thirty regional territories. My challenge was to bring the sales and overall performance numbers up as quickly as possible."

Action. "To do so, I met with the twenty-person sales staff, jointly established ten aggressive goals for the next six to twelve months, and developed a promotional strategy to increase customer awareness of our products, which included incentives for new purchases within a stated period of time."

Result. "Within ninety days, sales were up by 15 percent, and by year's end we were second in the nation with $1.2 million in sales."

Most clients should be encouraged to write at least six to ten work experience stories to describe their key accomplishments. And they should have at least one story for each skill that is central to their next job target, as well as one to three stories for each position they have held. (These may overlap.) Using the skill labels on Authentic Vocation Worksheet 4 can help trigger ideas for clients as to what stories to write. They can develop their stories on Authentic Vocation Worksheet 5 in the Career Coach's Toolbox (p. 344).

Traditional and New Types of Career Paths

In the old world of work that governed prior to the 1980s, typically employees moved in a vertical career path through their organization. This path was referred to as the "career ladder." As they were promoted, they (usually men) moved up one rung at a time until, at the top, they retired with the proverbial gold watch. Sales representative becomes senior sales rep, sales manager, regional manager, and ultimately national sales manager in this ladder-like progression.

Though some workers still progress using the ladder-type approach, other career paths have become more common in the past two decades, where at least ten career changes are typical during one's professional life. Following are some of the new types of career paths.

1. **Zigzag career path.** Here, the worker's job, career, and educational choices do not follow in a traditional or logical order. For example, a woman may begin with a degree in business, get a first job doing commission sales for a pharmaceutical

firm, then study Web design and work for an advertising firm doing Web-based surveys for a while. After a six-month parental leave/sabbatical to have a child, she may then pursue a home-based business in an entirely unrelated field to allow her the flexibility she needs to be home with her infant. This pattern no longer carries the stigma of instability it once did and works well for lifelong learners with varying interests.

2. **Portfolio career path.** For many people, divergent interests preclude their being satisfied with just one job or role. The portfolio career path allows them to pursue multiple positions at once that together pay well enough to meet their financial needs. Such an approach also provides "psychic income"—the fulfillment of making a contribution or doing "good work" in the world. It also often allows them to give back to their profession or community. This model can also be used by would-be entrepreneurs as a transitional strategy—that is, working part-time evenings and weekends in an entrepreneurial venture and keeping a "day job" either full-time or part-time until the business can support them (assuming that their primary employer's policies do not prohibit "moonlighting"). Fig. 11 illustrates this approach.

Figure 11: Portfolio Career

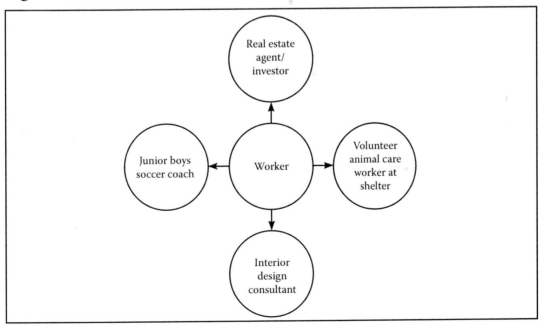

3. **Lateral career paths.** Here, employees move logically but in a horizontal fashion, either through a matrixed organization (where functions cross over and reporting is both horizontal and vertical) or through one or more industries or functions.

   - **Lateral through industries.** For example, a marketing/communications director may work for five years in the transportation industry, then move to a parallel position in a financial services firm and later to an engineering consulting firm, doing the same function in each company but changing the context to maintain his interest and professional challenge.

   - **Lateral through functions.** After eight years as quality manager in a multinational lumber products company, an employee might be transferred to a position as operations manager of a troubled region to assist in a turnaround effort; two years later after the turnaround has been implemented she may shift to project manager for a new manufacturing certification initiative the company is implementing. These positions are all within the same corporation, and may or may not require a geographical move.

4. **"Pro-tirement."** Dr. Frederick Hudson, founder of The Hudson Institute (www. hudsoninstitute.com) coined the term "pro-tirement" to define the active lifestyle of today's retirement-age people. In the new world of work, people who are sixty-five or older are no longer required to retire—in fact, recent legislation allows seniors up to age seventy to retain their Social Security income while earning unlimited income from work. Clients who have accumulated sufficient assets through work and/or investments to sufficiently fund their postemployment lifestyle, but still desire to be active—whether in paid work or volunteer activities— may seek out a career coach to help them plan this so-called third half of their life or "third age."

KEY COACHING CONCEPTS

1. Our clients' work and other experience can tell us much about their personality and drive, and can form the basis for some key coaching questions.

2. Experience can best be communicated through the use of Work Experience Stories, using the three elements of context, action, and results.

3. The related exercises suggested in his chapter to catalog clients' experience can help shift the client to focusing on achievement, contributions, and strengths, resulting in higher levels of confidence, enthusiasm, and energy for taking action.

4. In addition to the vertical, ladder-like career path that characterized the old workplace, new career paths include the zigzag path, the portfolio career path, the lateral path, and "pro-tirement."

9

Authentic Vocation™ Factor 6: Job/Career Targets

"IT IS NOT ENOUGH TO BE BUSY...THE QUESTION IS: WHAT ARE WE BUSY ABOUT?"
—*Henry David Thoreau*

To this point we have used the Authentic Vocation process primarily to help engage clients in self-exploration and self-discovery, to clarify their life purpose, values, motivators, interests, skills, and the experience they wish to leverage. As we move to Authentic Vocation Factor 6, "Job/Career Targets," we may find our clients asking us to guide them toward viable job or career options or even to advise them. This is primarily a career counseling or consulting role, not pure coaching. It is vital that we create an appropriate balance between offering a few useful tips and having clients do the work to discover their Authentic Vocation. Remember, career coaching is all about them, not us!

We can suggest to clients at this stage that they adopt an attitude of curiosity. This is an opportunity for them to think beyond all that they have done and been so far. What larger part of them is being called forth in this transition? This is a part of the career discovery journey where clients can feel free to try on different possible jobs or careers, as though they were throwing spaghetti at the wall to see what sticks.

This phase can feel very scary to clients. Often they will say things like, "I wonder if I'm going crazy; I seem to have a different idea every week." Or, "Won't I ever figure out what I'm supposed to be when I grow up?" It's the in-between stage of any transition, what I have called the "sorting-out" phase in my prior books on transition (available at www.careercoachinstitute.com).[29] As a career coach, your job is to reassure clients as they go through this stage.

First, reassure them that this feeling of being scattered and unsure is normal. Trying on a variety of professional roles—most of which will ultimately be rejected—is a prerequisite to deciding on the one the client will ultimately choose.

Second, encourage them to capture all the job ads that interest them, notes from informational interviews or books and articles they have read, ideas that occur to them in the middle of the night or in off hours, and so on. Whether they stuff scraps of paper into a manila envelope, organize the data in a three-ring binder, or create an electronic file on their computer, the point is to collect these seemingly unrelated ideas and review them again in four to six weeks. The patterns that emerge—as well as how obvious the new career direction becomes—are often quite amazing.

Selecting Job Targets

Between the skill/experience myopia we talked about in chapter 8 and the rapidly changing career paths, clients often feel more limited than they need to about what other jobs are possible for them. A beginning approach you can take to broaden their perspective and develop job search targets is to identify the logical options based on clients' prior positions and experience. That is, if they were working in a medium- to large-sized organization and were going to be promoted, what would the next logical position up the ladder be (even if the ladder has turned into a spiral, a patchwork quilt, or something else)?

Example: Mary has been an account representative and sales rep with progressively larger territories and diverse products, so logical next steps would be national account rep, sales rep with other similar companies or sales manager in her current company.

Secondly, you want to look beyond merely what steps are logical to how the client can rearrange her "building blocks"—that is, her responses to the first five factors of Authentic Vocation—to form new career shapes.

> *Example*: Mary's building blocks include (1) life purpose: making the world a better place through promoting and selling environmentally friendly products and services; (2) values: integrity, social responsibility, and authenticity; (3) motivators: mentoring, seeing tangible results of her work; (4) skills and abilities: working with people, sales, developing marketing campaigns, resourcefulness, and follow-through; and (5) work experience in consumer products sales and marketing.

Arranging her building blocks, Mary could be a sales manager or a Web designer for consumer products companies. She might also consider targeting a position as customer relations manager, a self-employed marketing consultant, or an entrepreneur who owns a company with a new, socially responsible product.

If clients are unsure what these logical building blocks are, you can suggest that they visit the O*Net database at http://online.onetcenter.org/ or the Occupational Outlook Handbook at http://www.bls.gov/oco/ to learn more.

As an alternative to the building blocks approach, coaches can help clients explore options elsewhere on the supply chain: manufacturing transfers the product to the wholesalers who sell to businesses that sell to the ultimate customer as retailers. If a client has experience in the manufacturing of a product, other job/career targets can be the distribution or retail side of the business—as well as consulting or working in a government agency that regulates that industry. So exploring other possibilities along the supply chain is another way to use the same raw material but create a different finished product.

Throughout this process, we want to ask probing questions to help generate more possibilities for applying clients' talents. Here are a few to consider:

- "What do you really want to do?"
- "When you were a child, what were some of your favorite pastimes?"
- "As a child, what did you dream of being when you grew up?"
- "What would you do if you didn't care what other people thought?"
- "What would you do if you couldn't fail?"
- "What if you had no limits?"
- "What if money were no object?"

Other lists of such questions are provided in part 3.

The "Ideal Day Exercise" in the Career Coach's Toolbox (p. 359) can be quite helpful to clients striving to fill in the details of their ideal job targets. This exercise can complement the more analytical techniques that appear in this chapter.

Useful Resources for Job and Career Information

When looking for ideas about what kind of work to pursue, clients often find it helpful to begin by perusing the classified help wanted ads in the Sunday newspaper (print or online) and noticing which positions sound interesting or seem appealing to them in some way. If they are looking for a new job within their current company, reviewing the internal postings of open positions can also be helpful. It is important for them to realize that the purpose of this exercise is not to apply for the jobs posted (at least not now!), but rather to notice which ones—in whole or in part—contain the kinds of activities and responsibilities that they want in their next job.

Also at this stage clients should be gathering names of key individuals (e.g., company managers or CEOs) in their target industries with whom they can conduct informational interviews to learn more. (Informational interviews are discussed in detail in chapter 22.)

By using these resources and Authentic Vocation Worksheet 6 in the Career Coach's Toolbox (p. 346), your clients should be able to generate a list of at least fifteen to twenty types of jobs they might consider—or at a minimum, would be willing to do some further research on to determine feasibility and match with their interests and skills. This is a critical stage, so be sure that clients regularly check in with you so that they don't get overwhelmed or frustrated with the exploration process.

Key goal – it keeps open-mind, esp. if financially constrained.

KEY COACHING CONCEPTS

1. When clients are apprehensive or frustrated about constantly generating new job and career options, reassure them that this is normal at this stage, and encourage them to capture the seemingly random ideas, thoughts, and information they are noticing at this time.

2. Five approaches to helping clients broaden their options for their next job or career include (a) logical next steps, (b) building blocks, (c) supply chain, (d) coaching questions to reveal what they really want to do, and (e) the "Ideal Day Exercise" (p. 359).

10

Authentic Vocation™ Factor 7: Work Environment

"I'M A GREAT BELIEVER IN LUCK, AND I FIND THE HARDER I WORK THE MORE I HAVE OF IT."
—*Thomas Jefferson*

Why is having the right work environment important in developing one's Authentic Vocation? When clients are attempting to apply their talents in a culture that conflicts with their life purpose or does not allow them to use their optimum work style, they will not be as productive or as satisfied as they could be, and ultimately they will not stay in the position.

Listed below are seven key components of the work environment to explore with clients (included also in Authentic Vocation Worksheet 7, "Work Environment," in the Career Coach's Toolbox on p. 348).

1. **Geographic location.** Where would the client like to work – in the state and city where she lives or somewhere else altogether? Perhaps this is a perfect time to explore relocating. Would she like to work in an office or outdoors? In an urban or rural setting? At home? Would she like to travel as part of her work?

2. **Pace.** Does the client enjoy an environment that is bustling and busy, or does she prefer an environment with a peaceful, slower pace? How many hours does she want to work each week? How many days per week or month?

3. **Support.** One way for the client to avoid burnout is to develop a supportive environment—one in which she has a sense of significance, autonomy, challenge, and support and in which there are relatively few unmanageable work stressors. This may be provided by the values and culture of the organization (see item 7 below), a company mentoring program, a new employee orientation, or a boss that is caring and concerned. Conversely, some clients like a lot of independence—the less direction, the better. A recent survey of more than one thousand employees found that employees who have less supportive workplaces feel more overworked.[30]

4. **Compensation.** How much money does the client want to earn in her ideal job? Which fringe benefits are important? The client may want to complete Authentic Vocation Worksheet 10: "Wants/Needs Analysis," in the Career Coach's Toolbox (p. 382) to trigger ideas about desired benefits and other job factors.

5. **Company size.** It is also important to evaluate whether the client works best alone, with one or two co-owners, or in a large company setting. To help determine the optimal work setting, refer to the profiles of the "solo worker," "the partner," and the "team personality" detailed in Authentic Vocation Worksheet 7 on page 348.

   Clients with a team personality type should also consider how large a company they wish to work for. Though the team dynamic is manifested in both the ten-person company and the thousand-person company, the day-to-day experience in those two organizations will be quite different.

6. **Primary function.** The client needs to evaluate whether she prefers to work primarily with people, with data, or with things. Her hobbies and past jobs can

provide clues here: What activities have given her the most joy—those involving interaction with people, working with data or information, or working on things with her hands?

7. **Organizational culture.** Culture, or "how we do things around here," is a final factor in work environment. Does the client prefer a company that is conservative or radical, socially conscious or not, employee oriented or bottom line/results oriented? Does she prefer that the company have a clear vision and mission, or that it "go with the flow"?

Evaluating Culture

Author Daniel Goleman, in *Working with Emotional Intelligence,* calls the relationship with one's direct supervisor the most important component of employee satisfaction. In addition, the culture of a company and employees' sense of "fit" within it are also critical in employee satisfaction and retention.[31] In short, if they feel like they fit into the culture, they will stay with the company longer.

By *culture* we simply mean what makes one company feel different than another. It includes such things as behavior patterns, standards, values, overall "feel" of the organization, as well as everything the company does and everything it makes. Employees can make a sounder job choice by exploring and identifying the organizational culture before starting a job.

Following are a few ideas on evaluating culture you can pass along to clients for use in either informational interviews or job interviews.

Client Tips: Evaluating a Company's Culture

- Ask some pre-interview questions to determine the company's culture and whether it appears to be a fit
- If you are a manager or executive, ask members of the team you would be joining to participate in the interview process

- Ask to interview one or two people in the company that are not part of the formal hiring process to ask questions about culture only, not the job itself

- Take advantage of any available software, web sites, publications or testing that matches employee values with company values and culture

- Ask hypothetical questions such as, "What would happen if..." or, "What would the company do if...?" and listen carefully to both what is said and what is unsaid. What values are apparent?

- Seek out sources that rank companies such as national and local business magazines that publish an annual list of the "best companies to work for"

- Consult the 100 Best Companies for Working Mothers List at http://www.workingmother.com/?service=vpage/109, for insights into organizational culture for working parents

- Do a "scouting trip" of the company both during business hours and non-business hours: What do you notice about how people appear, what they are wearing, what their energy is? Is the parking lot full on the weekend, perhaps indicating long work hours?

- Do a Web search on the company to see if they appear in any interesting articles or unexpected places

Entrepreneurship

One of the fastest-growing forms of work today is entrepreneurship—owning your own business. As a career coach, you may be asked to guide someone who wants to start his or her own business, or at least wants to explore that as an option. You may choose to develop your own expertise in this area (though you will need additional training to do so), or you may partner with a coach who specializes in business start-ups and working with entrepreneurs. But initially, you can at least help your clients determine whether or not entrepreneurship is a potential fit for them, using the "Entrepreneurial Quiz" in the Career Coach's Toolbox (p. 351).

To learn how to coach clients who wish to become entrepreneurs, consider the Career Coach Institute home study course, "Coaching the Entrepreneurial Client," available at www.careercoachinstitute.com

Telecommuting and Home-Based Work Options

As people get busier and try to balance the conflicting life demands, flexible work options such as telecommuting (aka teleworking) are of increasing interest. Teleworkers work from home and off-site locations at least part of the time. They use telephone, fax and internet to stay in contact with bosses, customers, and colleagues. Some of your clients may wish to pursue telework as an option. According to the national telephone survey data collected by Telework America (www.workingfromanywhere.org):

- The number of Americans whose employer allows them to work remotely at least one day per month increased 63 percent, from 7.6 million in 2004 to 12.4 million in 2006, according to a recent report issued by WorldatWork. In total, the sum of teleworkers (both employed and self-employed) working remotely at least one day per month has risen 10 percent from 26.1 million in 2005 to 28.7 million in 2006.[32]

- Thirty-nine percent of the workers who do not currently work remotely are interested in teleworking—and 13 percent of those workers would consider the ability to telework an important influence when making a decision to accept another job.[33]

- Roughly 20 percent of the American workforce is currently engaged in Telework.[34]

Clients who want to consider teleworking should know the relevant factors involved.

First, teleworking is not appropriate for every job. Some job activities do not lend themselves to telework. Organizations need to analyze the job activity, not the job title, to determine suitability to telework. The key is to find jobs with at least a portion of the work that can be done as well or better away from the office—taking advantage of technology and getting away from the distractions and interruptions experienced in the typical office.

Second, teleworking isn't for every worker. Just as being selective about the job activity is important, it's equally important to limit telework to employees who have the job knowledge/skills, personality, self-motivation, and home setting that will allow them to work effectively at home or elsewhere away from the office.

For some success stories of people who are teleworking and some resource links to teleworking opportunities, see www.telework101.com.

Key Coaching Concepts

1. The seven key aspects to be considered in Authentic Vocation Factor 7, "Work Environment," include geographic location, pace, support, compensation, company size, primary function, and organizational culture.
2. In evaluating a company's culture, several factors need to be considered including behavior patterns, standards, values, overall "feel" of the organization, as well as everything the company does and everything it makes.
3. Entrepreneurship is a growing trend; if clients indicate interest in starting their own business, we can help them determine whether they have the entrepreneurial personality.
4. Your guidance for clients who are considering teleworking should include two questions: (a) Is teleworking appropriate for the job? and (b) Is telework right for this client?

11

Authentic Vocation™ Factor 8: Business Reality

"MONEY IS A TERRIBLE MASTER BUT AN EXCELLENT SERVANT."
—*P.T. Barnum*

Once our clients have identified the kinds of work that will fulfill them emotionally, they then need to filter their ideas through "business reality," which asks tough questions such as: "Can this occupation support you financially? Does it allow you to sustain the life-style to which you are, or would like to be, accustomed?"

Business reality is placed last in the Authentic Vocation model by design. If we allow our clients to become overly focused on income potential and viability of their desired work too early in the process, their creativity will be stifled. In *The Artist's Way*, author Julia Cameron points out that many times artists (which can be anyone, not just gifted painters or musicians) become blocked because they are overly concerned about commercial sales potential for their creative output.[35]

We will get the best results if we help clients allow their ideas to flow freely first (as clients explore Authentic Vocation Factors 1 through 7), and only then - after the creative ideas have been expressed - should they deal with income potential and other aspects of business reality. (An exception is where clients have an urgent need for income.) In some cases the statistics will indicate that an occupation cannot support the client. Rather than giving up, we can encourage the client to apply a creative approach: Could this job become one element of a portfolio career? Or could strategic negotiation increase the compensation far beyond the averages due to what the client brings to the table, or by combining the duties of two positions?

We need to focus on four tasks at this stage:

1. **Determining market need.** Does the work the client wants to do meet a need in the business/work world?

2. **Evaluating financial feasibility.** Base on the client's needs and goals, are the job targets financially realistic?

3. **Measuring job targets for viability.** Are there enough potential or actual positions to make the job targets viable for a full-scale job search?

4. **Understanding the job search time frame.** Is the client prepared, both mentally and financially, for the realistic length of his or her job search?

Determining Market Need

For some clients, market need is so obvious as not to preclude the need for extensive inquiry. If a client's job targets clearly fall within one of the ten primary functional areas of the organization we examined in The Career Transition Report (see chapter 6), and there is a plethora of help wanted ads for that type of work each week, market need is clearly present. For example, there is nearly always a need for sales representatives, accountants, human resource professionals, and some information technology positions. *Can what you do in the past be reframed to apply to other occupations?*

Even for these seemingly obvious needs, however, it is still advisable for clients to check the latest data in the Occupational Outlook Handbook (OOH) (http://www.bls.gov/oco/) and similar sources to see whether the occupation is expected to grow—and at what pace—remain stagnant, or decline in the coming years. Regional and statewide occupational data from web sites such as Career Guide to Industries (http://www.bls.gov/oco/cg/) and America's Career Infonet (http://www.acinet.org/acinet/), as well as the opinions of leaders within the industry, can supplement the OOH data and assure clients that they are making a viable choice.

Clients in midcareer often present a different type of challenge. They do not seem to quite fit into the standard boxes represented by traditional job descriptions. By this point they have completed their formal education and initial job(s) after graduation, have accumulated some work experience, and have proven themselves according to the external standards of success. That is, they often have a family as well as investments, a home, one or more automobiles, and other trappings of prosperity. The problem is, these clients have become bored, fed up, unchallenged or burned out on doing what has constituted their livelihood so far. There's another part of themselves that wants to emerge, a talent or skill thus far untapped in their professional life. In my experience working with dozens of midlife career changers, the most satisfying work for clients in the second half of their life often combines—in creative and many times unexpected ways—the talents they have exhibited in their first few jobs plus the additional part of themselves that is trying to emerge.

My own career path is one example of this. As I chose my first few jobs, they drew upon my organizational and business skills, which I enjoyed using. My twelve years in the legal field was part of that competency focus that characterizes most people's initial positions. But the time came when merely excelling with those skills began to feel empty. I needed something more in my work. The creative part of me that had previously found expression when I studied music and dabbled in art in college, or when I prepared a gourmet meal for a dinner party, was not finding expression in my work. It was only when I discovered consulting—and later coaching and coach training—and began doing that work as an entrepreneur that I found satisfaction. The strategic planning, marketing, writing, and curriculum development satisfied my creative urge, while the financial and business responsibilities fulfilled the analytical side of my talents.

When working with midcareer clients, often the best approach for articulating a desired career and evaluating the need in the workplace or business market for it is to encourage a "both/and" approach. Perhaps, instead of choosing something entirely different from one's prior work as a next step (and failing to draw on the wealth in that experience), one can find a way to combine that with the untapped skill set in a new position—and then propose it to a firm that has a need for it. So rather than "either this or that," clients can combine both and create a win-win result. Clients increase their satisfaction and avoid compromising their financial goals, and the employer has fulfilled a previously unmet need. Benefits to corporations in these cases can include savings in human capital expenditure, since many times one person ends up filling two roles that would have otherwise required two separate employees. The acid test of whether a newly designed job targets meets a need is ultimately whether one or more firms respond positively to a proposal submitted by the client offering that blend of abilities and services. For more on this subject, see chapter 22.

Evaluating Financial Feasibility

Next, we help clients examine whether the job will provide the salary and benefits as well as growth opportunities to meet their needs. Fortunately, there is ample free information readily available on the Internet. We can also suggest that they ask key questions in informational interviews with people working in the industry to determine typical pay ranges for their desired job(s).

The following Web sites should help clients determine salary ranges for the type of work they are seeking:

- http://online.wsj.com/careers
- www.jobsmart.org
- www.abbott-langer.com
- www.wageweb.com
- www.salary.com
- http://www.bls.gov/OES/
- www.rileyguide.com
- http://www.bls.gov/oco/
- http://blogs.payscale.com/ask_dr_salary/

A fee-based service to which you can subscribe, or ask for a per-client report regarding salary data, is Pay Scale, www.payscale.com.

In addition, clients seeking employment in a specific geographic location may want to consult a salary calculator program to make any regional cost-of-living adjustments to the industry averages. (See, for example, http://www.homefair.com/calc/salcalc.html.)

Measuring Job Targets for Viability

Once clients have chosen at least three to five target jobs (or careers) that seem interesting, each needs to be evaluated for viability. Clients may find the target is too specialized (and therefore too small a pool of potential employers), or too large with a lot of openings and options—but too many to strategically pursue. Clients should then complete the form below in Fig. 12 to determine each job target's opportunity.

Figure 12: Formula for Measuring Job Targets

For each target, determine:	_____
Desired company size:	_____
Desired position/job/function/role:	_____
Desired geographic area:	_____
Size of target market:	_____
a. Total number of organizations	_____
b. Number of probable positions fitting desired criteria in each organization:	_____
a x b. Total number of probable and suitable positions	_____

Source: Adapted from Kate Wendleton, *Targeting the Job You Want* (Franklin Lakes, NJ: Career Press, 2000).

This information and other data used for refining targets can be obtained through:

- Industry associations

- Trade publications, magazines
- www.hoovers.com
- Labor market information for your local area (contact your State Labor Department or State Employment Department)
- U.S. Department of Labor Web sites; see http://www.dol.gov/
- ERISS: www.usworks.com; select target city or region
- Local chamber of commerce
- State and local Economic Development Department

Kate Wendleton of the Five O'Clock Club offers a rule of thumb for the viability of a job target: "A target list of 200 positions in a healthy market results in seven interviews that result in one job offer."[36] So if there are fewer than two hundred potential positions within a client's target, the target may need to be refined or expanded.

Understanding the Job Search Time Frame

Most people just beginning their job search—particularly if it is due to an unexpected layoff—underestimate how long it will likely take for them to become re-employed. While there are exceptions, as a general rule the average length of a job search for a professional or manager is three to six months, regardless of the economy or other factors. Another commonly cited guideline is that it often takes as much as one month for every $10,000 of income/salary the candidate was making to find gainful employment.

In addition, the following factors can significantly affect the length of candidates' search, however, and may provide openings for coaching to shorten the search.

Rate 1.5

Clients' clarity on their job/career target. If your clients come to you already knowing what kind(s) of work they want to do, the exploration process will be fairly short. In fact, the work can begin with designing a job search marketing plan, one or more resumes, and coaching them in the execution of their search. The reality is that clients who are that clear about what they want to do rarely seek career coaching; they can conduct a successful search on their own. But market changes such as the recent decline of the information technology and Internet fields can test the resourcefulness of even people who have clear job targets.

Geographic scope/limits. This factor includes two types of clients. First are clients who are open to relocating anywhere within the U.S. or another broad geographical area. Their search may be shortened because recruiters with a national scope can more easily place such a candidate, and there are more total possibilities available to them. However, conducting the search itself—particularly the aspects that deal with targeted contacts to companies and individuals—can be overwhelming unless clients select two or three cities, states, or regions that are their top preferences and focus them first.

The second type are clients who are absolutely committed to staying where they are—or, even more difficult, clients who have moved to a city for life-style reasons and now want to get a job there. This may be due to having children close to finishing high school, community ties, family in the area, or just a preference to stay where they are. The length of the search is usually prolonged because the pool of available possibilities is much smaller for these clients. Conversely, the execution of the search is more manageable due to this smaller pool.

Even the latter type of client can sometimes have delightful results. I worked with an information technology manager in Orange County, California, who had just built a lovely beachfront house and did not want to move despite her recent layoff. In fact, she said she wanted a job within two miles of where she lived—and this in a part of the country where commutes of an hour or more are not uncommon! Within just three months, she was hired into an IT manager position with a leading Internet firm that needed her exact expertise, and the position was in fact located within two miles of her home!

Job searches in the same field versus a career change. When clients are seeking a position within an industry in which they have experience, the job search time tends to be shortened for several reasons. First, they know the companies to approach, have a network in the industry and area, and will be favorably considered by screeners when applying for published openings—assuming the industry is hiring. Career changers, on the other hand, typically need to rely on the unpublished job market for their opportunities, and will often spend more coaching time clarifying their goals. For these reasons, their job search time is usually (but not always) longer than that of other clients.

Size of existing network of contacts. It is not necessarily true that the larger the client's network, the sooner the job search is completed. But when clients have a substantial network of contacts both within and outside their target industries, it does facilitate the process of getting connected with the right people for both published and unpublished openings. Even then, however, clients may need to be coached about how to most strategically utilize their network, as we will explore in chapter 22.

network in target area

Marketability of clients' skills. Are your clients' skills and background marketable in the current climate? In other words, is there a demand for what they have to offer? The more demand there is, generally speaking, the shorter the search (it can literally be a matter of days instead of months to complete a search in some cases!). Of course, the reality is that when a company downsizes, reorganizes, closes a division, or otherwise eliminates a long-standing function from its business, the skills of those workers may be outmoded in today's marketplace. I once facilitated a series of job search workshops for employees of the Forms Division in a major paper-manufacturing firm when that division was eliminated. Many of the men who worked there had twenty-five to thirty years with the company and literally did not know what else to do—yet the skills that had been desirable in that company for so many years had no real market value with other companies. Retraining was an option for some, early retirement for others.

Market and economic conditions. The conditions of the job marketplace and the economy of the local area and country where the candidate is searching, as well as the global economy, all have an impact on the length of the search. During prosperous times, when there are more jobs available than candidates to fill them, openings are filled quickly. During recessions or other economic downturns (whether global or limited to one industry or type of work), it takes longer for a candidate to find suitable employment because there is greatly increased competition for each opening. With the aging of the Baby Boom generation, some retiring and many continuing to work, skilled worker shortages are cropping up in unprecedented numbers in some sectors of the economy also.

Clients' attitude, self-confidence, and personality style. Clients to some extent influence how long their search will take based on whether they are optimistic or pessimistic, confident or unsure, and even introverted or extroverted. A pessimistic, "poor me" attitude will be noticed subliminally—if not overtly—by interviewers and networking contacts alike, making the candidate less desirable. Conversely, an enthusiastic, "can-do" attitude is contagious and makes people want to hire a person with such an outlook.

Clients who are introverted and have difficulty picking up the phone to call people they do not know can be successful in their job search but may find that the search takes longer. We'll talk in chapter 20 about some ways to adjust the job search plan for this variable, but in my experience extroverted, gregarious clients generally have an easier time with the job search and find a job faster than those that lack these qualities.

Financial reserves and/or severance. Clients' ability to sustain themselves during the transition period can make a huge difference in how aggressive they are in their search. There's nothing like needing to make next month's mortgage payment to stimulate job search activity! Yet many clients who received a generous severance package, affording them the luxury of a few months off, will take the time off. While I would not discourage taking a mini-sabbatical, clients also need to be aware that a recent gap on their resume may be perceived as a liability. Screeners often jump to the conclusion that the job seeker has been searching throughout the time gap and has been unsuccessful so far. When clients decide to exercise this option, they need to be aware of the potential consequences. We will discuss a strategy to counter the negative perception in chapter 24.

Support by family and friends. Are clients' family members supportive of their job search, or continually asking when they will get back to work? Do your clients have friends or a support group from whom they can draw encouragement and with whom they can share ideas during the "emotional roller coaster" of being between jobs? I always became wary when a client's spouse wanted to talk with me or meet with me midway through the client's search; it was usually a clear sign that the spouse is applying more pressure than is appropriate on the client, which - even if well intentioned - does not help the client meet his or her goals.

Amount of effort and commitment invested. Looking for a job takes time. In fact, with unemployed clients, their job search *is* their job until they find a new position. As a general rule, unemployed clients (or full-time job seekers) should spend four to six hours each day on their search, and employed clients (part-time job seekers) should spend one to two hours each day and at least a half-day each weekend in job search activities. Clients who apply these levels of effort should find work within the three- to six-month average search time. Those who exert only a half-hearted effort or spend half of each unemployed day playing golf or watching soap operas on television can extend their search time dramatically.

Failing the Test

You may be wondering what happens when clients' desired job or career targets don't pass the business reality test. Does that mean they must give up on the quest for greater satisfaction, even fulfillment, on the job? Of course not. Here again, your coaching skills can make the difference between clients finding a way to pursue their passion and letting it die on the vine.

For example, Dave wanted to leave his job as a production manager to be a stand-up comedian. Stand-up comedy, like acting and music performing, is a field in which people tend to become highly successful or spend years struggling. The first approach to take in such cases is to probe in order to discover the essence of what appeals to clients about their desired occupation. Do they want to have the opportunity to "work the crowd" and be in the spotlight? Do they desire to lighten up what has been a serious, tedious life-style? Do they feel they have a calling to do this type of work? These questions often reveal an urge that could be expressed in a number of ways. Dave could become a humorous motivational speaker if his essential goal were to get in front of people and share his sense of humor. He might even be able to bring more humor into his current position and experience increased satisfaction as more of his true self is revealed.

Alternatively, if Dave says that stand-up comedy is truly the occupation he wants, and anything else would be a compromise, we move into what we call Level 1 coaching (described in part 3) and brainstorm possible ways to achieve his goal. Could he start doing stand-up at night while maintaining his production job? Who could he choose as a mentor to help him get started and learn the basics of the business? These and other logistical considerations could allow Dave to make a gradual transition into the job of his dreams and learn as he goes how successful he can be. The point is, we as coaches must often be creative and help clients go beyond stereotypes and initial obstacles if they are to create the job of their dreams and make a living doing it.

Authentic Vocation Profile   p. 357

Once you have completed your coaching with a client on all 8 elements of Authentic Vocation, an added service is to compile their results – along with results of any assessments you may have administered, summaries from online sources regarding outlook on top 5 career choices, and other relevant data – into a booklet or pdf report you can call the "Authentic Vocation Profile." A sample appears on p. 357. (The author acknowledges CCI Instructor and Master Certified Career Coach Valerie McClure for this wonderful addition to the Authentic Vocation work!)

KEY COACHING CONCEPTS

1. Business reality asks clients, among other things, "Can this occupation support you financially? Does it allow you to sustain the life-style to which you are, or would like to be, accustomed?"

2. There are four key considerations in using the business reality filter:

    • Does the work the client wants to do meet a need in the business/work world?

    • Are the job targets the client has selected financially feasible?

    • Are there enough potential or actual positions to make the job targets viable for a full-scale job search?

    • Is the client prepared, both mentally and financially, for the realistic length of his or her job search?

3. Once you finish all eight Authentic Vocation Worksheets and the coaching on them with a client, you can provide an Authentic Vocation Profile to summarize the results of this and any related work, including assessment results.

PART THREE

QUANTUMSHIFT!
COACHING PRINCIPLES

12

The QuantumShift!™ Coaching Model: Getting to Aha!

"CHANGE COMES TO OUR LIVES NOT ONLY FROM SHIFTS IN OUR INNER NEEDS, BUT ALSO FROM SHIFTS IN OUR EXTERNAL CIRCUMSTANCES... WHEN WE RESPECT THE NATURAL CYCLES OF LIFE, WE FIND THAT EACH OF LIFE'S STAGES HAS A SPIRITUAL DIMENSION."
—*Jack Kornfield,* A Path with Heart

Now that coaching as a profession is coming into its own, a plethora of coaching models exists. At this writing there are hundreds of coach training schools, each with its own approach to coaching. So, you may be wondering, why do we need yet another model? And where does QuantumShift! coaching fit into the mix? The answer: it provides the structure, methods, and techniques by which we help our clients access their Authentic Vocation (and can also be used by coaches in other disciplines to elicit desired solutions from clients too!).

At Career Coach Institute (CCI) we use the definition of coaching, the ethical standards, and the competencies established by the International Coach Federation (ICF), as described in chapters 1 and 2 (modified for the career coaching context), as standards for our coach training. Merely adhering to ICF's universal definition and standards, however, does not delineate a specific coaching approach or model. Many of the commonly used models of coaching today work on the level of "effects" or behavior only. For example, a client comes into a coaching session and says he is worried about being able to pay next month's mortgage. Many coaches would address the issue by exploring possible issues at a surface level only. They would brainstorm with the client about his budget, where he could cut expenses, how to get a raise in pay or bring in more income from other sources, and the like.

While this approach may in some ways be useful, it is nevertheless superficial; it does not address deeper systemic issues within the client's belief system. If, for example, we could help our client identify his belief that he deserves only enough money to survive – and then transform that belief – that could automatically solve the problem of paying the mortgage, and conceivably every other financial challenge the person is facing. QuantumShift! Coaching (QSC) is a deeper, more lasting, fundamental, and broad-reaching transformation than merely problem solving to find a solution to the current issue. The immediate situation, we believe, is usually a symptom of a belief-based coaching issue, and working at the deeper level will create a higher impact for clients. And when they "get it," the shift that occurs—a *quantum* shift—is immediate and usually permanent. After that, if it is still necessary, the surface-level brainstorming and problem solving can be done—we call it Level 1 coaching—but it has more meaning because it is within the context of the larger change.

Quantum shifts, also known as quantum leaps, or jumps, in quantum physics refer to unexpected sudden moves to another state of being. When an electron is about to make a quantum leap to a new orbit, it puts out temporary feelers toward its own future stability by trying out—all at once—all the possible new orbits into which it might eventually settle. These temporary feelers are called "virtual transitions," and the actual transition of the electron into its new, permanent home a "real transition." [37]

The behavior of electrons as they "try on" new orbits and then make a sudden leap parallels human behavior as we explore options prior to making a dramatic shift in our behavior or beliefs or career. In much the same way we might try out a new idea by throwing out imaginary scenarios depicting their many possible consequences.

The discovery of quantum physics completely turned the former paradigm—Newtonian physics—on its ear. And QuantumShift! coaching does that with former coaching paradigms, too.

The QSC model (see fig. 13) is deceptively simple in theory: it outlines three key coaching competencies, each of which is used during a complete coaching session. We begin by establishing rapport with the client (whether a new client or as a continuation of an ongoing client relationship) and the agenda or issue to be discussed in the coaching session. The majority of the remaining time is spent using the second competency: exploring and elaborating upon the issue the client has raised, using a wide variety of techniques. The third competency or phase of the session is eliciting a plan for action, in which the client determines at least one step he or she is going to execute in the coming week.

Figure 13: QuantumShift!™ Model

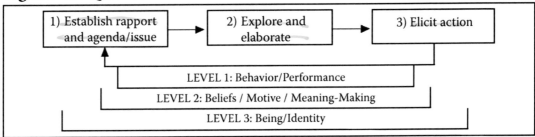

As alluded to earlier, there are three levels of QuantumShift! Coaching, adding a second dimension to the use of the three coaching competencies. Level 1 deals with behavior, performance, and the surface level of effects. Level 2 works at the level of beliefs, motivation, and other thought systems that undergird our daily activities. And Level 3 involves our identity, our views of our inner self, and who we are. Each level will be explored in detail in its later chapters.

Perhaps the difference between QuantumShift! and other coaching methods can be made more apparent with an example. John was a member of a project team, but at team meetings he sat quietly, did not offer ideas, folded his arms, and looked away during the discussions. A coach using Level 1 coaching would try to change his withdrawn behavior and train him in communication techniques and effective body language. A QuantumShift! coach using Level 2 coaching would explore his beliefs about being on a team, see if anything is demotivating him about being on the team or how the team is approaching the project, and perhaps administer an assessment dealing with team dynamics, styles of interacting, and the like. Going even deeper, a QuantumShift! coach using Level 3 coaching would probe how John views himself vis-à-vis the team and what kind of person he perceives himself to be. The coach might use a 360-degree assessment or other personality evaluation tool to increase John's awareness about his own natural strengths and weaknesses, and ask, "Who do you need to be in order to make involvement on the team more engaging for you?"

Keep in mind that QuantumShift! coaching isn't quite as simple as it initially appears. The following chapters will further help you distinguish differences between coaching styles by isolating specific elements of the model for individual treatment.

The Role and Results of QuantumShift! Coaching

Of course the real proof in the effectiveness of QuantumShift! coaching lies in its results. Both on the personal level and in the organizational context, QuantumShift! coaching can have a dramatic effect, especially as part of a blended learning approach. A successful coach will help clients clarify their goals and streamline their job search process, resulting in a career move that is more satisfying.

When a company is considering implementing coaching, whether through the use of external coaches or an internal manager-as-coach or a coaching staff approach, it is often because it is noticing performance problems. Perhaps productivity is off, morale is lower than desired, error rates are up in the production line, or they want to increase the amount of claims processed or widgets produced per employee dollar paid. While coaching can help with these issues, there are other reasons for bringing in coaches, too. Fully 86 percent of companies hire coaches to sharpen the leadership skills of high potentials, and 72 percent hire them to correct management behavior problems, according to recent industry research.[38]

In our experience organizations frequently make one or more of the following three mistakes when considering using coaching:

1. **Relying unduly on training.** They send the individuals involved to a training session, thinking content provided in a classroom setting will fix the problem. No follow-up intervention is attempted.

2. **Failing to identify and leverage strengths.** They fail to assess the strengths or natural abilities of their employees and match them to the best job to maximize their contribution to the firm. Instead, they focus on individuals' weaknesses and try to improve them—which, as Marcus Buckingham and Donald O. Clifton point out in *Now Discover Your Strengths,* will never create optimum performance.[39]

3. **Settling for surface-level performance coaching.** They bring in coaches that use "performance coaching," one form of the surface-level coaching described above. Even when that coaching seems to resolve the current situation, other problems crop up in its wake. Each situation then requires separate coaching efforts, resulting in higher costs for the company and a never-ending stream of coaching needs. (Can you see how QuantumShift! coaches tend to make themselves obsolete faster than others?)

The QuantumShift! alternative to the first mistake is to combine training with coaching. A research study written by Professional Certified Career Coach™ Denise Bane, Ph.D., found that when training is combined with coaching, individuals increase their productivity by an average of 88 percent, compared to 22.4 percent with training alone.[40] That's quite a difference! And in another recent study of three thousand companies by the University of Pennsylvania, 10 percent of revenues invested in capital improvements increased productivity by 3.9 percent, versus an 8.5 percent increase from a similar investment in developing human capital.[41]

Regarding mistake 2, QuantumShift! coaching draws on the concept of strengths. It uses an appreciative approach to inquire into what is working well, what employees like in their job and what they would like to do more of, and helps match natural abilities with a fulfilling job.

Levels 2 and 3 of the QSC model directly address mistake 3 by probing into beliefs, motivations, and identity, when appropriate, to facilitate systemic change at both the individual and organizational levels.

Three Principles of QuantumShift! Coaching

The QSC model draws on three key principles from quantum physics. In this new world of physics, as in some Eastern philosophies such as Buddhism, the relationship between cause and effect is not always linear. For example, the Buddhists talk about "not doing" as sometimes being the best type of action to take. In *Zen Mind, Beginner's Mind,* Shunryu Suzuki writes, "In calmness there should be activity; in activity there should be calmness. Actually, they are the same thing."[42] This does not make sense to our rational Western mind, but if we practice meditation, martial arts, or similar disciplines, perhaps we can discover its meaning. With that in mind, let's examine the three core QSC principles.

1. **Change occurs discontinuously, and its source is unpredictable.** As you learn coaching techniques and begin working with clients, you may expect that clients' most significant changes will come directly from your brilliant coaching questions, or from their doing a certain activity that you have suggested. And that may happen! But just as often, the changes clients need to make actually occur due to an offhand comment they hear while carrying out their daily tasks, or a thought that occurs to them while they are driving to work. That is not to say that you had no role in their transformation, just that the path to change is not necessarily linear. When people set their intention toward change, a series of events and people are drawn into their life because of that intention. Yet it is not just one of those people or events that causes the transformation, but the combination of them—or something else seemingly unrelated—that causes the client to shift.

    An example from my own life a few years ago was the transition that led to my founding Career Coach Institute. I had spent the previous year feeling lost in my professional life. Though outwardly successful, I was no longer challenged by what I had been doing as senior vice president in a career management firm. I needed something more creative, more flexible (since my husband had just retired), and over which I had a greater sense of ownership than the salaried job offered. After attending many personal growth workshops, reading dozens of books, and enrolling in a business coach training program, I still felt unclear about what was next for me. I also took a teleleader training course that equipped me to lead classes over the phone.

As my husband and I drove back from our Thanksgiving holiday with my family, I was trying to develop topics to offer as teleclasses to complete my teleleader certification. Suddenly, like a bolt of lightning, it struck me: I could combine my years of experience in career development with teleclasses and coach training and have a one-of-a-kind career coach training school. I knew instinctively that it was the kind of inspiration that constitutes a "calling," as Gregg LeVoy describes it in his book, *Callings*.[43] Yet it wasn't anything my husband said, anything my coach at the time did, or anything else that was causally related in time that led to my epiphany; it was a combination of those things and some quiet time to think and reflect. This is an example of principle 1 in action.

2. **We create, or at least heavily influence, our own reality and thus create a "coaching space."** Scientists have actually observed that a particle will change its entire nature and turn into a wave when they begin watching its activity. The observer is somehow connected to the particle in a way not previously understood.[44] This applies in coaching in that by our merely coming together with a client, a third space, which we refer to as the "coach space," is created—and that is where our interaction occurs. It is co-created by the coach and client as the session proceeds. New ideas, insights, and results then emerge that would not have occurred by just sitting and thinking about the issue, keeping a journal, or doing other individual activities without a coach.

3. **Be open to synchronicity!** As coaches we need to expect synchronicity, or "meaningful coincidence," to occur in our work with clients. In doing so, what appears impossible becomes possible by combining the power of dedicated intention with an openness to how it manifests. (For more on synchronicity, see chapter 20.) According to Joseph Jaworski in *Synchronicity: The Inner Path of Leadership*,

It's critical that you focus on the result and not get attached to any particular process for achieving the result. When we are in the process of creating something, we must have the flexibility of mind to move with what needs to be done. What allows this to happen is precisely the fact that we're not attached to how things should be done. It's a little bit like sailing. If you're focused on your course rather than your destination, you're in big trouble. If you were to be blown off course, you would never simply return to the course you were on. No one would sail that way. Rather, you would focus on the destination and set a new course. But that's the way we live our lives. We get attached to our assumptions about how things should get done.[45]

We will explore how to get behind assumptions as we delve further into the QSC model.

Desired Outcomes of Successful Career Coaching

As we use the QSC model in our coaching, we seek to achieve four ultimate outcomes for clients:

1. **Enhanced self-awareness.** One goal is to facilitate clients' process of knowing themselves better, particularly in comparison with personality styles other than their own (e.g., using one or more assessments). Clients will also bring to conscious awareness previously unconscious beliefs, motivations, and principles that would otherwise keep them on "automatic pilot" in making decisions. Greater self-awareness leads to more conscious choices in every aspect of life, including career.

2. **Clarity of purpose and goals.** As you have read, life purpose is the foundation of Authentic Vocation, and we believe it is the secret to finding fulfillment in one's work. QuantumShift! coaching is in part designed to increase clients' clarity regarding their life purpose. In addition, as an organizing principle it leads to clearer long- and short-term goals.

3. **Increased career self-management.** In today's turbulent work climate, workers must manage their own career and exercise career self-management as though

they were self-employed. This is the only kind of "job security" that exists today. QuantumShift! career coaching is the equivalent of teaching people how to fish, rather than handing them a fish, so they can manage their career for a lifetime, not just during this transition.

4. **Overall improved quality of life**. As clients' fulfillment at work increases, it is certain to spill over into other areas of their life. And as life purpose is used as a filter to determine which life roles to increase and which to decrease, work/life balance also improves and with it, quality of life. So in a very real sense, participating in QuantumShift! career coaching betters the quality of one's overall life experience.

KEY COACHING CONCEPTS

1. The QuantumShift Coaching model includes three competencies: (a) establish rapport and the agenda, (b) exploring and elaborating on the issue, and (c) eliciting action.

2. There are three levels of QSC—Level 1: behavior and performance; Level 2: beliefs and motivators; and Level 3: identity and sense of self.

3. Companies seeking to incorporate coaching often make one or more of three mistakes: (a) relying unduly on training; (b) failing to identify and leverage strengths; and (c) settling for surface-level performance coaching.

4. QuantumShift! coaching is based on three principles: (a) change occurs discontinuously, and its source is unpredictable; (b) we create, or at least heavily influence, a new own reality through the "coaching space,"; and (c) be open to synchronicity!

5. Career coaching should achieve four desired outcomes: (a) enhanced self-awareness; (b) clarity regarding life purpose and goals; (c) increased career self-management; and (d) overall improved quality of life.

13

Initiating the Coaching Relationship

"NO MATTER HOW LONG YOU'VE BEEN LOOKING FOR IT, SUCCESS USUALLY FINDS YOU BEFORE YOU'RE READY."
—*Barbara Sher,* Wishcraft

So it's happened: a prospective client has called you to inquire about your coaching services. What do you do next? While this chapter is not a primer on sales skills, it is about handling clients from inquiry to commencement of coaching. The best coaches don't "sell" their skills per se, but instead instill a sense within their clients and prospects that they understand their needs and can help them meet their needs or solve their stated problems.

Let's explore some common reasons people would call a career coach. Your job at this point is both to understand and identify prospects' needs and to dig deeper (yes, it starts here) to help them see underlying issues and/or broader solutions than they may initially anticipate. Typically, prospects contact a coach because they:

- Have been laid off (or "made redundant")
- Dislike their job
- Dislike their career and want to explore a change
- Want to make more money
- Need a new resume
- Have a job search liability which they need help in overcoming

- Have never conducted a job search (either "fell into" each job or have been with one company their entire career)
- Want to advance/get a promotion
- Want to start their own business
- Are overstressed and want some relief

In each case, we want to ask more about their stated needs, how they believe coaching will be beneficial, and whether our services are appropriate for them. The ICF competencies require that we not misrepresent our services, and that we refer inappropriate clients to another coach or service provider. Fig. 14 illustrates the process that we go through as we decide whether or not a match exists.

It is during this initial conversation with the new client when we need to define career coaching, simply, and clarify how it is different from other roles such as therapy, career counseling, and consulting (review chapter 1 for more details). It is also a good time to outline the respective roles of coach and client, to be further elaborated in a written coaching agreement.

The prospective client may have both questions to ask and what in sales jargon are called "objections," or reasons they may not want to buy ("It's too costly," "I'm not sure I have the time," "Maybe now is not the right time," "I need to interview other coaches, too," etc.). The professional career coach simply addresses these objections one at a time and suggests a coaching program or package that will meet the client's needs for a reasonable fee.

Most career coaches charge on a monthly basis, no less than US $300 per month and upwards of US $2500 per month if working with executive clients or in a technical specialty area. That fee can include three or four half-hour coaching sessions, once a week (some coaches work a three-week month), as well as assessments, workbooks or books with relevant information to the coaching process, access to a networking group if the coach offers one, e-mail between sessions, and the like. (NOTE: as bo-

Figure 14: Determining the Match Between Prospect and Coach

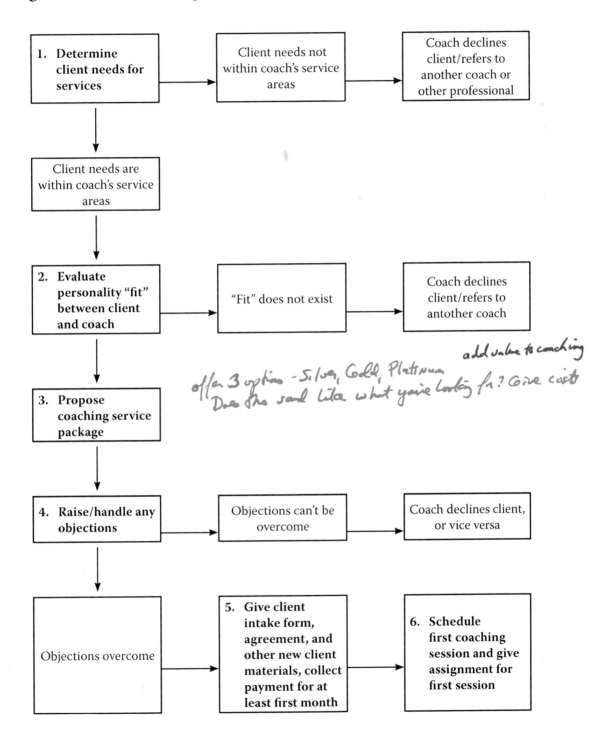

nus just for readers of this book, visit the following link to obtain your free Fee Setting Calculator to determine the hourly and monthly fees that will ensure you can pay your overhead, pay your net income, and make a profit in your business: www.careercoachinstitute.com/feesettingformula.html)

Most coaches, regardless of specialty, request a ninety-day minimum commitment from the client. The work may continue for more or less time than that (and if shorter, a prorated refund may be appropriate). But that gets both client and coach into a committed relationship and gives enough time to work through both the stated issues and their implications.

Newer models of delivering coaching services – which I call "Career Coaching 2.0" – which minimize live phone time and serve a wider range of clients use an "infopreneur" (information entrepreneur) approach, versus offering coaching services as a standalone service. Such strategies as "coaching gyms," membership programs, information products and other innovative approaches are described in a 9-step system in the author's related book, *Career Infopreneur's Success Roadmap* (High Flight Press 2007) available at www.careercoachinstitute.com.

The New Client Materials Packet

Once the prospect has agreed to become a client, some type of written agreement and other initial forms should be provided. With corporate clients, a written contract will be required. With individual clients, use of a written agreement is recommended, both to clarify all aspects of the coaching relationship and to help ease clients' foray into the coaching relationship. In addition, written agreements facilitate resolution if there is ever a misunderstanding about any aspect of the engagement.

One special note at this stage concerning corporate clients: when hired by a corporation to work with employees within the organization, special care must be taken to clarify who the client is and to whom you owe confidentiality. Several coaching agreement forms that can be customized to your needs are provided in the Career

Coach's Toolbox (pp. 362-367). *Caveat*: please have an attorney review the form you choose before using it to ensure that it satisfies the legal standards of your jurisdiction. Several states in the U.S. have much stricter standards than others regarding how coaches must represent themselves to the public. With some client populations, you may also want to include hold-harmless or disclaimer provisions to protect you from unintended liability.

In addition to the agreement itself, you may include in the new client materials packet a welcome letter and a set of policies or guidelines your firm uses (if not outlined in the agreement) in the event a session must be postponed or missed for whatever reason. Tools from the Career Coach's Toolbox such as "What Do Career Coaches Do?" (p. 387), Job Satisfaction Inventory (p. 314), and "What is Authentic Vocation?" (p. 385) can also be included, along with the Coaching Intake Form (p. 368) with instructions for the client to follow. Finally, if any assessments are to be administered at the outset of the coaching, instructions on completing them online or on paper can be another item included in the new client materials packet. Most professional career coaches now provide their new client materials packet, as well as other client materials, electronically for ease of transmission and response. We recommend this practice.

The Intake Session

One of the initial issues you will need to decide as a policy for your practice is how you will structure the intake session with your new clients. There are no hard-and-fast rules on this now; however, there are a few protocols that most coaches follow.

Prior to the intake coaching session—during initial conversation with the client—you probably gained a sense of how coachable he is. That is, is he mentally healthy? Is he open to the process? Can you help him with the issues he presents? and so on. The "Are You Coachable?" worksheet in the Career Coach's Toolbox (p. 361) can help you and your clients decide whether coaching is the appropriate intervention at this time for the issues they are facing.

Length of Intake Session

Most coaches choose one of the following two formats in the intake session:

1. **Same length as regular session.** The coach discusses the coaching process with clients when they sign up and asks them to review the contract, if there is one, as well as complete a Coaching Intake Form and review any other materials prior to the first session. The first and subsequent sessions are each twenty to thirty minutes in length. No additional fee is charged for the intake session in this scenario.

2. **Extended session.** The coach holds a one- to two-hour intake session in which to explain the coaching process, gets the coaching agreement signed, reviews any initial intake forms and/or assessments that clients have completed, and set goals/desired outcomes for the coaching interaction. This session is typically charged at a rate equaling 50 percent of one month's coaching in addition to regular coaching charges for the balance of the sessions that month.

Coaches may choose format 1 because they find that their clients are resistant to paying an additional fee for the intake session. Or, they may simply prefer to start with the standard session length, using the first session to discuss the intake form and give clients an immediate coaching experience. Coaches who prefer format 2 use it as a "stick" strategy in that they believe that the longer session creates a more solid rapport at the outset. They also will frequently discuss the results of an assessment here to give clients an immediate experience with the coaching process.

Virtual or Face-to-Face

Another decision for you to make here is whether to hold the intake session face-to-face or over the phone. For local clients you may prefer to hold an initial face-to-face session so that you get more of a sense of the person, his or her personality, and so on. For corporate clients, where you need to establish a rapport with both employees and their manager (who may be paying your fees), a face-to-face meeting may make the process go more smoothly and facilitate an effective interaction. The logistical issue in meeting face-to-face with individual clients is that you will need a professional space to hold the meeting. While some coaches meet new clients in a coffee shop or restaurant, privacy there is limited. Renting office space may be prohibitively expensive for a beginning coach. One alternative is office sharing or using the facilities of an executive suite where you can rent meeting space on an as-needed basis. In some cases, you can meet at a client company's facility.

If you decide not to hold a face-to-face intake session, or when clients are in distant locations, you may wish to request a photo of them (and share yours with them) so that you both have visual images to complement the audio impressions you get through the telecoaching.

The Intake Form
As you begin coaching with new clients, you will want them to complete an Intake Form. This form gives them a chance to tell you about themselves, and to communicate the most important issues on which they want to focus during the coaching interaction. A sample Intake Form is provided in the Career Coach's Toolbox (p. 368), which you are free to use with your clients if you wish.

One way to automate your intake process so that you have an easily accessible record is to use client-tracking software. Such software is affordable and often offers not only automated client intake, but also invoicing, client session preparation forms, payment history, tracking of marketing and practice-building activity, and continuing education tracking if you are working toward certification.

Benchmarks for a Successful Intake Session
When you have finished an intake session, how do you know it has met your client's needs? What skills do you need to apply to be effective in this part of the coaching interaction? Here is what our coaches have noticed:
- Clients feel excited about moving forward—and may express it
- When a rapport is established, clients feel comfortable sharing their issues

- Clients get a taste of what coaching is – and look forward to more
- The coach gains a better sense of clients' primary issues and personality style
- Coach and client come to agreement at the end of the intake session on the goals they will be focusing on throughout the coaching interaction (a kind of informal coaching plan)

The Coaching Plan

One final part of building the initial relationship is the development of a Coaching Plan. Listed as one of the ICF coaching core competencies, a Coaching Plan is an agreed-upon set of goals and objectives, based on a client's stated needs and desired outcomes, on which the client will work on throughout the coaching relationship. It can be formal or informal, depending on whether you are working with individual clients or within an organization, where periodic reporting may be required. The Coaching Plan is co-created by you and the client, ideally with the client being the one who takes the lead and records it, using the "Coaching Plan Worksheet " provided in the Career Coach's Toolbox (p. 373) and providing a copy to the coach after the session.

There are a number of advantages of having a Coaching Plan. First, it provides a structural bridge for taking clients from where they are to where they want to be. "If you fail to plan, you plan to fail," as the old adage goes. It is a point of reference at the beginning, middle, and end of the coaching relationship to remind clients what their goals are (or were), update them as the process unfolds, and see what they have accomplished when the coaching is completed. A Coaching Plan differs from the intake form/process in that it:

- Integrates the goals, desires, concerns, and perceived barriers stated on the intake form into a specific plan for development
- May draw on the results of one or more assessments, focusing on areas of desired development
- States specific outcomes to be achieved through the coaching interaction
- Is shorter than the intake form, usually just a page in length

- May be articulated for corporate clients at the outset of the coaching process, and for individual clients, after two to three sessions, once a rapport is clearly established and their most important goals become clearer

Benchmarking Clients' Current Situation

To formulate a Coaching Plan, clients must first have a sense of where they currently stand regarding the issues on which they want coaching. Numerous tools are available to assist them, including the "Ideal Day Wheel," a sample of which is shown in fig. 15. In this exercise clients imagine they are watching two movies—the first is of their current job and life-style, describing a typical day from awakening to bedtime, and the second is of their "ideal day," including work and personal aspects. From this narrative, two contrasting wheels can be developed that are divided proportionally by time spent on each type of task or activity during the day, now and in the ideal scenario.

Figure 15: Ideal Day Wheel

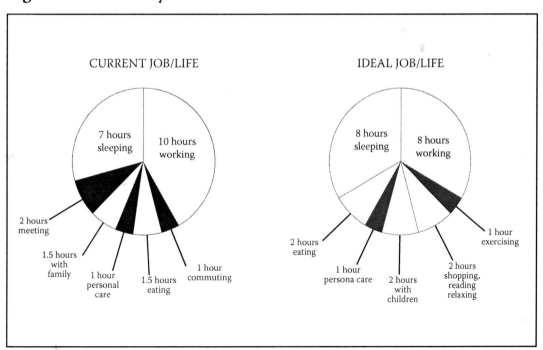

Another exercise that specifically addresses work is included in the Career Coach's Toolbox is the "Professional Balance Wheel" (p. 360) and the "Ideal Day Exercise" (p. 359).

Key Elements of a Coaching Plan

The three critical elements of a Coaching Plan are goals, action steps, and results.

1. **Goals.** Goals are the desired changes clients would like to make during the coaching interaction. They should be:

   - **Specific.** Goals should be specific enough to describe what clients will do and when they will do it, and they should be quantifiable.

   - **Realistic.** Goals should be "just out of reach, but not out of sight." That is, they should provide a stretch for the client but not be overly ambitious.

   - **Measurable.** Clients should be able to point to a specific result to know that the goal has been achieved. Any progress toward an overall goal should be observable so that it can be acknowledged. Setting a timeline is usually advised.

   - **Self-reliant.** Clients will sometimes set goals that depend on others for their achievement. For example, if their goal is to get a promotion within their department or company, that goal depends on someone giving them a good performance review, another person vacating his or her job, and someone deciding that the client fits that job.

When clients set these "other-dependent" goals, the coach should help him/her to determine the essence of the goal and reformulate it in those terms. The essence of the goal in the example above may be more money, gain more responsibility, get away from a difficult co-worker, or any number of other things. If the goal is stated in those terms, it has more than one possible way to be achieved—and it leaves room for synchronicity to occur.

The goals element answers the following questions:

   - "What do I want to change in my life in the next three to six months?"

- "What do I want to improve?"
- "What is in my way that I need to overcome?"

2. **Action steps.** Once the goals are clarified, we then help clients describe the action steps leading to their achievement. For example, if the goal is to move to a coastal town and have viable work there, initial actions steps might include:
   - Listing the criteria for the ideal location (small or large town, East vs. West Coast—or abroad, etc.)
   - Listing three to five towns that fit the stated criteria
   - Contacting each towns' chamber of commerce (via Internet, phone or "snail mail") for relevant information about them
   - Identifying Web sites that include job openings and company information for those areas

The action steps element answers the following questions:

- "What specific actions will I take to achieve my goals?"
- "Which action steps are most urgent [i.e., must be done first] and which are less urgent?" (helps clients prioritize)
- "If I need more resources, information, or contacts to achieve my goals, where will I find them?"

3. **Results.** Without concrete results there is no evidence of success. This is the payoff for achieving the goal! Some of the possible types of results might include measurable changes in behavior (e.g., instead of avoiding making phone calls to prospective employers, the client makes five phone calls per day); specific dates for completion; numbers of interviews, letters sent, resumes submitted, and so on. For example, if a client's goal is to find a job that pays $10,000 more per year, the result may be more financial peace of mind, a more secure retirement, the ability to improve his or her life-style or increase investments, and so on.

The results element answers the questions,

- "What is the payoff for completing the action steps?"

- "How will achieving this goal help me fulfill my long-term or lifetime goals?"
- "What will I have after completing this goal that I don't have now?"

Implementing the Coaching Plan

Of course, once the Coaching Plan is formulated, the next step is its implementation. Once a goal has been established, action steps and results should be identified immediately. After a week or two—or even several months later—clients may find that their goals have shifted and that, as a result, the Coaching Plan needs to be changed. That's fine as long as they are not avoiding making the changes they initially desired. Adjusting the Coaching Plan as appropriate as time goes on is one of the ICF core coaching competencies.

Your role as coach in implementing the Coaching Plan is to:

- Be supportive
- Encourage clients to "go for their dream"
- Help guide clients to the people, resources, and information they need to achieve it
- Hold clients accountable for the results they said they wanted
- Keep records of the clients' progress (minimal or more detailed depending on your coaching style)
- Confront clients, as necessary, when they fail to take the actions they agreed to take

KEY COACHING CONCEPTS

1. When prospects call to inquire about coaching, your first step is to determine whether you and the prospect are a good fit. To do so, you must (a) determine the prospect's needs, (b) assess his or her personality, (c) propose coaching services to meet his or her needs, and (d) address any objections. You can then (e) provide the prospect with a new client materials packet and (f) schedule the first session.

2. Using a tool to determine whether clients are coachable is an optional step at the outset of the coaching relationship.

3. It is advisable to use a written coaching agreement so that both parties are clear on their roles and responsibilities.

4. Two initial decisions you will need to make regarding intake sessions are length and whether they are to be done over the phone or face-to-face.

5. Following the intake session, you and your clients should co-create a Coaching Plan that outlines the goals, action steps, and results to be obtained from the coaching work.

6. The goals set in the coaching plan should be: (a) specific, (b) realistic, (c) measurable, and (d) self-reliant.

14

Three Core Coaching Competencies: the 3 "E's" of Successful Coaching

"THE DIFFERENCE BETWEEN WHAT WE DO AND WHAT WE ARE CAPABLE OF DOING WOULD SUFFICE TO SOLVE MOST OF THE WORLD'S PROBLEMS."
—*Mohandas Gandhi*

You will recall that in the QuantumShift!™ coaching model, there are three core coaching competencies. These competencies also constitute the three phases of a successful coaching call or session: (1) establishing rapport and the agenda or issue to be discussed; (2) exploring and elaborating on the agenda or issue; and (3) eliciting action. In this chapter we will examine each of these in depth.

Phase 1: Establishing Rapport and the Agenda or Issue

This first phase of a telephone coaching session—usually the first two to five minutes of your coaching call—is critical to the success of the session overall. It sets the tone for the rest of the interaction and can determine whether it will be focused or unfocused, effective or not.

You must be "fully present" as the call begins and use strategies that will successfully help clients determine what they want to focus on. Otherwise, the call can end up being a mere conversation instead of a coaching interaction.

Preparing for the Call

Being fully present with your clients means you are undistracted, focused, and centered directly on the individual. Here are some practices that can help you to prepare for your coaching calls:

- Before making a call, close your eyes and take a few deep breaths; have a picture of a peaceful nature scene or some other device in your work area that you can look at before you take a call

- Consciously put aside any mental distractions from events that have just happened (including your last client call); if necessary, close your eyes as you pick up the phone to eliminate all visual input and concentrate on the client's voice

- Ensure that your work area is quiet and free from noise that would detract from the quality of the coaching session; if you work from home, be sure to turn off any music that you may have been listening to, as well as the television, and log off the Internet; if you have children, be sure they are being cared for in another room

- Have a glass of water nearby

- Clear your desk of everything except the client's file, a pad and pen (or a clean screen on your computer) for jotting down notes, and your calendar, for scheduling the next session

- Put a smile in your mind that carries through your voice as you answer the phone

- Visualize an image that is calming for you: floating in warm water, sitting by the ocean, walking through the woods, etc.

- Have an object such as a special stone, container, or crystal on your desk that you can physically touch to center yourself

- Repeat a simple saying or thought such as "I open myself to serve my client" or "I now prepare myself to access my Inner Wisdom" just before the call

You may think of other things you can do to help you concentrate on the coaching session. On the other hand, some new coaches find that they want to avoid too much preparation because it makes them anxious—that is fine too.

Phase 1a: Establishing Rapport on the Phone

Both you and your client will immediately pick up verbal and nonverbal cues from each other as the call begins, if you are listening for them. Imagine yourself starting a coaching call. Do you act differently if the client is talking quickly, seems excited, appears depressed, or is distracted? If you sense these sorts of behavior, you can ask the client about it in a neutral way. For example: "I notice you're talking very quickly today. What is happening?" or, "You sound distracted. Are you prepared to continue with our session now?"

Once any initial issues are addressed, the following questions are other ways to establish rapport:

- "How are you today?"
- "How has your week been?"
- "What has been happening in your life that you'd like to share?"

In the first coaching call, establishing rapport is often different than in subsequent sessions because you do not know the client, their personality, sense of humor, and so on. This will be especially true if you do not conduct an extended intake session. You may feel the need to make a good impression as you continue to set the tone for the coaching interaction. In subsequent calls you have an ongoing relationship with the client, which grows with each session. In each you may need to catch up a bit on the past week's activities, how the client has done with the assignment/action steps from the last session, and so on. But the rapport building will probably take less time in the subsequent sessions because you have a relationship established.

Indicators That Rapport Has Been Established

We know that rapport has successfully been established when we notice that:

- Clients seem receptive to coaching
- Clients lack defensiveness
- Extroverted clients begin processing out loud, talking through the issue and possible solutions

- Clients seem eager to share what has been happening
- Clients have completed the work assigned or committed to in the previous session
- You feel a flow or rhythm with them

What If Rapport Is Not There?

There may be some calls where you immediately sense that something is being left unsaid, or you find it difficult to create rapport. Perhaps the client is facing a challenge, has an issue he wants to discuss with you, or is just plain distracted by children, an ongoing event at work, or other issues. Despite your natural tendency to the contrary, avoid taking it personally. Most likely, the client's issue is not about you. And even if it is, you now have a forum to discuss it. It is worse when clients just stop keeping their appointments without explaining why. Here are some things you can do in this situation:

- Ask the client if there is something he wishes to discuss
- Say something like, "It sounds like you're busy right now. Is this a good time to talk, or should we reschedule?"

If the client is not following up/doing his/her work, ask, "What could we do to make this more valuable for you?" Or, "What's in the way of your following through?"

Phase 1b: Establishing the Agenda or Issue to Be Discussed

The second objective or phase may involve nothing more than asking a question. Or, in other cases it may require isolating one issue out of a long series of initial statements the client makes.

One way to ensure that the issue is isolated before the session begins is to use the "Coaching Call Preparation Form" provided in the Career Coach's Toolbox (pp. 375). You would provide this worksheet to clients prior to their session, asking them to complete and return it to you twenty-four hours before the session. (For information on how to download electronic files from the Career Coach's Toolbox, see p.

313.) If a more urgent issue arises, you can shift the focus of the session. Clients get an opportunity to recap their week's activities and determine what they want to discuss. This can be particularly helpful for clients who have a tendency to ramble and not stay on one topic during their coaching sessions.

Following are some suggested questions to ask to determine the agenda or issue to discuss:

- "We have about X minutes today; what would you like to focus on?"
- "In the time we have today, what's the most important thing we could talk about that might make a big difference in the upcoming week?"
- After the client shares what has been happening: "You've mentioned several possible issues for us to discuss. Which one would you like to focus on first?" Or, "Which one seems most urgent now?"
- "What would be the best use of our time today?"
- "How would you like to spend our time today?"
- "What issue did you bring to the session from your pre-work?"
- "How can we use the time we have to make a difference for you?"

What to Do When Clients Do Not Have an Issue

The pre-session worksheet may minimize the number of times the client comes to the call without an issue. But sometimes the client just may not have anything pressing to discuss, and you may need to generate some questions to stimulate more ideas. Plus, once you have been coaching a client for a few weeks or months, there are times when it is helpful to recap, summarize, and otherwise recognize progress—as well as take the coaching to a new level. Following are some questions that might help in this situation:

- "Would today be a good time to summarize what we've accomplished in our coaching so far?"
- "Is there an area of your life in which you would like to have better results?"
- "What are five things you'd like to accomplish in the next six months?"
- "How is not having an issue perfect for you right now?"

- "Is there anything you have been wanting to say, either to me or another person, but haven't?"

You could also administer an assessment and use that as a basis for some future goals, a new Coaching Plan, or other developmental objectives.

Indicators That the Agenda/Issue is Established

We know the agenda or issue is sufficiently clear when the client has mentioned one or more challenges for discussion and appears ready to proceed with the rest of the coaching session.

Phase 2: Explore and Elaborate on the Agenda or Issue

Phase 2 usually constitutes the largest amount of time spent during a coaching session. Though of course you will want to begin by exploring the issues as stated by the client, there will usually be underlying issues that will be rich for exploration, particularly as you move into coaching levels 2 and 3. These may include clients':

- Motivations (in this situation and in their life overall)
- Assumptions about their current situation and/or how the world works
- Issues that, for them, are not open to question (That's just the way it is)
- Beliefs about behaviors, situations, and so on
- Priorities among competing issues
- Mental models derived from multiple beliefs and conclusions including their worldview, where those views originated, whether they are useful now, and what needs to change
- Awareness of their own behavior—and of other styles of learning and behavior (as described in various assessments as well as through coaching and observation)
- Values and motivators vis-à-vis the issues that are the subject of the coaching

"Blind Spots"

What happens if you see a coaching issue and the client doesn't want to explore it?

We call such issues "blind spots" because only the coach is aware of the issue. Two of the ICF coaching competencies are demonstrating respect for clients' perceptions, learning style, and personal being and asking permission to coach clients in sensitive and new areas.[46] So if the client is reluctant—or downright unwilling—to discuss an issue, we must honor that. However, there are some coaching techniques we can use to pry open these closed doors:

- Ask the client, "Are you willing to explore your resistance to this issue?" or, "Do I have your permission to ask a few more questions on this topic?"
- Use the "Reflective Model of Elaboration" outlined below and ask the client if she hears the issue as you restate it to her
- Say such things as, "You may not be tracking with me on this, since I think it is a blind spot for you, but what else might be going on here?"

This kind of blind spot can be uncomfortable for clients until they, too, can see the issue. What's important is that they understand what is blocking them. If you feel the need or think you need more clarity about an issue, beware of falling into the trap of trying to solve the problem yourself. Let the client do it! A good question to ask the client here is, "What do you need to be clearer about to resolve this issue?"

The "Reflective Model of Elaboration": Hear, Restate, Inquire

Active listening is another ICF core competency. It refers to the ability to listen to more than the client's words, "to focus completely on what the client is saying and is not saying, to understand the meaning of what is said in the context of the client's desires, and to support client self-expression."[47] The Reflective Model of Elaboration is a variation of active listening in which the coach takes an active role in fleshing out what the client has shared. The coach: (1) listens to ("hears") what the client says; then (2) restates it back to the client (hopefully offering a deeper or different perspective on the statement); and finally (3) inquires as to any inconsistencies the coach notices or other areas in which the coach senses the need to further explore the issue. The following example illustrates how this works.

Example

The client is trying to decide what to do as part of a team doing a corporate consulting intervention, but it is one of a series that management authorized but did not act on. The client is concerned about the reaction of the employees "in the trenches" to the information she will be delivering.

Coach:	How could you as a team member helping on this assignment get this information to upper management?"
Client:	That's what I've got to figure out. I'm working with the VP of construction and trying to decide what kinds of things we could do or avoid doing for the people in the trenches to make sure we don't; have to deal with this again.
Coach:	Do you have a solution?
Client:	Yes, one agreement on the front end that we will implement is that if I see an area where they're shooting themselves in the foot, I can raise it. I have unofficial license to do so.
Coach:	So you've already asked for permission on that up front. What would keep you from doing it?
Client:	Nothing – I guess I have permission, now that you say it.
Coach:	Sounds like you have the answer.
Client:	I got off track on the emotional issues.
Coach:	What will you do in the following week?
Client:	Talk to the HR manager and tell him my thoughts because I know him better; then I'll follow his lead.
Coach:	OK, please let me know how it goes.

Coaching Questions to Ask to Explore and/or Elaborate on an Issue

In exploring and elaborating on an issue, what questions you use will depend on whether you take a Level 1, 2, or 3 approach. (Levels are discussed individually in the following chapters.)

For Level 1:

- "What have you tried already?"
- "What else could you do?"
- "Are there more options besides the two you?"
- "Could you say more about that?"
- "Which is more urgent now?"
- "Is anything in your way?"
- If clients say they do not know: "If you did know, what would it look (or sound or feel) like?"
- "What would you be doing differently if...?"
- "Has this ever happened before? What worked then?"
- "What has to happen for X to occur?"
- "Do you know anyone who has done this that you could talk to?"

For Level 2:

- "What really matters to you in this situation?"
- "What is important about that?"
- "Where is your energy regarding this?"
- "Why does it matter?"
- "What's your intention?" or, "What's motivating you?"
- "How does that serve your purpose?"
- "Is there any part of you that feels [e.g., scared, uncertain]?"
- "If there were one thing you could do to shift this situation, what would it be?"
- "What must you let go of here?"
- "What if that weren't the truth?"
- "What's underneath the [e.g., stress]?"
- "What are you not willing to look at here?"

For Level 3:

- "What beliefs would a [e.g., successful] person hold about himself or herself?"
- "If you were to achieve this state, what would be happening in you that would be [e.g., irresistibly compelling]?"
- "What if [e.g., pleasing people] weren't necessary/important?"
- "What kind of a person would you have to be to achieve X?"
- "Is there something that makes a [e.g., successful] person fundamentally different from you?"
- "If this were the perfect environment for you to learn what you need to know about yourself, what would be the lesson?"
- "Who is the authentic/essential you?"
- "How would your life change if you were more [e.g., compassionate]?"
- "What is beneath your [e.g., overcommitment]?"
- "What are you firmly attached to here?"

Remember that you don't have to understand clients' situations to help them unless you are problem solving, so avoid "fact-finding" or "information-gathering" questions. (See chapter 15 on Level 1 coaching for details.)

Avoiding "Interrogation"

One danger of spending the entire second part of your coaching interaction asking one question after another is that clients can end up feeling like they are being interrogated. This does not further your rapport and can make clients defensive (or worse: they may withdraw from coaching). To avoid this, try mixing up your coaching techniques: along with asking questions, give clients feedback, state your observations, solicit (or, on select occasions, introduce) ideas, reaffirm what they are saying, restate what they have said, and so on. This actualizes the coaching competency of "dancing in the moment," being present yet flexible as the situation requires. When we do this, a rhythm develops between coach and client much like that between dance partners or tennis players. Each party's next move flows from the other's.

Indicators That Exploration and/or Elaboration Are Successful

We know that we have explored and elaborated on issues long enough when:

- Clients seem complete regarding the issue
- Clients have an "aha!" experience
- Clients know what to do next
- Clients have resolved the issue they brought to the issue (or others that arose during the session)
- Clients understand themselves and/or the situation better and can move forward
- Clients reiterate what they are going to do
- Clients exhibit excitement

Phase 3: Eliciting Action

After we have helped clients amplify the issue they wished to discuss, we then need to draw the session to a close. Even when clients have not yet finished processing their issue, it is important to keep your sessions within the stated time limits. This models good time management for clients.

Eliciting action may — but need not — refer to clients' taking physical action. Action steps to which the client agrees take may be things like noticing situations in which a problematic behavior shows up or thoughts or beliefs that are going through their mind at that time. Perhaps the action step will be to reflect on an idea. Or, consider this example from a recent session I had with one of my clients: to avoid spending time on petty issues unrelated to her strategic goals, she put a sign in her work area that said "Think Big!" to remind her to keep her thoughts on what is important.

This coaching competency cannot be overemphasized, because clients will take with them the tone and feeling of this phase of the coaching call as they go into the week. Will they leave the session excited or lackadaisical? Energized or depressed? Action oriented or overwhelmed? The way you handle this phase of the session is vital to the session's success.

Testing Action for Viability

It is critical that the action agreed upon be one or more steps that clients are not only planning toward, but prepared to do, capable of doing, and willing to do. We call this "PCW" for *prepared, capable,* and *willing:*

- **Prepared.** Clients are clear on what they will do, feel ready to do it, and are excited to do it, and the timing is right. They are prepared to get into action immediately.

- **Capable.** Clients have the necessary skills to do the agreed-upon action, or if not, they know what resources (people, books, courses, etc.) to consult to gain the needed competency.

- **Willing.** Clients are willing to proceed. This is stronger than mere wanting; clients freely choose a desired action. At a minimum, they have given themselves permission, and at most, they have established a highly motivated commitment to move forward.

When clients are reluctant to state or commit to an action step, many times it is because one or more of these elements are absent. And as a result, they are unlikely to follow through.

One aspect of being prepared that can make clients reluctant to act is simply lack of clarity about how to take the issue discussed during the interaction to the next step. Clients may want you to suggest an action step, or claim not to know what they are taking with them from the session to do in the next week. In this situation you might ask something like, "If you did know, what would it be?"—a great question for shifting perspective. Or, "Have you considered doing X?"—which is not the same as the advice-giving question, "I think you should do X," but can still help clients past blind spots as well as help you bring the session to a successful conclusion.

Remember that clients' sense of what constitutes a reasonable plan of action may be bigger or smaller than what you feel is appropriate. It is usually best, however, to let them assume the level of commitment they believe is realistic, and if they either far exceed it or fail to make much progress, the scope of the following week's action can be adjusted accordingly—or the barriers can be explored.

Coaching Questions to Elicit Action

The following questions can bring the session to conclusion and move clients toward action:

- "Based on our discussion today, what's your next step?" (lets clients clarify/ summarize)
- "With all we have talked about, summarize what will happen next. What's one thing you could [or will] do?"
- "If there were one thing you could do right now that would make a difference, what would it be?"
- "What are you going to do next week?" or, "What specific actions are you going to take?"
- "Could you summarize what you're taking away from our session? Can you set a time frame for that?"

And then, to follow up:

- "Is there anything to prevent you from...?"
- "Is anything in your way?"
- "Do you need to know or learn anything new to implement this plan?"
- "Based on our discussion, are we on the right track? How do you know?"
- "How would you like to end our session today?"
- "Do you have any final questions that I might help you with before we end our session?"

If you're running short on time, a great question to ask is, "If there were one thing you could do in the next week to take this issue further, what would it be?"

One of our coaching competencies is to help clients "do it now," as appropriate. So in suitable situations, immediately starting to role-play or do what they have suggested during the session can begin the shift – and the implementation.

Indicators That the Eliciting Action Is Successful

You know the eliciting action phase of the coaching session has been successful when:

- Clients knows what to do next, and are prepared, capable, and willing to do it
- Clients are excited!
- Clients want to end the session so they can get started
- Clients seem complete and have no further questions right now

---

KEY COACHING CONCEPTS

1. Prior to a coaching call, the coach must become focused, centered, and prepared for the call, using one or more techniques from the suggested list.
2. Phase 1a, establishing rapport, occurs in the first few minutes of the coaching call and sets the tone for the rest of the session.
3. If rapport seems to be difficult to establish, it can help to ask clients whether there is something they need to say.
4. Phase 1b, establishing the agenda or issue to be discussed, should be determined after rapport has been established. The pre-session worksheet can help with clients who tend to ramble.
5. Phase 2, exploring and elaborating on an issue, constitutes the bulk of the coaching session.
6. The Reflective Model of Elaboration can help clients overcome blind spots and/or shift perspective.
7. One trap to avoid during phase 2 is interrogating the client; mixing up coaching techniques can help.
8. Phase 3, eliciting action—conducted as the session draws to a close—is critical because clients take the feeling they have at the end of the session into their week.
9. To test actions for viability, we need to inquire whether clients are prepared, capable, and willing to do the agreed-upon actions.

15

Level 1 Coaching: Changing Performance and Behavior for the Better

"Insanity is doing the same thing over and over and expecting a different result."
—*Albert Einstein*

We continue our discussion of coaching skills with Level 1 of the Quantum-Shift! coaching model. You may have had the impression from our earlier overview that Level 1 is undesirable as a coaching style. In fact, it is quite useful. And it is the simplest coaching technique, which is why we begin here. However, the old adage "if all you have is a hammer, everything is a nail" applies here. If you have no other tools in your toolkit besides Level 1, your coaching will fall short in many situations.

What Level 1 Coaching Does

Level 1 coaching works at the level of behavior and performance to effect change. Each situation or environment in which the behavior appears must be separately addressed at this level. This is the first rung of author Chris Argyris' "Ladder of Inference"[48] (described in more detail in chapter 16). Level 1 coaching:

- Works to change behavior
- Solves problems
- Tries to improve performance
- Focuses on observable data
- Leads to specific action steps
- Prioritizes goals and actions to be taken

Level 1 coaching is easiest because many of us are accustomed to problem solving, goal setting, and prioritizing for ourselves. Consultants who enter the CCI training program to become coaches are often experts on this level. The shift for them—and for each of us—is to learn to be neutral and unattached to any ideas we may submit to clients. In the coaching environment, we are not "experts" in the subjects our clients are raising—no matter how much experience we may have with them – because clients must come to the solution that is right for them. Rather, we cultivate our expertise in the coaching process itself. Focusing on our role as catalyst and facilitator helps us avoid becoming attached to our clients' outcomes.

What Level 1 Coaching Does Not Do:
- Does not address motivation 2
- Does not inquire into the interpretation of facts 2
- Does not explore beliefs 2
- Does not question identity 3
- Does not ask why something is important 3

Premises of Level 1 Coaching:
- The objective is to change behavior, eliminate "problems," and/or resolve dilemmas at the behavior level
- Performance improvement is a primary focus
- Beliefs, assumptions, motives, meaning, or interpretation of situations are not mentioned; they are irrelevant to behavioral change in the Level 1 paradigm

Level 1 Coaching Techniques

When coaching at Level 1, we need to have at our disposal not only the appropriate questions to ask (such as those listed in chapter 14), but also a variety of other coaching techniques necessary to help clients resolve their issues. Following are some representative Level 1 techniques.

1. **Using "Cartesian Coordinates."** To help you fully address all aspects of problems that clients want to solve, you can use the Cartesian Coordinates method described in fig. 16 to assure that "no rock remains unturned." Otherwise, clients' actions may have unanticipated and unintended consequences. For example, Sue could not seem to decide whether to leave her job as a financial analyst—which she was enjoying less than she did at first—and felt drawn to become a consultant to companies analyzing merger or acquisition targets. A coach using the Cartesian Coordinates method would first ask Sue, "What would happen if you left?" and invite Sue to list her answers.

Figure 16: Cartesian Coordinates

THEOREM	CONVERSE
AB	-AB
Example:	*Example:*
What would happen if you did?	What wouldn't happen if you did?
INVERSE	NON-MIRROR IMAGE REVERSE
A-B	-A-B
Example:	*Example:*
What would happen if you didn't?	What wouldn't happen if you didn't?

The second question would be, "What wouldn't happen if you left?" In other words, what would Sue miss out on if she started her own business now? She would lose any appreciation on her stock options and/or pension plan, and she may have less job security, at least in terms of regular paycheck. If the business climate were such that mergers and acquisitions were on the rise and she were well connected in her industry, perhaps she would lean in favor of the decision to leave. But perhaps she would have to give up profit-sharing, bonuses, or stock options at her current employer by leaving at this time. Those factors must also be considered.

The third question would be, "What would happen if you didn't leave?" That is, if Sue stayed in her job, what would the benefits be? And finally, "What wouldn't happen if you didn't?" While she would retain the financial benefits listed above, she would also likely continue to struggle with her lack of satisfaction in her current job. If she stayed, what opportunities would she be missing out on?

The Cartesian Coordinates method helps put all the relevant criteria before your clients. They can then evaluate those criteria, consult their inner resources, and make their decision.

2. **Drawing on past successes.** Here, you help clients recall past situations where they have successfully managed a similar issue and leverage that success here. For instance, when clients are finding it hard to become self-motivated to make the contact calls they need to make in their job search campaign, you can ask whether there was any other time in their past when they were motivated to take necessary steps toward a goal. If so, how did they find that motivation, and are there any parallels they can draw or skills they can build upon from that experience in the current challenge?

3. **Finding an expert.** Ask clients whether they know anyone who has successfully solved a similar problem whom they could contact for advice or input. Even if they do not know such an individual personally, can they identify role models or industry experts and develop a way to approach them?

4. **Shifting perspective.** Though a somewhat advanced skill, this can be used skillfully at Level 1. For example, you might ask the client, "What if you were the coach? What would you ask now?" Or, "What if you were someone else in the scenario? How would that person see the situation differently?"
    What if money wasn't an issue?

Traps in Level 1 Coaching

Since most of us have some experience with problem solving, we often make assumptions or fall into certain traps when learning coaching techniques. Here are some common ones:

- **Gathering information to solve the problem yourself.** Information-gathering questions to elicit details about the situation are common among new coaches. Remember that you do not have to know all the details or fully understand the situation to coach the person about it. In fact, having a lot of experience with similar issues can interfere: you still cannot see through the client's eyes. Coaching is all about the clients. Instead of gathering information, simply ask neutral questions to lead them to their next insight. Contrast the two examples in fig. 17 .

Notice how the client stays more neutral in the right-hand column and how the topics discussed go an entirely different direction than when the coach feels the need to get all the details, as in the left column. (For future reference: many of the questions in the right-hand column also illustrate the impact of Level 2 coaching.)

- **Giving advice or assuming a consulting role.** No matter how intelligent or well informed or even well intentioned you are, giving advice has no place in coaching. Giving advice is telling clients what you would do, or what they should do, or otherwise submitting an idea that you want them to implement. You may also be a subject matter expert or perhaps a consultant, but here you are a coach. When you give clients your ideas or advice, the dynamic shifts to *your* best answer, rather than theirs. And even if the idea is brilliant, clients have less ownership than if they had discovered it themselves through your provocative questions. In fig. 17, if the coach began to tell the client that he "should" take an assertiveness class, told a story about a similar situation and what the coach did and suggested the client do the same, or something similar, that would be inappropriate advice giving. Whether we are coaching at Level 1 or another level, it is best to avoid advising clients on how to resolve their issues or reach their goals. *remain unattached to the decision*

Figure 17: Information-Gathering vs. Coaching

INFORMATION GATHERING	COACHING
Coach: What would you like to discuss today?	**Coach:** What would you like to focus on today?
Client: I'm having trouble with my supervisor at work.	**Client:** I'm having trouble with my supervisor at work.
Coach: What kind of trouble is it?	**Coach:** What makes this an important issue for you?
Client: She supports other employees in going "over my head" in getting things approved.	**Client:** I'm feeling undermined by him.
Coach: Give me an example.	**Coach:** On what evidence do you base that statement?
Client: Well, yesterday Mary went to my boss and asked my boss, Dan, to approve the new course she wants to teach next term. Dan did so, even though that is my responsibility because I'm Mary's direct supervisor.	**Client:** He approves requests from employees who report directly to me.
	Coach: What do you want?
	Client: To have my authority recognized.
Coach: What kind of course was it?	**Coach:** What if authority wasn't so important to you?
Client: Organizational Development Principles for the Pharmaceutical Industry.	**Client:** [Pauses to think.] I might feel less resentful.
Coach: What are some of the main points the course covers?	**Coach:** What else?
	Client: I would be able to concentrate better.
Client: How to set up an OD plan, things to watch out for, who the key players are, stuff like that.	**Coach:** So would you like to work on authority being less important, or your relationship with your supervisor?
Coach: What kind of paperwork should Mary have done instead?	**Client:** Both. I think it has to do with how I communicate with him.
Client: She should have filled out a Request for Course Approval, Form 101A, and submitted it to me in due course.	**Coach:** And what do you want to be different in your communication?
	Client: I need to be more assertive.
Coach: Could you suggest that she do that next time?	**Coach:** So what step would you like to take between now and next time to move in that direction?
Client: Yes, I guess so.	**Client:** I'll script out what I'd like to say to him.

KEY COACHING CONCEPTS

1. Level 1 coaching works at the level of behavior and performance to facilitate change.
2. Level 1 coaching does not inquire into beliefs, assumptions, motives, meaning, interpretation of situations, or similar issues.
3. Coaching techniques to use at Level 1 include using "Cartesian Coordinates," drawing on past successes, finding an expert, and shifting perspective.
4. Traps in Level 1 coaching include gathering information to solve the problem yourself, and giving advice.

16

Level 2 Coaching: Honing in on Beliefs, Perspective and Motivation

"SOMETIMES I'VE BELIEVED AS MANY AS SIX IMPOSSIBLE THINGS BEFORE BREAKFAST."
—*Lewis Carroll,* Alice in Wonderland

L evel 2 coaching takes us one level deeper than Level 1 to the underlying beliefs, motivators, and unconscious programming that drive our clients' behavior. It can be described as working with clients to help them access their unconscious programming and consciously change it when desired. This will result in clients' behavior and other effects of this programming changing automatically. Note that we do not impose this change on our clients; we ask questions that invite them to explore issues and then we honor their response, whether they wish to proceed or not.

Level 2 issues often underlie stated Level 1 issues and affect clients' lives in ways that they do not always understand. For example, we might have a client who has had a series of unsatisfying jobs, had a boss who berates him, and has a salary below the market rate. Delving into this behavioral pattern may reveal a Level 2 issue such as a feeling that success is undeserved; that is, that the client believes that work is supposed to be hard. This feeling may have originated in his childhood socioeconomic circumstances, messages that he internalized from other significant influences in his life, or from some other source. If the client can consciously change these beliefs through coaching, he will be able to avoid repeating this undesirable pattern in his next job.

What Level 2 Coaching Does

Unlike the more superficial coaching of Level 1, Level 2 coaching:

- Inquires into what clients' motivation is (directly or indirectly)
- Solicits clients' interpretation of events
- Explores clients' beliefs about a situation
- Challenges or test assumptions clients have made for validation
- Asks why an issue or goal is important to the client

What Level 2 Coaching Does Not Do:

- Does not work to change behavior
- Does not try to solve surface-level problems
- Does not try to improve performance (at least not directly)
- Does not focus on observable data—except for indicators of clients' feelings and perceptions
- Does not prioritize goals and actions to be taken
- Does not question basic assumptions regarding clients' identity

Premises for Level 2 Coaching:

- The purpose of Level 2 coaching is to change beliefs, assumptions, and clients' worldview
- As clients' unconscious programming is changed, their behavior and performance will change automatically
- Level 2 coaching questions explore beliefs, assumptions, motives, meaning, and interpretation of situations

Principles of Level 2 Coaching

As we have discussed, attempting change at Level 1 (the level of behavior and performance) requires multiple interventions, because changing a behavior in one situation does not carry over to another. It's like an old container that is too full and begins to leak: plugging one hole will simply force the liquid to come out another, and the holes—new situations in which the behavior is manifested—are endless. So it is with Level 1 coaching.

Please note once again: we are not saying never to use Level 1 coaching. There can be a place for so-called problem solving in the coaching process, but it usually occurs after the Level 2 or Level 3 work has been done. Then clients are conscious of their motivations, choosing their assumptions and beliefs rather than being driven by them—this is when Level 1 coaching can have the greatest impact.

Traps in Level 2 Coaching

Whereas one trap to avoid in Level 1 coaching is giving advice or answers (which is the role of consulting), in Level 2 coaching our challenge is to avoid providing "armchair" therapy. Most therapy involves:

- Delving into the past more than the present or future
- Working with what was, in order to change what is now
- Focusing on clients' feelings and emotions
- Leading clients through psychotherapeutic methods, with the therapist directing the process

By contrast, skillful Level 2 coaching involves:

- Concentrating on the present and future more than the past, working with what is and what could be, not what was
- Focusing on clients' beliefs, assumptions, and motives, helping clients test and examine them to bring them to conscious awareness
- Letting clients set the session agenda, asking skillful questions and providing provocative feedback to help them broaden their awareness to implement change

The Ladder of Inference

In *Theory in Practice,* noted business writers Chris Argyris and Donald Schön have articulated a model for problem solving and understanding human behavior they call the "Ladder of Inference," as depicted in fig. 18.[49] Each of us climbs the ladder each time we interact with another person or have an impactful experience. It is a frequently used mental pathway that, with each step up the ladder, creates increased abstraction and distortion. With the abstraction, the person becomes more removed from the initial experience. Misguided beliefs and significant misunderstandings often result, and they become more and more complex as they are applied within an organizational or family system. As each experience occurs, we draw inferences about it that become our assumptions, conclusions, and beliefs. Our inferences interact with those of our boss, family members, and others. No one is really dealing with actual facts or data, but rather each other's inferences.

Figure 18: Ladder of Inference - Level 2

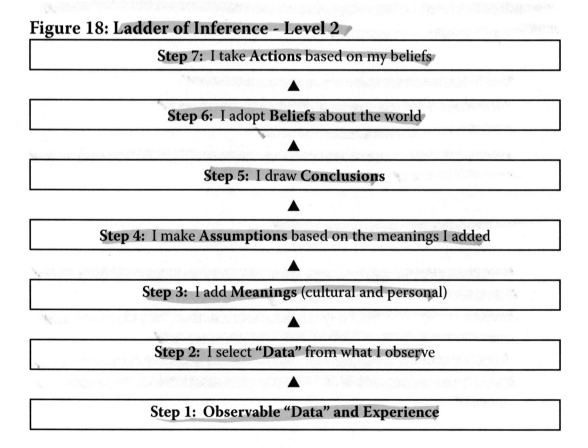

Step 7: I take **Actions** based on my beliefs

▲

Step 6: I adopt **Beliefs** about the world

▲

Step 5: I draw **Conclusions**

▲

Step 4: I make **Assumptions** based on the meanings I added

▲

Step 3: I add **Meanings** (cultural and personal)

▲

Step 2: I select **"Data"** from what I observe

▲

Step 1: Observable **"Data" and Experience**

Here is an example of the Ladder of Inference at work.

Example

Data:	You are making a presentation to a group of colleagues.
Meanings:	Most of them are engaged and alert, except for Ann, who seems to be bored.
Data:	She turns her eyes away from you and puts her hand to her mouth. She doesn't ask questions until you're finished, and then suggests that the group should ask for a more expanded report.
Meanings:	In this group, such a comment usually means the group should move on to the next item on the agenda…
Group Conclusions:	Everyone starts to do so.
Your Assumptions:	You think, "Ann must think I'm incompetent, which is a shame, because my ideas are just what she needs in her business."
Conclusions:	"In fact, she has never liked my ideas…She must hold a grudge against me for something."
Beliefs and Actions:	By the time you sit down again, you have decided you won't include anything in the report that she can use, justifying your behavior by the "fact" that she wouldn't read it, or even if she did may use it against you.

The Ladder of Inference is a powerful tool in coaching. Clients move up the ladder with lightning speed, usually unconsciously, and without questioning the assumptions they make and the meaning they attach to otherwise neutral behavior and events. They are often reluctant to communicate their conclusions to us because the conclusions are based on "real data" and the "truth" is obvious—right?

As skilled coaches who understand the ladder, we can analyze and challenge assumptions, conclusions, and beliefs by asking questions such as these:

- "Do you think I'm stupid?" (very direct approach)
- "On what data do you base that conclusion?"
- "Have you noticed this behavior in yourself or someone else before, and if so, did it always mean the same thing?"
- "What meaning did you attribute to the event or behavior when it first occurred?"
- "What other meanings are possible for this behavior?"
- "What conclusions did you draw about that analysis?"
- "What other conclusions could you draw?"
- "What beliefs do you hold, or need to hold, to maintain this conclusion?"
- "What beliefs would you need to have to view this situation differently?"
- "Even if your belief were true, do you have other options for action steps here?"

Theory vs. Practice

An important aspect of Argyris's ladder is the distinction between what individuals say is important to them and what they actually do, or what Argyris and Schön call "espoused theory" as opposed to "theory in use." Bringing these two things into congruence is a primary focus of Level 2 coaching. Following are two examples provided by Argyris and Schön.

espoused—what you say
Theory in use — what you do

Example 1

A teacher who believes that she has a class of "stupid" students will communicate expectations such that the children behave stupidly. She confirms her theory by asking them questions and eliciting stupid answers or puts them in situations where they behave stupidly. The theory-in-use is self-fulfilling. (This principle has been referred to in psychology as the Pygmalion Effect.)

Example 2

A manager who believes his subordinates are passive, dependent and require authoritarian guidance rewards dependent and submissive behavior. He tests his theory by posing challenges for employees and eliciting dependent outcomes. In order to break this congruency, the teacher or manager would need to engage in open loop learning in which they deliberately disconfirm their theory-in-use.[50]

Similarly, our beliefs about our clients greatly affect our coaching interactions. Clients' beliefs and assumptions about us and the people and situations they encounter in turn affect the quality of their lives and relationships. If they can get "unstuck" from those underlying conclusions and the beliefs they form, they can more consciously direct their mental energy to have more of what they want in their lives. Following is an example of Level 2 coaching from a real-life situation.

Coaching Example: Level 2 Coaching at Work

Jenny discussed with her coach her anxiety about an upcoming campaign meeting. She very much wanted to convey a sense of power and confidence despite her slight appearance. In prior meetings with the campaign committee, her input as campaign manager was ignored. The meetings got off track as everyone expressed their own ideas. To avoid a repeat occurrence, she had planned to wear her "power" suit to the meeting, arrive early, and sit at the head of the table to be in a controlling position.

Her coach asked her, "What's important about being in control and powerful here?" Despite feeling that the behavioral issues of what to wear and where to sit was the place to focus, Jenny agreed to reflect on the question, but in fact turned it around: "What if power were not so important to me?" She determined that she:

- Did not have to feel pressured to find a clean blouse to wear with her power suit
- Would not care about control but instead would focus on working together with the committee to obtain positive outcomes

- Would be much less stressed about the meeting and in general

The outcome? She wore jeans to the meeting, arrived late (not intentionally, but she didn't obsess about it), sat in a side chair instead of at the head of the table, listened to other people's suggestions and took notes, accepted constructive criticism of the plan she created, made adjustments to the plan, and left the meeting with a smile! And, as a postscript, her candidate won the election.

Level 2 Coaching Techniques

When we're working at Level 2, we are bringing the unconscious beliefs to consciousness. It is as though we were establishing a new habit or pattern of thinking. And, as with learning any new habit or skill, we need to marshal all our mental, physical, emotional, spiritual, and social resources to implement change. Marshall Goldsmith, for example, described in the *Wall Street Journal* as one of the top ten executive coaches in the world, refuses to work with an executive unless his or her entire team is involved. Those close to the executive are asked to give input at regular intervals and fully participate in supporting the executive in making the changes he or she desires. We can learn from this principle!

The following techniques can augment our questions and help move the Level 2 coaching process toward a QuantumShift! in our clients.

1. **Visualization.** Most work in corporations today draws primarily on the left brain: analytical processes, thinking (vs. feeling), logic, and objectivity. To make changes in our beliefs and foundational assumptions, we need to invite the right brain (our creative, intuitive aspects) to participate, too! Visualization is simply forming a mental picture (as though we were watching a movie) of our desired state and reinforcing it frequently (at least daily; hourly is better). The most effective visualization is done when we are not distracted, quiet, undisturbed, and focused. Sitting quietly with our eyes closed is best. Whether it is a guided meditation such as the "Symbol Meditation" in the Career Coach's Toolbox (p.

319) or reflecting on a positive image for the future in which we embody a desired state, visualization is one way of directing the mind to work powerfully to create the change we want. An exercise we can suggest to our clients is for them to visualize themselves as having already achieved their goal. The best visualization allows clients to place themselves in that vision, to see, hear, and feel it as their own. This accelerates its manifestation.

2. **Role-modeling.** Related to, but slightly different from, visualization is role-modeling, in which we find a person who exhibits the trait we want or who has made the change we want to make. We then pattern ourselves after this person. He or she can be dead or alive, someone we know personally, have read about, or have seen in movies or on television. What's important is that in every respect, he or she embodies the change we want to make. We may visualize or imagine that the person is standing in front of us, and as he or she turns away we notice there is a zipper running down the person's back. We unzip the zipper, step into the person's skin, and experience the world through his or her eyes, ears, and mind. What do we notice? This is a powerful exercise—be sure your clients are ready for it!

3. **Affirmations.** Psychologists tell us that that it takes at least twenty-one consecutive days of repetition of a new behavior before we can say it has become a habit (that is, it has reached the unconscious level where we do not have to think about doing it any more). Whether clients are trying to change a problematic behavior or find a more fulfilling job, affirmations—properly used—engage both the left and right brain while activating the power of synchronicity to create the desired state. An affirmation must be
   - Short (one sentence is ideal)
   - Stated in the present tense ("I am" vs. "I will")
   - Repeated several times each day

One easy way clients can use affirmations is to write them on 3x5" cards or sticky notes and put them on their bathroom and car mirrors, desk, refrigerator, phone, and anywhere else they will be regularly during the day. Examples might include, "I am now moving toward my ideal job" or, "I am now releasing everything that isn't exactly what I want."

4. **Support groups or "Master Mind" teams.** Let's face it: most of us will not make a change if we are left on our own. We need to build some accountability into our change process! The "Master Mind" concept as conceived by Napoleon Hill is that when two or more people gather together with a common purpose (including a coach and client), something greater than the sum of the parts emerges.[51] These weekly meetings can be held in person—over breakfast or lunch—or via phone on a bridge or conference call line. Usually the participants celebrate each other's successes, articulate desired goals, and support each other through challenges. Such support can make a big difference in each member's ability to achieve his or her goals. You may want to sponsor such a group and charge members a nominal fee to be part of a support or networking group that you facilitate to help them stay on track! Alternatively, clients may wish to choose an "accountability partner" or "success partner" with whom they check in daily (and vice versa) to reinforce commitments to their goals.

5. **Meditating on a "power" question.** Many times, we can't reason our way out of our present state. Albert Einstein once said that we cannot solve a problem in the same state of mind that created it. And often during the process of exploring a new career direction or making a personal change, taking action for the sake of "doing something" isn't appropriate. Meditating on a power question such as, "What do I really want?" or, "What do I want my life to mean?" can lead to some powerful insights. The insights become more powerful by staying with the question through the course of a week or two without feeling the need to find a specific answer. Even looking into the need for an answer can be helpful.

6. **Journal writing.** One final practice that can be useful as clients are exploring Level 2 issues is free-form journal writing. One of the best resources on this topic

is Julia Cameron's *The Artist's Way*.[52] Aimed at creative people who feel blocked, her concept of "morning pages"—writing three pages of rambling, spontaneous thoughts each morning and periodically reading back through them—can help increase our clients' clarity about repeating patterns in their life.

Sample questions to use when coaching at Level 2 are listed in chapter 14.

KEY COACHING CONCEPTS

1. Level 2 coaching works at the level of beliefs, assumptions, motives, meaning, or interpretation of situations to facilitate change.
2. Level 2 coaching does not do problem solving, focus on action steps, or delve into clients' identity.
3. The "Ladder of Inference" explains how observable data are distorted through a series of assumptions and conclusions that ultimately form one's worldview.
4. Level 2 coaching should not be confused with, or colored by, therapeutic techniques such as inventorying the past, focusing on clients' feelings instead of beliefs, and being overly directive in the process.
5. In addition to asking effective questions, other Level 2 coaching techniques include visualization, role-modeling, affirmations, support groups, meditating on a power question, and journal writing.

17

Level 3 Coaching: Shifting Personal Identity for Lasting Change

"FOR SELF IS A SEA BOUNDLESS AND MEASURELESS.
SAY NOT, 'I HAVE FOUND THE TRUTH,' BUT RATHER, 'I HAVE FOUND A
   TRUTH.'
SAY NOT, 'I HAVE FOUND THE PATH OF THE SOUL.' SAY RATHER, 'I HAVE
   MET THE SOUL WALKING UPON MY PATH.'
FOR THE SOUL WALKS UPON ALL PATHS.
THE SOUL WALKS NOT UPON A LINE, NEITHER DOES IT GROW LIKE A
   REED.
THE SOUL UNFOLDS ITSELF, LIKE A LOTUS OF COUNTLESS PETALS."
—*Kahlil Gibran,* The Prophet

Level 3 adds yet another step to the Ladder of Inference described in chapter 16. Here, we explore how to clarify and transform our very identity, the self as it is expressed in the world. As the quotation above illustrates, often what we have believed to be "the truth" about ourselves turns out to be just "a truth," one of may possible ways of viewing who we are. When a shift happens at Level 3, clients' beliefs and behaviors tend to change automatically as a result.

A parallel can be made between the three levels of coaching and a computer:

- Level 1 is like the output a software program produces (e.g., a font in a document)

- Level 2 is like the software program itself (e.g., the default settings for a document that are automatically applied to every document created within one program)

- Level 3 is like the operating system, such as Windows®, which is hard-wired to impose certain features on documents created in any program. If a change is made at this level, it automatically impacts the software program and the output from the program, including fonts in a document.

What Level 3 Coaching Does

Level 3 coaching has several purposes. It:

- Delves into identity (directly)

- Questions beliefs clients holds about themselves

- Seeks personal transformation

- Asks about what is important about an aspect of one's self-concept or a personal trait and whether it still serves the client's best interests

What Level 3 Coaching Does Not Do:

- Does not try to improve performance (directly)

- Does not focus on observable data

- Does not lead to specific action steps

- Does not prioritize goals and actions to be taken—except those regarding core beliefs about self

Premises of Level 3 Coaching:

- The Level 3 coaching objective is to change clients' very identity, or how they view themselves

- Personal transformation is the focus

- Level 3 coaching does not problem-solve; to the extent it deals with beliefs, these are beliefs about clients themselves, not a situation

Figure 19: Ladder of Inference - Level 3

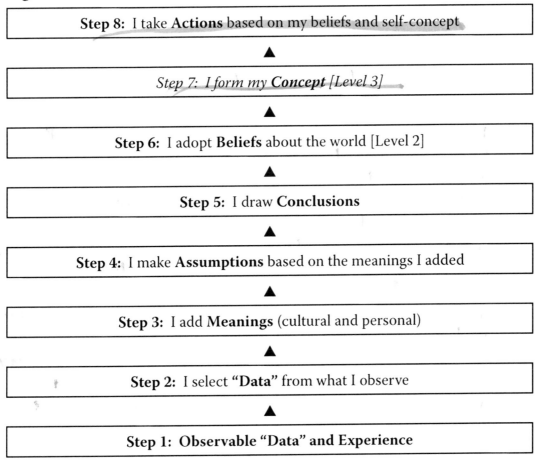

Step 8: I take **Actions** based on my beliefs and self-concept

▲

*Step 7: I form my **Concept** [Level 3]*

▲

Step 6: I adopt **Beliefs** about the world [Level 2]

▲

Step 5: I draw **Conclusions**

▲

Step 4: I make **Assumptions** based on the meanings I added

▲

Step 3: I add **Meanings** (cultural and personal)

▲

Step 2: I select **"Data"** from what I observe

▲

Step 1: Observable "Data" and Experience

Level 3 Coaching Techniques

You will notice in fig. 19 that another step, step 7, has been added to the Ladder of Inference. This is the area on which Level 3 focuses. Building upon our beliefs (step 6), we form our self-concept—the basis for our everyday actions.

Often in coaching sessions, coaches—and sometimes clients—realize that they (the clients) have internalized an aspect of themselves, from an observable life experience, that is not accurate (and often never was). This is because their selective perception of the event led to erroneous conclusions, which in turn coalesced to form their self-concept. Level 3 coaching can help unravel these sorts of complex and deep-seated issues, which often contribute to dissatisfaction at work and/or clients' seeming inability to pursue their dream job.

In the sometimes confusing task of differentiating between Level 2 and Level 3 issues, it helps to remember that Level 3 issues:

- Go beyond beliefs about how the world works to beliefs about oneself
- Often bring up emotion
- May be deep-seated—clients may hang onto them and defend their position
- Can often be stated by beginning with "I am a person who..." or, "I am the kind of person who..."
- May have been true at one time (e.g., in childhood) but are now inaccurate, irrelevant, or need to be changed to match current reality
- May be painful
- May involve clients seeing a given characteristic or principle as "the only way to be" (coaching and/or assessments can reveal others)
- May take some time to internalize—however, when the QuantumShift! happens, the aspect of self that was blocking them becomes obvious
- Could be a blind spot that the coach can see more clearly than the client

Coaching at Level 3 is illustrated in the following example.

Coaching Example: Level 3 Coaching at Work

Dave states that his challenge is to reduce the number of projects he has going at one time. He says he always seems to be overbooked. Asked how long this has been an issue, he says, "Forever." He believes that what is needed is better prioritization; however, upon further inquiry, it seems that the issue has more to do with his inability to say no. What might the Level 3 aspect of this issue be? That is, what does Dave appear to believe about himself that may be the source of this behavior? Start by asking Dave to say, "I am a person who..." as in:

- "I am a person who doesn't turn people down"
- "I am a person who needs to please everyone"
- "I am a person who wants to be liked"
- "I am a person who is afraid of missing out on opportunities"
- "I am a person who is good at starting things but cannot follow through"

As we continue to coach Dave, we would first bring these issues to conscious awareness; then determine whether or not he wants to change. If he does, we ask what beliefs he wishes to hold instead. We might ask, "What beliefs would a person who felt he had the right amount of work for him embrace?" We then work to shift his beliefs (see "Transforming Beliefs" below).

Traps in Level 3 Coaching

Issues of style or personality type can be confused with Level 3 issues. For example, someone whose type according to the *Myers-Briggs Type Indicator*® assessment (available at www.cpp.com as well as through Career Coach Institute) is ISTJ (Introversion, Sensing, Thinking, Judging) may state that he struggles with an extreme need for structure and organization. According to type theory, simply opening his perspective to the strengths and characteristics of that type and of others with similar preferences may allow him to soften his approach in some situations. However, this may or may not be a true Level 3 issue, depending on whether he believes his style is the only way he can be, or whether he can choose. The degree of attachment to the behavior or how stuck a person is in that behavior will help determine whether it is a Level 3 issue or not.

Level 3 coaching is not therapy. As described in chapter 16, most therapy explores the depths of the past—including childhood and even birth experiences—to find the root cause of the issue. Coaching generally does not dwell on the past. Instead, it finds leverage for change in the present. While we may ask when a belief began, we would then immediately shift to the present to ask clients whether that long-standing belief still serves them.

Coaches who become concerned when clients display emotion or raise issues stemming from childhood are often afraid that they will uncover more than they can handle. We will discuss handling strong emotions in chapter 19. But, as with Level 2, we need to keep our focus on staying neutral by inviting clients to explore their reactions and asking them how they want to move forward. This will keep us in the coaching role, rather than the therapist role, and empower clients to leverage their experience to their benefit.

Transforming Level 3 Beliefs

When coaching at Level 3, you may wish to use some of the sample questions provided in chapter 14, along with others you develop, to explore your clients' identity. Level 3 questions are powerful in the way they reveal identity issues to clients. Then comes the follow-up task of integrating the desired transformation. Once clients raise an issue of identity, it can be helpful to list the beliefs that support that identity. Often, one core belief has many other beliefs connected to it.

Next, clients can list the beliefs that would characterize a person who had the traits they desired. These are often the opposite of their current beliefs. This might be a good idea for people who feel they always have to please people, like Dave in the example above. Fig. 20 lists some of the sorts of beliefs Dave could move toward.

To integrate these beliefs will require consistent repetition through affirmations, visualization, and similar processes we described in chapter 16. Often, simply becoming aware of the broad-based impacts of the belief causes an immediate QuantumShift! Other times it takes days or weeks to completely embrace the new beliefs as part of one's identity.

Figure 20: Current vs. Future Beliefs

Current Belief	Future Belief
If I say yes, people will like me.	If I say no, people will honor my integrity and boundaries.
I must please everyone in my life, at all costs.	I can't please veryone in my life; I will act in congruity with what's right for me.
I'm not enough; doing things defines who I am.	My beingness defines who I am; I am enough.
If I do enough different things, I'll fool people into thinking I'm successful and I won't have to worry about falling.	I can trust myself to excel at what I choose.

KEY COACHING CONCEPTS:

1. Level 3 coaching works at the level of identity to facilitate transformation. It adds another step to the Ladder of Inference: our self-concept.
2. Level 3 coaching does not problem-solve, focus on action steps, or delve into clients' assumptions about the situation itself.
3. Level 3 issues should not be mistaken for issues of style or personality type. Furthermore, Level 3 coaching is not therapy.
4. Besides asking powerful questions, Level 3 coaching should articulate the desired beliefs or state of mind that clients want to move toward. It also includes repetition to integrate those beliefs into clients' identity.

18

The Role of Intuition and Deep Listening in Coaching

"THE CREATIVE IS THE PLACE WHERE NO ONE ELSE HAS EVER BEEN. YOU HAVE TO LEAVE THE CITY OF YOUR COMFORT AND GO INTO THE WILDERNESS OF YOUR INTUITION."
—*Alan Alda*

One of the ICF coaching core competencies is listening to one's intuition. However, clients' acceptance of coaches' reliance on his or her intuition varies widely in different contexts.

Intuition: Practical Insight or Mystery?

Intuition as defined by *Webster's Dictionary* is "the capacity of knowing without the use of rational processes; keen insight." Of course, in the corporate world, knowing has traditionally been valued only if it comes through rational (or analytical) processes. If it could not be explained and documented, it was discarded. Thankfully, that view is changing.

As early as the 1980s, books on using intuition in management were being circulated among executives. Laura Day's *Practical Intuition* has taken the mystery out of intuition[53]—no longer is it the sole province of women or the specially gifted; now it can be used by anyone who takes the time to recognize how intuition manifests for him or her. However, when it comes to coaching, it is not a matter of either using intellect or intuition, but rather of combining both in a strategic way as the coaching interaction calls for it. Adding an awareness of your intuition to your coaching tool-kit will enhance your effectiveness and, many times, will lead to the breakthroughs your clients are seeking.

How Intuition Manifests

Intuition is a very individual thing: each of us experiences it differently. Here are a few of the ways in which it can emerge. Which ones characterize your unique conduit for intuition?

- As a passing thought or image in waking hours—often seemingly unrelated to what is being said
- In a dream that conveys a message our intuition is trying to give us about an particular issue
- As a physical sensation, such as tingling, tension, heat, or cold in a part of the body
- As a "gut feeling" that something is "not quite right" or is "out of sync" with what's being said—or conversely, that it is in sync and authentic
- As an "aha!" or a sudden realization, often at seemingly the wrong time

Intuition or Your Own Agenda?

Confusing the issue somewhat is the fact that it is not always clear whether you are acting on intuition or from a personal agenda. There are no hard-and-fast rules to know the difference, but it is a matter of gaining experience with your own intuition and having the courage to follow it. It may not be intuition if:

- The proposed idea or solution would harm anyone else, or be done at his or her expense
- The insight is the "logical" answer (though it still may be valid)
- It comes from a self-centered agenda
- It results from overanalyzing
- It expresses a personal projection or a personal prejudice

On the other hand, intuition often:

- Does not make logical sense
- Contemplates something that you would not have thought of naturally
- Urges you to take some little step (e.g., call someone you do not normally talk to, attend a new kind of event, or drive home a different way than usual), without your knowing where that step will lead
- Involves an element of trust, a leap of faith
- Comes to you—you do not go to it

Knowing When to Share Intuitive Insights

Once you have a flash of intuition, as a coach you must then decide what to do with it. Do you share it? If so, how? When should you not? The answers may depend on the nature of the hunch. If, for example, you suddenly got an image of one person abusing another as a client was talking, that would be much more sensitive to voice than would simply an insight into the client's emotional or motivational underpinnings of the issue being discussed.

You also need to be aware of clients' mental and emotional state. If they are relatively fragile, we may be less likely to share significant insights with them than if they were strong. On the other hand, it may be your intuitive sense that helps them move to a position of strength. If you do decide to share, it is best to ease into it with the client to see if you are on track. You might say, "I'm getting a sense that..." or, "Does that resonate with you?" The client will usually know immediately whether or not that issue has relevance to what he or she is discussing.

Deep Listening

In chapter 14, we introduced the Reflective Model of Elaboration as a variation on active listening, one of our core competencies. We will now introduce a more advanced form of listening called "deep listening." In this methodology, the coach tests assumptions, heeds intuitive hunches, and draws distinctions between facts and the interpretation of facts.

Active listening (Level 1) and deep listening (Level 2) are compared in fig. 21. After reviewing the chart, complete the exercise in fig. 22..

Figure 21: Level 1 versus Level 2 Listening

Level 1(Active)	Level 2 (Deep)
Takes facts at face value	Listens beneath/beyond the facts to discern espoused theory vs. theory in use
Focuses on problem-solving right away, generating options for solutions	Focuses on testing assumptions beneath facts, bringing unconscious beliefs to awareness - and only then generating options for solutions
Active listening: "Summarizes, paraphrases, reiterates, mirrors back what client has said to ensure clarity and understanding" (ICF Competencies)	Goes beyond active listening to "deep" listening: "Distinguishes between the words, the tone of voice, and the body language"; "Helps clients to see the different, interrelated factors that affect them and their behaviors (e.g., thoughts, emotions, body, background)" (ICF Competencies)
Stays with client's perspective on the situation	Seeks openings which will shift client's perspective, perhaps to the other person/ people involved in client's situation, to someone with different beliefs or thinking patterns, or a meta-perspective
Asks client to choose among several options	Asks client to see themes and underlying patterns among a set of options or behaviors

Figure 22: Facts Versus Interpretations

As you read the statements in the following scenario, try to determine which are facts and which are interpretations of facts. How would you approach the situation differently if you were listening from Level 1 as opposed to Level 2? Then look at the answers below.

Scenario: Susie went to Coach John because she wanted to change jobs. Her company's profit margins had deteriorated from positive to negative in the past six months, and she was afraid that they would be laying people off soon. She said to John, "I just know that I'll be the first to go since I was hired just six months ago when everything was going fine." She then launched into a long story about her best friend, Jill, and how Jill's company treated her when they started having financial problems. "I know that if it can happen to Jill—she's an overachiever if I ever saw one—then it could happen to me, too. I'd better get my resume updated and start sending out copies."

Facts:

companies profit margins deteriorated in past 6 months
Susie was hired 6 months ago.

Interpretations:

deterioration of profit margins results in layoffs
LIFO
if Jill can be let go, so can Susie is Susie not as good.

Level 1 questions:

Sounds like you're worried you'll be laid off + you want to preclude that by finding new job.
Question re: resume update

Level 2 questions:

Other possibility other than layoffs
*Concern re: not good enough.

ANSWERS:

Facts:

• Susie's company has experienced a deterioration of their profit margins
• Susie was hired six months ago
• Susie wants to change jobs

Interpretations:
- Susie's company will be laying off people soon
- Susie will be one of the people to be laid off
- This is just like what Jill's company did to her
- Jill, unlike Susie, is an overachiever
- Overachievers do not get laid off

Susie's interpretations may in fact be incorrect: Jill may not have actually been treated poorly; her being an overachiever may also be an interpretation. Level 1 listening might yield these questions: "What is your best plan of action given these facts?" and, "Would it be better to work less and start job searching now, or to invest even more energy into your current job?" Level 2 listening might prompt you to go deeper and ask, "What's important about your friend being an overachiever?" "Is that even true?" "How do you know what process will be used in deciding who will be laid off?"

Applying Deep Listening in Coaching

Much of coaching involves asking powerful questions to help increase clients' awareness, clarity, and well-being. But other techniques such as the following, stemming from Level 2 listening, can also have a significant impact.

Bottom-Lining

Bottom-lining as defined by the ICF is to "understand the essence of the client's communication and help the client get there rather than engaging in long descriptive stories."[54] This skill calls for not only the ability to listen deeply for this "essence" level of communication, but also the confidence to interrupt clients' stories to short-cut the process. The skillful coach will preview this possibility with clients during the initial session(s), or in their client welcome materials, so that they will not view this technique as rude or disrespectful. Bottom-lining can allow the coaching to be successful more quickly. It keeps the client from rambling on about things that take up time but do not move the coaching forward and allows the coaching session to be devoted to the core aspects of the client's issue. Using bottom-lining, a coach might ask:

- "What are you saying here?"
- "Can you summarize your point in telling this story?"
- "Are you sure this is how you want to spend your coaching time today, or do think we could get to the point and do some further exploration?"

Providing Feedback

Feedback sometimes has a negative connotation, as in "May I give you some feedback?" (as you grit your teeth and wait for the bad news). When we facilitate coaching practice sessions for our coaches-in-training at Career Coach Institute, we are careful to balance positive comments with suggestions for improvement. That allows the coaches to think of feedback in a more neutral way than they may have otherwise. Feedback may consist of observations, intuitive insights, and other statements you make to clients regarding what they have shared. Of course, you can only give meaningful feedback if you are listening carefully, making connections between the client's statements, and doing some interpreting of what he or she is saying.

The inherent risk in giving feedback is that it is easy to impose your own meaning on clients' statements in a way that is not in alignment with their meaning. You must be sure to get their response and to ensure that they do not say "yes, that's true" just to please the coach.

Exploring Stretch Goals or Challenges

There may be times when your deep listening reveals an apparent barrier in clients' perception. They may not believe they can make any more than X number of phone calls in a week, or they may have become accustomed to working at a level of performance that is beneath their capability. This often happens when clients are not living their Authentic Vocation and feel unable to bring their "whole self" to work.

When you sense this may be limiting clients' perception of their options and possibilities, or even sabotaging their ability to advance in their career, you can explore with them the possibility of formulating a stretch goal that challenges them to a new level of performance, risk taking, or commitment. Stretch goals should challenge clients beyond their current comfort level but not be so aggressive as to set them up for failure. Just like the goals formulated in the Coaching Plan, the stretch goal should be "just out of reach, but not out of sight." If a client's goal was to begin an exercise program, an appropriate goal would be to go to the gym three times a week and spend twenty minutes on the treadmill; an inappropriate goal would be to work out two hours per day, seven days per week.

Discerning Subtleties of Client Communication

Another alternative to questioning focuses on discerning. Discerning is simply making distinctions between such things as:

- Words and tone of voice
- Stated and real priorities
- Stated and actual values
- Facts and interpretations
- Words and meanings
- Thoughts, feelings, and actions
- Foreground and background
- Trivial and significant issues
- Situational and recurring behaviors
- Immediate and long-term goals/needs/issues

We might practice discerning by providing feedback, sharing observations, or asking questions such as, "Is it X or Y?" or, "Are you saying...?"

"Between the Lines" Issues

In our experience with career coaching clients, there are a few "classic" issues that you are likely to encounter as you listen deeply to clients' needs. Following are four examples and some strategies for addressing them.

1. **Guilt/feeling undeserving/self-criticism.** The client feels as though he should have done something to avoid being laid off or believes he is not worth more than a certain (under market) salary—or even that he doesn't deserve to do work he loves! Even if these sorts of beliefs do not serve clients, they may hold hard and fast to them because they are comfortable—the beliefs may have been with them for most of their life. To address this challenging issue, it is critical first to ask clients if they are willing to explore and face it (the ICF competency of asking permission to coach clients in sensitive, new areas[55]). If so, asking clients what they are giving up or losing out on by holding these beliefs (maybe even having them write this out), as well as what alternative beliefs might serve them better, may help them become open to changing these beliefs. That process is most often done successfully through:

   - Repeating a short affirmation (e.g., "I deserve to be fulfilled in my work"), with emotion

   - Visualizing how doing fulfilling work would look, feel, and be

   - Using "The Witness," a technique by which we imagine we are observing ourselves from the outside, noticing when we engage in behavior that indicates that we don't feel we deserve X, and slowly but surely catching ourselves until we can integrate the new beliefs and, in turn, behaviors

   - Writing out a dialogue between one's "internal critic" and the grounded or "authentic" self. Writing the statements down sometimes makes them seem silly, inappropriate, or downright incorrect, which allows clients to overcome guilt and similar issues by recognizing, and choosing to change, overly critical inner dialogue.

2. **Perfectionism/workaholism.** Whenever clients exhibit extraordinarily high standards for themselves—manifested in working long hours, taking little or no vacation, working on weekends and holidays, and/or having difficulties with finding time for self or family—the coach should inquire as to whether they believe they are workaholics. Overwork is one of the most common issues among

workers today. Much recent research has been done to distinguish workaholics from people who work hard because they love what they do. Key differentiating factors are that those working with passion may work overtime or weekends but also have a happy family life, are aware of appropriate boundaries between work and home/personal life, and are actually very happy with their lives. Workaholics, on the other hand, live for the recognition of their overachievements, often engaging in overwork to escape an unhappy family life or difficult personal issues. For more on this topic, see *Working Ourselves to Death* by Diane Fassel.[56] The workaholic may need therapy (either instead of, or in conjunction with, coaching) to address the mental and emotional issues that underlie this addictive behavior, so a referral should be considered.

When, on the other hand, perfectionist tendencies have led clients to work harder than they need to simply to meet their own high standards, coaching techniques such as the following can be very helpful:

- Ask clients to define success for themselves (versus external standards)
- Query, "How do you know when you have done or accomplished enough?"
- Probe clients' openness to having different standards for different projects
- Delve into clients' desired balance between work and personal life

3. **Fear.** Fear is, of course, a common reaction to any new experience as well as to any change or transition. Such experiences take people into uncharted territory— and outside their comfort zone. What most of us tend to do when faced with fear is either to resist it or try to ignore it. It is as though it were a "monster in the closet" – we hope if we just ignore it long enough, it will die or disappear. What happens instead is that it occupies an undue amount of our mental energy and distracts us from our daily activities—not to mention that it holds us back from doing what we need to do in order to grow!

The secret to dealing with fear is to face it, as expressed in the title of Susan Jeffers's book *Feel the Fear and Do It Anyway*.[57] In fact, we encourage you to take your clients even further than that: suggest that they embrace the fear! You might ask a question such as, "What if this fear were a friend—what would it want you to know?" or, "What is the message in the fear?" Our body and mind are wise, and we normally will not feel fear unless there is some good reason for it. Rather than let it stop us, we can face it, have a dialogue with it, and "get" the message it wants us to hear. After having considered the best case/worst case scenarios, we can then make our decision whether to move forward into the unfamiliar action step that the fear has warned us about.

4. **Career as identity.** Contrary to what some believe, we are not what we do. Many men and women who define themselves by their job title feel as though they have lost their identity when they lose their job. Probing coaching questions like the following can reveal the fallacy in this way of thinking:

   - "Who were you before you were a [e.g., vice president]?"
   - "What characteristics do you have that do not depend on work for expression?"
   - "Who is the 'you' that is asking these questions?"

One exercise for such clients is to have them talk to some of their friends about how they view them. It can be very revealing for clients to hear how others describe their strengths and personality assets in terms that do not involve work.

KEY COACHING CONCEPTS

1. A good definition of intuition is "the capacity of knowing without the use of rational processes; keen insight."

2. Intuition can manifest in many ways, each of which is unique to the individual. However, intuition will never suggest that one person harm another.

3. Deep listening is an advanced listening skill beyond active listening or the Reflective Model of Elaboration.

4. Some techniques to augment deep listening include bottom-lining, providing feedback, setting stretch goals, and discerning.

5. Some common "between the lines" issues among career coaching clients include guilt/feeling undeserving, perfectionism, fear, and career as identity.

19

Advanced Coaching Skills

"To know what is happening, push less, open out and be
 aware.
 See without staring. Listen quietly rather than listening
 hard.
Use intuition and reflection rather than trying to figure
 things out.
The more you can let go of trying, and the more open and
 receptive you become, the more easily you will know what
 is happening."
—*John Heider,* The Tao of Leadership

Progressing in expertise as a coach is not usually a linear process. It is not necessarily true, therefore, that someone who has been coaching ten years is better at it than someone who has been coaching for five years. But coaches who have continued to learn and grow, using the self-awareness building process of "listen quietly rather than listening hard" as described above, will continually become better at what they do.

This chapter explores the key coaching skills that add nuances to the use of the basic QuantumShift! coaching model we have described thus far. These skills are:

- Shifting perspective
- Identifying and eliminating self-defeating behaviors
- Handling strong client emotions
- Powerful questioning
- Communicating clearly
- Celebrating successes
- Maintaining client focus
- Being client-centered
- Ending the coaching relationship

Shifting Perspective

The dictionary defines *perspective* as "a mental view of the relationship of aspects of a subject to each other and to a whole" and "an idea of the relative importance of things." Both definitions are relevant in the coaching context. In Level 2 coaching, we test whether clients can separate themselves from the people and situations in their lives, and even from their beliefs and assumptions. Developing the ability to see a situation not just through the lens of their own viewpoint, but also from the perspective of co-workers, a spouse, a prospective employer, or even their coach is a sign of high self-awareness.

Fig. 23 provides some examples of opposing, or complementary, perspectives. If the client's perspective as expressed falls on one side of the continuum, it may be useful to explore the perspective on the other side to help find an answer.

Coaching Questions to Shift Perspective

In helping clients shift their perspective, we first ask questions to identify their current perspective. We then test to see if they can also articulate other people's views or other filters through which they might look at the situation. Here are some sample questions to ask for this purpose:

- "If you were X [the other person in the situation], what would you want/feel/ need/say?"

Figure 23: Sample Opposing Perspectives

Short-term	Long-term
Immediate	Distant
Limitation	Possibility
Weakness	Strength
Big picture	Current issue
Behavior	Motivation
Motivation	Identity
Who you are	Who you could be
People	Things
Individual	Family
Monocultural	Multicultural/diverse
Black and white	Shades of gray
Right and wrong	Situational ethics
National	Global
Selfish	Selfless
Visual	Auditory
Analytical	Intuitive
Constant problems	Lessons to be learned
Me	Them
Challenge	Opportunity
Old	Young
Male	Female
Conservative	Progressive
Positive	Negative
Small	Large
Pessimistic	Optimistic
Limited	Unlimited

- If the client says they're stuck:
  - "What's important about getting unstuck?"
  - "If you were advising yourself, what would you suggest for getting unstuck?"
  - "How is it perfect for you to feel stuck right now?"
  - "If you weren't stuck, what would you do next?"

- "If you were the coach, what question would you ask right now?"
- "What powerful question would your 'wise self' ask right now?"
- "If that weren't true, what else could it be?"
- "What if X were not so important to you?
- "How does that serve your life purpose?"
- "How else could you view this situation?"
- "What would you do if you knew you couldn't fail?"
- "Is there a broader perspective here?"
- "You've talked about yourself; what about the others involved?"
- "I hear your analytical self speaking; what does your intuition say?"
- "What if you gave up your 'script' around this?"
- "If you didn't have to blame X, what else might be possible?"
- "What's beneath the [e.g., stress, fear, guilt]? If it weren't that, what else could it be?"

Other Perspective-Shifting Techniques

In addition to these powerful perspective-shifting questions, at least two other techniques can also help clients see a situation from another vantage point.

1. **Reframing.** When clients make a statement reflecting a particular perspective, reframing through the use of a perspective-shifting question can create an immediate shift, as seen in the following examples:

Client:	"I just don't know how I'll make next month's mortgage payment."
Coach:	"What could you do to stop living month-to-month?"
Client:	"I'm just too stubborn to work for someone else."
Coach:	"How could your stubbornness be used as an asset?" (e.g., as an entrepreneur)

What if ___ was no object?
What if power wasn't so important to you?

Client:	"It just seems like I can either make good money or do work I enjoy."
Coach:	"How could you have both?"

2. **Feedback.** Simply by stating what you observe, you may help clients see the absurdity or "stuckness" of what they are saying. To take feedback one step further, use it to communicate a broader perspective that inspires clients to make a shift. In the first example above we illustrate how this can be done. A broader perspective is just one kind of different perspective, but it is critical that as you listen to your clients you mentally step back to see whether there might be a larger aspect to what they are saying. This kind of "dancing in the moment" demonstrates yet another of our coaching competencies. We must learn to be both present and flexible to facilitate transformation and discovery in our clients.

Identifying and Eliminating Self-Defeating Behaviors

Nearly all of us engage in activities each day that either waste our time or drain our energy. The problem is, we're often unaware of them, but we tolerate them day in and day out and then wonder why we are not making faster progress toward our goals.

When clients raise this issue – or when you suspect that examining it may be a way for them to reduce their stress level – you might ask them to keep a log of all of their activities for at least a week. Initially, they should just list the time of day and what they are doing—from when they wake up in the morning until they go to bed at night. Then later they can come back and evaluate their activities to determine what was time or energy well spent, and what was not.

It often becomes amazingly clear from this "time log" exercise what is getting in the way of clients' fulfilling their career, job change, or other professional (or personal) goals. Sometimes, even the people with whom we spend time can be what wastes our time and/or drains our energy most, so we want our clients to be on the lookout for that, as well as self-defeating behaviors and activities!

Eliminating a behavior or activity by itself is not enough, though, since that leaves an empty space or vacuum that must be replaced with something else that aligns with one's purpose, goals, and intention. So the next step is to encourage clients to identify what actions, behaviors, or activities, however small or seemingly insignificant, would contribute to their being more focused and more purposeful, and to their having more time and energy available to fulfill their goals. Clients can then track how many days during a month they engage in that behavior, and keep another time log after working with the new behavior for a while to see if they engage in fewer time-wasting and energy-draining activities.

Handling Client Emotions

Periodically during our coaching experience, clients will express strong emotions such as fear, anger, frustration, tears, sadness, and pain. Depending on how comfortable we are personally with expressing emotion, this situation may be something we approach with ease or trepidation. Factoring in our clients' comfort level—high or low—with their feelings makes the situation more complex yet.

What is important to realize about strong emotions is that they are communicating important information about the client. An effective coach will have developed the ability to be present with clients even during these challenging times, knowing that working through the emotions will help in their transformation.

What Not to Do When Strong Emotions Arise

Here is a list of ways not to react when clients display strong emotions:

- Ignore these displays
- Ask them why they feel that way (you don't need to know the cause of the feeling, but simply help them embrace it and move through it)
- Tell them they should not feel that way

- Tell them they should see a therapist (unless, of course, it keeps happening, and they cannot meaningfully participate in coaching)
- Encourage them to bury, ignore, or hide their feelings (from you or themselves)
- Confuse their emotions with your own issues, or get caught up in them

Strategies for Coaching When Strong Emotions Arise

Here are some techniques you may, instead, want to try:

- Mirror clients' intensity, pace, breathing, and language and then notice how it makes you feel, and what it tells you about their energy level and emotional state
- Focus more on simply "being there" with them, rather than "doing" something or moving them to an action plan
- Since many clients' tendency is to avoid emotions—and what lies beneath them—part of your role is to help them welcome the emotions and include them in their experience of life. You can even encourage clients to go deeper into the emotions and explore them with prompts such as the following:
    - "I sense some powerful emotions there. Can you describe them?"
    - "What are you not willing to explore?"
    - "Does this create any feeling in your body? What does it feel like?"
    - "What message is in this emotion [or experience]?"
    - "What is the gift in this emotion?"
    - "What would happen if you did what you fear most?"
    - "What would you miss out on if you ignored this message?"

Notice whether the emotions seem to be about the conflict between clients' stated goal or desire (e.g., to lose weight) and their actual behavior (e.g., overeating). Exploring that and asking clients whether that conflict is part of the issue can help them voice what they are feeling. You might use metaphors to help them see the emotions from a higher perspective by asking them, for example:

- To imagine they are floating above their situation and to share what they see

- To imagine that the situation is a lake into which they dive and then swim around in, exploring all aspects of the experience
- To imagine that they can rewrite their life from here on, free of the deep issues beneath these emotions—What would be different?
- If the emotion were an animal, what would it be?
- If the emotion were a color or shape, what would it be?

You might also use humor—judiciously—to help clients laugh at their own situation.

Powerful Questioning

Asking questions in coaching is powerful only when we bring a sense of artistry to it, rather than a mechanical approach. This difference is more easily felt than described, more perceived than observed. A similar example is students learning how to play a piano: some simply press the keys in a mechanical fashion as dictated by the musical score, whereas others make the instrument absolutely sing as they bring expression, soul, and feeling to the music.

We know a powerful question when we hear one—and sometimes when we ask one. But just what is it about a question that makes it powerful? Here are three distinctions that can make a difference:

- **Nonjudgmental vs. judgmental.** One key to powerful questions is whether or not they contain a judgment. It is the difference between "Don't you think you should do X?" (leading/judgmental) and "What are your options as you see them?" (nonjudgmental). Leading questions tend to contain judgments.
- **Short vs. long.** The more concise a question is, the less likely it will contain a judgment, include your own biases, and/or confuse the client. If you tend to think aloud, you may have a tendency to frame your questions as you talk, ending up with one long question or two or three questions in one. Instead, pause to take a breath, determine what you want to ask, and ask it simply and concisely. You'll be surprised how much it improves your coaching!
- **Open- vs. closed-ended.** Even in Level 1 coaching, we have learned to focus on asking open-ended questions to generate as many options as possible for resolving clients' issues. Closed-ended questions (those that can be answered "yes" or "no") tend to be weak, whereas open-ended questions are powerful. For example, "Did you notice how he talked down to you?" (closed-ended) versus "What did you notice?" (open-ended).

Blaming/Playing the Victim vs. Empowerment

Questions that encourage clients to bemoan their fate tend to look into the past and do not forward the session. Remember that as a coach your job is not to analyze clients' behavior! Instead, you can ask questions that empower them to look at the present and the future, as in the examples shown in fig. 24.

Figure 24: Two Types of Questions

Blaming/Victim	Empowerment
Why do you think you did that?	What lesson can you take forward for next time this happens?
What did your parents teach you about this?	What do you want your philosophy or governing principle to be here?
Why can't I seem to find jobs I like?	What would your ideal job be like?
Why am I so afraid to take a risk?	How can you embrace the message in your fear as a catalyst for forward action?
What happened then?	What is happening now?

Asking Questions That Reflect Clients' Language and/or Communication Style

Using your knowledge of clients' communication style (see fig. 25), you can reframe your question as appropriate, as illustrated in the following examples and their neurolinguistic designations:

- "How does that look to you?" (visual)
- "How does that sound to you?" (auditory)
- "How does that feel to you?" (kinesthetic)
- "What does that mean to you?" (auditory-digital)

Figure 25: Understanding Communication Styles Using Neurolinguistic Programming (NLP) Order

	VISUAL	AUDITORY
Common Characteristics	They memorize by seeing pictures. They often have trouble remembering verbal instructions because their mind tends to wander.	They typically are easily distracted by noise. They can repeat things back to you easialy, learn by listening, like music, and like to talk on the phone.
Describing to them	They are interested by how the program looks	Tone of voice and the words used are important
Commonly used words	• See • Look • Appear • View • Show • Imagine • Crystalize	• Hear • Listen • Sound • Tune in/out • Click • Ring a bell
Speech Pattern	Quickly grouped words	Lots of interruptions and 'uh', 'um', 'ah', etc
Processing Patterns	Quickly with minimum of detail	Will let you know unconsciously when they understand by changing the subject
Their Gifts	• Big Picture • Organized • Great planners • Get things done quickly • Great sellers • Visionaries	• Big Picture • Brilliant ideas • Little/no details • Inventors • Born leaders • Quality work • Good story tellers • Love telephone

Here are some other important techniques for asking powerful questions:

- **Bypass rephrasing and go directly to the question you want to ask next.** Though as a beginning coach you may have tended to do a lot of rephrasing of, or reflecting on, what the client was saying (using the Reflective Model of Elaboration), as you become more experienced you can increase your effectiveness by bypassing rephrasing. When tempted to say, "So what you're

Figure 25: Understanding Communication Styles Using Neurolinguistic Programming (NLP) Order (continued)

	KINESTHETIC	AUDITORY (DIGITAL)
Common Characteristics	They often talk slowly. They respond to physical rewards, and touching. They memorize by doing or walking through something.	This person spends a fair amount of time talking to themselves. They memorize by steps, procedures, and sequences.
Describing to them	They will be interested in a program that 'feels right' /"gut-feelings".	They will want to know if your program makes sense
Commonly used words	• Feel • Touch • Touch base • Get hold of • Comfortable • Catch on • Play, Together	• Sense • Experience • Understand • Think • Process • Decide • I Know
Speech Pattern	Deliberate phrasing	Long complicated sentences
Processing Patterns	Extensive detail	Will not give indication of understanding unless you ask
Their Gifts	• Love details • Creative • Work well with others • Patient • Loyal or devoted • Sensitive to people and environment • Supportive	• Problem solvers • Talent for 'figuring' it out • Work fast • Likes behind-the-scenes • Project planner

saying is..." or, "So what I'm hearing you say your options are is...," simply ask the question that would follow that statement for a more powerful question, such as, "What would you most enjoy doing?" or, "What else do you need to consider?"

- **Use optimal timing.** The right question asked at the wrong time becomes inappropriate, rather than powerful. How do you know when to ask a question? It's a combination of listening to your intuition, deep listening to hear what clients are saying, and determining why you are asking the question. Are you seeking to enhance clients' awareness, or do you need to know the answer for yourself? Remember, it is all about *them*—your agenda does not enter into the coaching process. Experience is also part of this, and the more you are "in the flow" with the client, the less you will need to consciously be aware of timing because it will naturally be right. Trying to plan questions may in fact throw the timing off.

- **Ask permission to coach in a sensitive area.** Clients may state this verbally ("I don't want to talk about X") or may simply become resistant, change the subject, or otherwise tell you nonverbally that they are uncomfortable talking about a particular issue. Certainly, whenever we explore Level 2 or 3 issues, there will be a level of discomfort—but we need to ask our clients' permission to walk through the door of behavior to motives, beliefs, interpretation, and identity. Asking permission may take one of the following forms:

  - "Do I have your permission to explore that area?"
  - "Would you like to go deeper into that issue now?"
  - How would you feel about seeing what else is there regarding that matter?"
  - "I notice that you may have some resistance; are you willing to explore it?"

The Flow of Powerful Questions

Combining all the elements above, we are now ready to explore how to formulate powerful questions. How do we know that our questions are effective in achieving our four desired career coaching outcomes for our clients, as outlined in chapter 12: enhanced self-awareness, clarity of purpose and goals, increased career self-management, and overall improved quality of life? And how do we continue to use questions, along with other coaching techniques such as feedback, observations, challenges, and role-modeling to further that process? The diagram in fig. 26 illustrates the result of unpowerful questions, which tend to elicit a "script" (the same old answer).

Contrast that with the diagram in fig. 27, which shows the progression of the use of powerful questions. Here, clients often pause to "process" or reflect on the question and their situation. When encouraged to share more, they begin developing insight. Then the process is repeated. At one of these levels, clients realize a pattern and/or shifts their beliefs or perceptions. The result is a QuantumShift!

Figure 26: Unpowerful Questioning

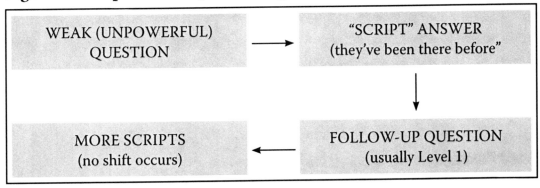

Figure 27: Powerful Questioning

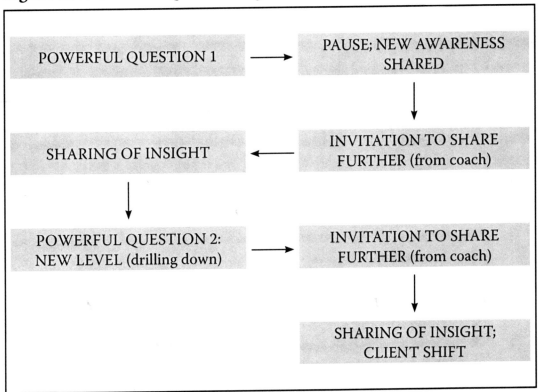

Communicating Clearly

Our coaching competencies include several approaches to clear and direct communication: direct feedback, reframing and introducing other perspectives, clear objectives, appropriate and respectful language, and appropriate use of metaphor and analogy. Since we have discussed several of these previously, we will address the last two of these aspects here.

Using Appropriate and Respectful Language

In our increasingly diverse culture, we must choose language that is both politically correct and culturally sensitive. This becomes more challenging as many of us work across international borders with clients in other countries.

Being *politically correct* means avoiding slang, stereotypes, colloquialisms, and offensive terms including racial slurs, derogatory or prejudicial language, or language that implies or states disapproval of life-style or sexual preferences. Being *culturally sensitive* refers to using terms that are clear and understandable based on the person's culture—for example, *trunk* in American English versus *boot* in British English. Cultural sensitivity has more to do with being understood, both in language and in customs, than offending someone. In addition, you need to avoid the following:

- Using absolutes (*always, never, all, every*)
- Generalizing—referring to the generic *they* or *people* and making untested assumptions about the world
- Referring to *you* or *they* when you mean yourself, as in, "When X happens, you feel like giving up"; point this out to clients when they do it
- Making broad "how it is" statements, as in, "That's just how engineers are," or, "It's the economy; there just aren't any jobs out there"
- Being inauthentic or hypocritical in any way (e.g., telling or encouraging the client to do something that you would not do yourself)

Using Metaphor and Analogy

Questions using metaphors—visual or other images—to explain clients' issues or experiences can be a powerful way to access a more holistic perspective on an issue than the more obvious question. For example, asking, "Do you feel like you're drifting at sea?" will be more powerful for some clients than, "Are you confused?" (especially if they're kinesthetic or highly visual in communication style). Analogy uses language creatively to draw parallels with clients' experiences. An example might be, "If the players in this situation were animals, what would they be?" or, "Is there any parallel between what you're experiencing and some event in nature? Describe it for me."

Coaching techniques using metaphor, analogy, and other images can also be used in a more suggestive way, as in the following examples:

- "Imagine you can rise above the situation in a helicopter and see the entire landscape. What do you see? What else? What colors? How fast are things moving? What are the most important or visible elements?"
- "Let's be a couple of miners, going deep into the earth to explore these beliefs further together. What do you notice as the elevator descends into the mine shaft? Where is the light coming from? Are there any creatures or other images that come to mind? What feelings do you feel? Let's go a bit deeper now, beginning to move toward the gold mine. The gold mine is where the answer to your dilemma lies. Now what do you feel? Where is it located in your body...?"

Roadblocks to Clear Communication

Most of us desire to communicate clearly and be understood. So what gets in our way?

- **Complex questions.** If you process your thoughts aloud and make up question(s) as you go, rather than taking a moment to pause, formulating the question you want to ask, and then asking it, you may confuse the client.
- **Lack of confidence.** When you lack confidence, you may hesitate, be unwilling to "tell it like it is," and so on, so your communication will be unclear. This may also prevent you from instilling confidence in your clients.
- **Lack of familiarity with clients' industry, job, or situation, as well as terminology.** If you don't know a lot about your clients' situation, you may feel the need to become more of an expert. But, learn only as much as you

need to know to coach them. Consider asking clients a generic coaching question and learn from them as they talk. Or, ask them to provide you with a job description or other summary of their background to complete the picture you have of them. Lack of industry knowledge can actually be an asset, as you bring more objectivity and open-mindedness to the commonly accepted paths of progression in an industry.

- **Either rushing or trying to slow clients' pace.** Indicators might include interrupting, taking long pauses, and so on. Masterful coaches will only move at a pace different from that of the client when there is a specific reason for it (e.g., when the client thinks slowly and analytically and the coach wants to "shake her up" by using a faster pace to generate new perspectives).

Other miscellaneous roadblocks can include:

- Getting emotionally caught up in the client's issue
- Mumbling; dropping your voice as you talk
- Inadequate time establishing rapport
- Failure to clear distractions from your mind before session
- Failure to follow through on promised tasks
- Taking excessive notes while coaching

Sometimes to communicate more clearly and be better understood, you may need to use a different communication style. For example, your client may stumble over a visual question she processes auditorily. Refer to fig. 25 for tips on language to use when reframing questions.

Measuring the Clarity of Your Communication

Perhaps one of the best ways to increase your awareness of how clear and effective your communication has been is to record—with the client's permission, of course—your coaching sessions. As you listen to the tape, or as you reflect on you coaching overall, you might ask yourself questions such as those listed in the exercises, "Evaluating Communication Clarity" in the Career Coach's Toolbox (p. 389).

Celebrating Successes

There are many ways to reward employees, as the title of Bob Nelson and Kenneth Blanchard's book *1001 Ways to Reward Employees* suggests—and each person likes to be rewarded in a different way.[58] Recognizing this fact can result in a shift. In considering rewards, however, we first want to be sure that clients are not taking the action just to satisfy us, or to get acknowledgement from us as their coach. While we may find it gratifying, it can create a codependency that stops their progress when the coaching ends. That said, here are some of the ways you may want to use to celebrate your clients' successes:

- Offer acknowledgment, appreciation
- Ask them how they could reward themselves
- Send clients free e-cards (emailed greeting cards) or inspirational messages
- Send flowers, balloons, or novelty items with your company name on it

Maintaining Client Focus

The final coaching competency discussed in this chapter is maintaining clients' focus. While goals seem quite palpable and important when set, over a period of weeks they can fade in priority—as can clients' commitment. Part of your role as coach is to help clients stay true to what they stated was important to them as you began the coaching—and to their changing priorities as the coaching continues.

One of your challenges as a coach is balancing accountability with support: keeping clients true to their goals but also supporting them as they progress. The dictionary definition of *accountability* is to be "responsible and answerable; being held to the task and required to follow through on what you have promised." Like feedback, accountability sometimes has a negative connotation—that of pointing out where the people (here, clients) have failed to keep their word. But in fact, accountability is a neutral concept. It simply means "to give an account"—to tell what worked and what did not and to learn from the results.

Holding clients accountable is more than babysitting, checking up on them, or even having them be accountable to you. They are in fact being held accountable to themselves—to do what they have promised. To hold clients accountable, ask them to articulate three things as part of their stated action step(s), as described in our Coaching Plan template:

- Actions to be taken
- A timeline
- The means to measure progress (or, if it is a reflective action, its value)

When Clients Do Not Do What They Promise

When clients do not follow through, the coach is put in the difficult position of needing to point this out and explore it. Yet, it is one of our coaching competencies to confront the client "positively." How do we do this? Here are some things you might say:

- "I noticed you didn't complete X" (the action the client intended to do at the close of your last session). "What are your observations about that?" Or, "What can you learn from this?" Or, "Has something prevented you from doing it?"
- "Based on your not doing what you set out to do, how do you want to redefine accountability in our relationship?" Or, "How can I help you be accountable to yourself around this issue?"
- "What's beneath your not following through here?"
- "Has this been a pattern? Does it pertain to a particular type of issue or to all issues?"
- "Imagine that you continue to not follow through on this [action/behavior/issue]. What will your life be like one year from now? Five years from now? Are you willing to accept those consequences?"

Becoming Client-Centered

One of the ICF coaching competencies is to develop a "coaching presence," one aspect of which is a focus on clients (we have explored many of the other aspects in previous chapters). Among the things that are involved in being client-centered are:

- Focusing our attention on clients exclusively during the session
- Showing genuine concern for clients and their welfare
- Being fully conscious and aware during the session
- Creating spontaneous relationships with clients
- Employing an open, flexible, confident style
- Using active and deep listening
- Adopting a neutral viewpoint, honoring clients' preferences and not judging
- Asking questions, being curious
- Being supportive
- Letting clients set the agenda
- Allowing clients to take responsibility for the depth they want to go to
- Being sensitive to clients' limits, not pushing them past those limits without their permission
- Relating observations as appropriate (and listening for content to observe)
- "Dancing in the moment"

One of the traps that can keep us from being client-centered is starting to pursue (even if inadvertently) our own agenda. We know that we are doing this if we start asking leading questions, miss nonverbal cues such as energy shifts, start to rephrase clients' statements, do more talking than listening, or begin planning our questions in advance.

If your agenda is getting in the way, you first want to acknowledge what is happening (to yourself first, to the client only if appropriate). You might then ask for a moment to take a breath and refocus, ask an open-ended question that will get the client talking about his or her agenda, or, if you are using a headset, get up and walk around to shift your energy unnoticeably. Then you can ask a question that will help your client refocus on his or her agenda.

We discourage extensive note taking during a coaching session, as it will distract you from both what is being said and not said. If you are concerned about missing important points, record your sessions, or learn to trust that you will remember what is important. Or, even better, ask clients to recap the important points and/or their "takeaways" after the call on the "After Coaching Call Reflection Form" in the Career Coach's Toolbox (p. 377), relieving you of the responsibility! After all, the coaching is for them, right?

Ending the Coaching Relationship

The savvy career coach will set expectations with clients at the outset that will encourage them to use the coach to manage their career in an ongoing way – as a "lifetime career management partner." While the intensity of the work may ebb and flow with clients' stage in their professional life, the relationship continues. Initial job change or career transition can be followed by coaching to help them successfully navigate the orientation or trial period, integrate into the company, achieve life/work balance, and prepare for the next intended promotion or job change.

If, however, the time comes that your clients decide that they no longer need your services, or for whatever reason they do not wish to renew their initial coaching commitment, there is an art to the ending process. Especially in career coaching, as opposed to other types of coaching, it is not so much "good-bye" as it is "farewell" or "adieu," since clients may return to work with you during a future career change or other work-related scenario. You should mark on your calendar the one-year anniversary of clients' starting a new job so that you can recontact them for possible assistance in preparing for a performance review and to see if the job still meets their needs. Ending this sequence of coaching, therefore, is more like a comma than of a period. So to end the relationship (for now) on the best of terms, here are a few tips:

- Review with clients their initial goals, as stated in the Coaching Plan. Were they achieved? Were new goals discovered that took their place?
- Ask clients to complete an evaluation of their coaching experience and return it to you within twenty-four hours, if possible

- Ask clients what surprised them, what disappointed them (if anything), and where they will go from here

- If clients have indicated any kind of dissatisfaction or disappointment, do what you can to make it right, including giving away additional sessions if need be, or otherwise correcting it. Dissatisfied customers tell ten people; satisfied customers usually only tell one.

- Invite clients to keep in touch with you as they become acclimated in their new position or situation and to feel free to contact you if they want or need further coaching—especially as they approach a performance review or possible promotion

As a career coach, you can envision and strive for a lifelong relationship with your clients. As career self-managers they will make numerous transitions during their lifetime. You can be their partner as they navigate their professional journey.

KEY COACHING CONCEPTS:

1. Shifting perspective means to see things in a different way.

2. To eliminate time and energy wasters, clients should keep a time log of their actual time spent during the day and evaluate what they can eliminate for more purposeful activity.

3. When clients express strong emotions, the best approach is to mirror their emotions, focusing on fully "being there," probing deeper into the emotions, and/or using humor.

4. Some keys to making questions more powerful include avoiding judgment, keeping questions short, using open-ended questions, asking empowering questions, honoring clients' communication style, bypassing rephrasing, using optimal timing, and asking permission to coach in sensitive areas.

5. It is critical to use appropriate language; that is, language that is politically correct and culturally sensitive.

6. Metaphor and analogy can better illustrate a point in some cases than stating the situation directly.

7. Maintaining a client focus requires a delicate balance between holding clients accountable and being supportive of them.

8. To be accountable, clients must state the desired action to be taken, a timeline, and a means to measure progress.

9. It is critical that you learn the techniques that allow you to stay focused on each client throughout each session.

10. When the time comes to end a coaching relationship, it should be more like a comma than a period, since clients may return to you for their next transition!

PART FOUR

JOB SEARCH
MECHANICS

Once job targets are identified:

Ask " What is the best approach to use to obtain my ideal job?"

20

Succeeding at the Job Search: Developing a Marketing Plan and Allowing for Synchronicity

"You are an individualized expression of the creative flow. There is something you can do that no one can do quite as uniquely as you. Somewhere there is a need for that special contribution. You are needed even as you have a need.... As you sit thinking, 'If I could only find a job,' some employer is at that very moment thinking, 'If only we could locate the right person for this opening!' Keep that vision of the orderly Universe. It is not a miracle that is needed to create a job for you but an expression of divine order in bringing you together with that which is looking for you."

—*Eric Butterworth,* Spiritual Economics

In part 4 we enter the realm of job search mechanics – helping clients take a strategic, marketing-oriented approach to their job search. At this stage, your clients should be wondering, "What is the best strategy to use to obtain my ideal job?" Key steps for you in helping them at this stage include using your QuantumShift!™ skills to:

- Get clients to think of themselves as a product to be marketed
- Assist them in designing a marketing strategy using an appropriate mix of published and unpublished sources
- Ensure that clients know how to identify appropriate openings and target companies
- Make certain they know how to use the strategies that will get them the best results depending on their goals
- Work with them to develop one or more resumes that will showcase their qualifications
- Discuss interviewing techniques, how to answer the most common questions, what questions to ask, how to dress for an interview, how to overcome liabilities, and the like
- Provide tools to help clients comprehensively evaluate the job offers they receive
- Assist them in negotiating the optimum compensation package

This is an area of career coaching that some coaches love and others dislike. Do you like to see quick results from your work? Do you enjoy pointing to tangible products from your day's activities? Then the job search mechanics aspect of career coaching may be a perfect fit. On the other hand, if you prefer the creativity of the career discovery and design process discussed in part 2 – and do not mind waiting for a QuantumShift! to occur – then you may want to leave the job search mechanics to someone else. To do so, you can partner with a coach and/or a professional resume writer who enjoys that work, or simply refer clients elsewhere when they are ready to launch their search.

One other difference between coaching the career design process and coaching job search mechanics is that your role in the latter is often one step closer to a consulting model (see fig. 28).

Figure 28: Career Coaching Continuum

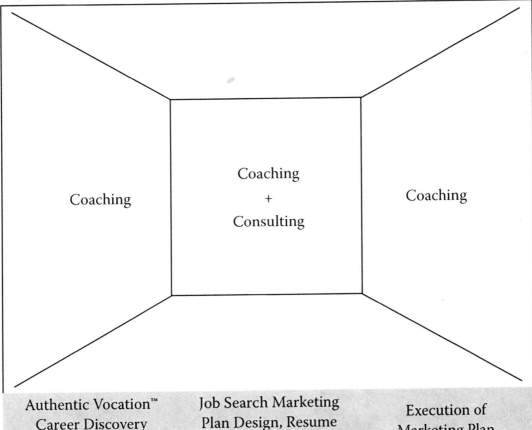

Clients need to internalize a huge volume of information about how the job search process works in order to be successful. Rather than spending the coaching sessions communicating this information in consulting or lecturing style, it usually works better to take one of the following approaches:

1. Offer regular teleclasses or live seminars, one to three hours in length, at which you communicate this information. Admit paid coaching clients at no charge as part of their coaching services package; consider inviting nonclients for a nominal fee as part of your marketing strategy.

2. Prepare sessions that can be made available on an audio program your Web site, in audio or video, so that clients can hear you discuss these topics.

3. Assign clients relevant reading – hard copy or electronic file – prior to broaching the next phase of their job search.[59]

Then, the coaching sessions themselves can be spent strategizing and applying the job search principles to their specific situation, with both coach and client having a common understanding of how resume design or answering common interview questions or evaluating a job offer should proceed.

Whether or not you decide to directly provide resume writing, interview coaching, negotiating assistance, and job search marketing plan coaching to your clients, you will nevertheless want to have a working knowledge of these topics. At the very least, you will be able to identify why some clients have become disillusioned with their job search – for example – if they have been relying exclusively on advertised openings in the Sunday newspaper and do not know how to access the unpublished market. And at best, you will want to know enough to spot-check the work of any subcontractors you may use so as to ensure that your clients are receiving the highest quality services.

Self As Product or "Brand"

We begin by exploring our job-searching mind-set. Successful job seekers think one way, unsuccessful ones think another. What is the difference? In today's competitive marketplace, it is no longer enough to think of oneself as a mere commodity hoping to be purchased by some company for a fair price. That is the approach of the unsuccessful job seeker.

Successful job seekers think of themselves as a brand, a niche product – one that needs to be marketed very specifically to the right target audience in order to result in the right mutual arrangement: the ideal job. Put yourself in the position of a marketer for a moment and imagine that you have been tasked with marketing a new software program designed for an industry-specific user group. What kinds of questions would you need to answer to market this product? Job seekers need to ask the following questions:

- "What are my assets?"
- "How am I different/better than other similar candidates?"
- "Where do I lack skills or attributes, and how will I manage employers' perceptions regarding these areas?"
- "Where are my customers (i.e., prospective employers) located?"
- "How can I best reach my customers?"

It may be helpful to have your clients write out their answers to these questions; these can be a useful reference to as they conduct their search.

One of the leading resources on personal branding in the job search is *Career Distinction: Stand Out by Building Your Brand*, by William Arruda and Kirsten Dixson (Wiley 2007). In it, the authors outline three key steps to building a personal brand: 1) extract (identifying the assets that will comprise your brand), 2) express (your personal communications plan), and 3) exude (managing your brand environment).

Designing the Marketing Plan: Job Search Strategy Mix

In guiding clients in launching their job search, you will also need to work with them to develop an appropriate mix of unpublished and published strategies that meet their needs. In the following two chapters, we will explore in detail how to approach both the published and the unpublished markets, including sample approach letters.

Even the idea of creating a marketing plan is a foreign concept to most job seekers. See what you already know about job search marketing by completing the quiz in fig. 29.

Figure 29: Job Search Marketing Quiz

TRUE OR FALSE STATEMENT	TRUE	FALSE
1. Most jobs are filled through advertised openings.		
2. A job seeker's chances of being hired through an Internet job board are over 75 percent.		
3. Submitting an unsolicited resume is the best way to get hired through an executive recruiter.		
4. The primary purpose of networking is to access published openings.		
5. Every job seeker should use both published and unpublished market strategies in their campaign.		
6. There's no point applying to advertised openings in trade journals; they're overused and usually flooded with applicants.		
7. It will reflect negatively on the job seeker if he/she sends an unsolicited letter requesting a meeting with a manager or CEO to learn more about their company and industry.		
8. Job fairs are a waste of time for people with experience in a targeted industry.		
9. To maximize exposure in the geographic area where the person wants to work, the best approach is to send out several hundred unsolicited resumes in a mass mailing directed to specific human resource professionals.		
10. Once a candidate gets their resume properly formatted with their work history and qualifications, he should use the same resume for each position he applies for, whether mailed, faxed or emailed.		

Believe it or not, every single one of those ten statements is false. How did you do? We will later discuss each of these principles in detail. In our experience, the typical scenario for a new job seeker works something like this: the candidate updates his resume, looks through the Sunday newspaper and peruses one or two of the large Internet job boards, submits his resume, perhaps attends a networking breakfast, and waits for the phone to ring or the e-mails to arrive. No results are forthcoming. What is wrong? This job seeker fails to understand that less than 20 percent of the job openings filled in a given year are ever published, and the percentage of placements that occur through job boards is significantly lower yet (as low as 1 percent for non-computer-related jobs).[60] And while people have typically heard that there is something called the "hidden job market," they usually don't know how to access it.

Following is a preview of the seven possible components of a diversified job search plan.

Published sources:

- *Help wanted ads* (newspapers, trade magazines): published openings from companies and recruiters
- *Recruiters/employment agencies:* professionals hiring on behalf of companies for specific positions
- *Internet job boards:* online services such as www.monster.com—and others that are industry-specific—that make published openings available to job seekers
- *Job fairs:* gatherings of employers seeking new staff—job seekers are invited to attend and distribute their resumes
  - industry job banks

Unpublished sources:

- *Networking* (various types): meeting with individuals in targeted companies and industries to discuss their needs and identify potential openings *including LinkedIn*
- *Direct targeted mailings:* customized approach letters to specific companies within target markets identifying a potential need and summarizing the candidate's background and ability to meet that need
- *News event-generated mailings:* targeted mailings to companies whose employees or firm appear in the news media describing recent events within the company indicating—often indirectly—a need for new employees

Tailoring Marketing Strategy to Client

As your clients prepare to initiate their search, it is important to set suitable goals for each marketing tactic to be used so that they have both a realistic approach and a way to gauge their progress. A representative marketing plan is available in Authentic Vocation Worksheet 9 in the Career Coach's Toolbox (p. 379). You will note that the marketing plan template includes targets for each type of job search tactic and columns for actual activities: letters sent, calls made, interviews generated, and offers received. It also provides space to designate the percentage of clients' activity to be spent in the published market versus the unpublished market.

Of course, those percentages and target numbers for each tactic will need to be customized to fit individual clients' specific situations. Following are a few examples.

- **Marketing for the introvert.** The natural tendency for most introverted clients is to respond primarily to advertised openings, sending unsolicited resumes to recruiters, surfing the job boards, and writing letters. Since they often excel at using the computer, they may tend to hide behind it. It is especially difficult for them to pick up the phone and call people they do not know and to meet with key people for informational interviews. One thing we can do is reduce the number of targeted networking meetings suggested for these clients. But we can also do some scripting and/or role-playing with them to increase their comfort level with networking and making follow-up calls to approach letters. Their search will be considerably more effective if they can stretch themselves to make the required calls and get face-to-face meetings with people.

- **Marketing for the career changer.** For when your clients making a change of industry or position, particularly when it is a wholesale career change, most of the published job market strategies will be of little use. Recruiters and screeners for advertised openings will, as a general rule, only consider candidates that have the requisite experience in the job and/or industry in which they seek to fill the position. Therefore, career-changing clients' marketing strategies will often rely almost solely on unpublished sources.

- **Marketing for the client with a large network.** In career coaching, we meet clients where they are. So when clients are well-networked within their industry and/or community, we want to encourage them to use that asset strategically in their search. Their marketing plan, therefore, might have a higher target number of networking contacts to make as compared to responding to advertised openings or submitting resumes to recruiters.

- **Marketing for the part-time versus full-time job seeker.** When we are working with clients who are looking for a job while currently employed (part-time job seekers), their number of target contacts each week should generally be half that of full-time job seekers who are not currently employed. Clients are often restricted in their search due to their current work environment (e.g., due to open cubicles or company monitoring of employee phone calls and/or Internet use), so that they cannot make networking or follow-up phone calls from work. In this case, we can suggest that they either reduce their target number of calls consider using/buying a cell phone to use for their search during their lunch hour or before or after work.

Note that in general, clients with characteristics opposite those of the examples will take the opposite approach. For example, an extroverted client would naturally use the strategies introverts may find difficult, so their marketing plan can be more balanced between published and unpublished sources.

Establishing the Ideal Job Vision

In addition to completing the marketing plan, clients also need to initiate their search with a clear vision of the key aspects of their ideal job. The "Ideal Job Template" and the "Ideal Day Exercise" in the Career Coach's Toolbox (pp. 352 and 359) begin this process. The Authentic Vocation Profile described at the end of chapter 11 will also help. In addition, clients/candidates should, at the outset of their search, fill in the "Wants" and "Needs" columns of "Authentic Vocation Worksheet 10" (p. 382) to indicate the items that would be desirable but not required and those that are non-negotiable. Then, when job offers come in, the features of each offer can be inserted in the right-hand columns and evaluated against the wants and needs in the left-hand columns to determine which offer best meets clients' criteria.

Organizing the Search

From the very beginning of clients' job search campaigns, they will need a system for managing their contacts. Not only does this allow them to maintain a proactive role in the process, but it also puts the information they will need to respond to a call or prepare for an interview at their fingertips. Depending on their comfort level with computer-based systems, they choose a low-tech or high-tech approach.

- **Low-Tech Approach:** A simple three-ring binder can serve as a way to organize the search. Client simply create a tickler file in the binder with index tabs for each month of the year and tabs numbered 1 to 31 for each day of the current month. The binder may also contain subject tabs by area of search, such as "networking contacts," "interviews," "banking industry information," and so on. To use the system, each time clients send an e-mail or letter responding to an ad or approaching a networking contact, they make a hard copy for the binder and file it under the date designated for follow-up. If desired, a second copy can be filed alphabetically by company (under another set of index tabs) so that it can be located easily when clients do not remember the follow-up date.

- **High-Tech Approach:** A number of software and Internet systems can streamline the contact management process during the job search.

    - Creating and using the "folders" feature in both Microsoft® Word® and the e-mail program of your choice (Eudora®, MS Outlook®, etc.) will keep job search correspondence organized. Whether clients designate the electronic folders by industry (e.g., "banking," "insurance," "financial software") or by marketing strategy (e.g., "responses to ads," "recruiter letters," "networking with alumni") or use another system they deem logical, the information will be more readily retrievable than a long list of documents that are not categorized.

    - Spreadsheet programs such as MS Excel® can be extremely useful for tracking the progress of each lead, or potential job opportunity. A separate spreadsheet can be used for each strategy, or it can be a long running spreadsheet in chronological order of approach with a column that designates the strategy used ("news event letter," "direct targeted letter," "response to ad," etc.).

    - Contact management programs such as ACT®, MS Access®, or MS Outlook will not only track contact names and dates, but can also be programmed to remind clients which contacts are ready for follow-up on a given date as they boot up their computer. Notes of each conversation and any related correspondence can also be preserved. However, ACT may be prohibitively expensive if the client is not in a sales job or other role for which the software could be used after the search is complete.

    - Automated calendar systems such as those offered by Blackberry®, PalmPilot, yahoo.com, google.com or MS Outlook can be used to track appointments and clients' "to do" list for their job search activities.

Special Tips for Career Changers

When your clients are seeking a career change, the one thing you can guarantee is that an approach relying on "Give me a chance. I know I can do the job! You won't be sorry..." will not be successful. It is unrealistic because an employer won't hire someone "on faith"—they have a lot to lose. For example, after the employer has made a substantial investment in the employee's training, they may find the individual has no real interest in the job or decides that it does not fit his or her needs—or, he or she may simply lack the transferable skills necessary to perform the job. For these clients, a better way to prove interest and capability to a prospective employer in a new job function or industry is to follow the tips below.

Client Tips: Networking for Career Changers

- Identify contacts in the industry through trade associations and personal networks
- Read the industry's trade journals to learn the terminology and trends in the industry
- Request any available industry information from trade associations (Associations Unlimited, available through any public or college library online, can be helpful here, as can Gales Encyclopedia of Associations and the Directory of Associations at http://www.marketingsource.com/associations/)
- Surf the Web for any pertinent information
- Join the local branch of any trade associations serving the industry, attend the meetings and chat with people there about the field
- Recharacterize accomplishments in a more generic format so that they demonstrate clear transferability outside the prior industry setting
- Take relevant courses or part-time jobs, or do volunteer work in the new industry/skill area
- Arrange and conduct informational interviews with these contacts
- Be increasingly clear about the type of work desired, and why you believe you will be successful
- Do not hesitate to make a proposal to an employer of interest
- Be persistent!

By taking these steps, your clients will be better positioned to make the career change they desire while meeting an employer's need.

Allowing for Synchronicity

> "The moment one definitely commits oneself, then Providence moves too. All sorts of things occur to help one that would otherwise never have occurred. A whole stream of events issues from the decision, raising in one's favor all manner of unforeseen incidents and meetings and material assistance, which no man could have dreamed would have come his way."
>
> —W. N. Murray, *The Scottish Himalayan Expedition*

There is a force at work within the job search that cannot be explained. People and information are brought into the job seeker's life seemingly by accident, when in fact they are a response of the physical world to the candidate's mentally stated goal. Some of my clients have shared with me that a book would literally fall off the shelf in the bookstore and into their hands, or they would suddenly find themselves next to the CEO of their dream employer on the airplane while flying home from a conference. While it may be tempting—and feel more comfortable—for clients to try to control the job search process and the people in it to fit their idea of how it should be, they will have even better results if they can stay somewhat open to the flow of synchronicity.

The term *synchronicity* was coined by Swiss psychologist Carl Jung to describe the "meaningful coincidence of two or more events, where something other than probability of chance is involved," and occurs when one is in pursuit of a dream or goal he or she is passionate about.[61]

In a recent issue of the *Career Development Quarterly,* a fascinating article appeared entitled "Coincidence, Happenstance, Serendipity, Fate, or the Hand of God: Case Studies in Synchronicity." In it, authors Mary Guindon and Fred Hanna, both professors at Johns Hopkins University, point out that:

> One tenet that has shaped the direction of career counseling is the view that career development is linear, progressive, and rational.... However, many counselors [and coaches] are aware that unknowable instances of coincidence, happenstance, and chance factors can play a significant role in career opportunities....We propose that these factors point to the nonlinear and acausal phenomenon of synchronicity.[62]

There are three types of synchronicity. The first involves a simultaneous coincidence of subjective psychic content with objective events. In one case study, Dan, who had become dissatisfied with his work as a newspaper reporter, worked with a career coach to increase his awareness of his skills and interests, and coincidentally re-membered a long-buried desire to own a small-town press. Then, despite a lack of money to buy such a business and an unwillingness to relocate due to his son's ongo-ing medical treatment needs for a serious illness, he struck up a conversation with an attorney at a parents' night at his son's school. The attorney had just acquired a now-defunct small press in settling a case, had no interest in running it but would welcome Dan's doing so, virtually eliminating the need for Dan to raise cash to pur-chase the business. Mere coincidence? Or synchronicity based on Dan's clear and long-standing desire that had just emerged for fulfillment?

The second type of synchronicity is the coincidence of a subjective psychic state with a dream or vision that later turns out to be analogous to circumstances that occur, "at a distance." Another case study followed Sarah, who was the breadwinner in her family and felt entirely incapable of leaving her job. She had a dream of a man dressed in black chasing her with a two-by-four board. She ran through a series of unfinished rooms splashed with color. At the same time, through networking she connected with an opportunity to develop programs for a church-affiliated school. The unfinished rooms had two-by-fours in them and paint cans of various colors.

Thirdly, synchronicity can occur as coincidence of a subjective psychic state with a dream or vision that later turns out to accurately reflect future events. One example is a woman who dreams of horses with riders wearing different colors galloping along a river. When the client moves from her current job at a university into a new position at another one, the school colors of both schools coincide exactly with the colors of the riders and horses in the dream.

In working with clients in transition, the opportunities they will explore and pursue may come directly from responding to an advertised opening, from networking, or from a casual conversation that leads to events foretold in a dream. Our job is to be open—and to encourage our clients to be open—to any and all avenues for input that will lead to their next step.

KEY COACHING CONCEPTS

1. Not all career coaches will offer services to assist clients with job search mechanics, but all career coaches should have a working knowledge of the best practices in the job search.
2. Clients need to learn to think of themselves as a "brand," a niche product that needs a customized marketing strategy to reach the ideal "customer," that is, an employer.
3. The job search marketing plan will use a carefully targeted mix of published and unpublished job search sources; it will need to be customized based on clients' personality style and goals.
4. Clients will need a way to track their contacts in her search, whether low-tech or high-tech.
5. Clients changing careers will need to make the effort to learn more about their target industries and positions as well as other special steps if their search is to be successful.
6. There are aspects of the job search process that have seemingly unknown or "mystical" origins; by being open to forces such as synchronicity, clients will connect with opportunities they may not have found through more tradition

21

Tactics for the Published Job Market: Finding Jobs with Ads, Recruiters, and the Internet

"LET ADVERTISERS SPEND THE SAME AMOUNT OF MONEY IMPROVING THEIR PRODUCT THAT THEY DO ON ADVERTISING AND THEY WOULDN'T HAVE TO ADVERTISE IT."
—*Will Rogers*

Often, the first thing people do when they are laid off (or, in some cultures, "made redundant") or feel dissatisfied enough to start looking for a new job is to start perusing the help wanted ads in the newspaper. While some people do get jobs through the ads and other related methods, these represent less than 20 percent of the total jobs filled in a given year.[63]

The "published job market" consists of newspaper ads (print and electronic), recruiters and employment agencies, Internet job banks, and job fairs. To guide our clients effectively, we must help them use each of these aspects of the published job market strategically in their overall campaign, devoting an appropriate amount of time to them in view of the typical returns they represent.

Newspaper Ads

Jane, a software engineer, applied for a job advertised in the *Wall Street Journal* that seemed tailor-made for her. It drew upon her certifications and training in specific program languages, and the company was located in the city where she lived. There was no phone number for follow-up, but when she had not heard anything from them in two weeks she called the number in the local phone book and got voicemail. "What's wrong with me?" she moaned. "I know I'm perfect for that job; why haven't they called me for an interview?"

Was something wrong with Jane? No, but many applicants immediately take it personally if they do not hear from the "perfect employer" within a few days of their application being submitted. Let's look at it from the other side of the desk: the human resources screener or recruiter. Responses to a help wanted ad placed in a local newspaper often number one hundred to five hundred or more, depending on the size of the metropolitan area covered. An ad in the *Wall Street Journal* or other national publication may draw in excess of one thousand responses for one opening. It takes screeners time to sort through these responses to get to a "short list" to interview. Job seekers must therefore not get discouraged if they do not hear back on a response to an ad, even if it seems to be a perfect fit.

For job seekers to obtain an interview from a response to an ad, the hiring manager, screener, or recruiter must view them as a very good fit for the job—though not necessarily a perfect fit. Often, a 70 percent match will qualify a candidate for an interview, especially if the company is having difficulty finding all the skills they desire in one candidate. For example, if an ad requests five years of experience in the industry, a bachelor's degree, good communication skills, and experience writing grant proposals, candidates could apply and expect favorable consideration even if they lacked the degree but possessed the remaining qualifications. The degree to which this "70 percent principle" is true will vary depending on the number of qualified candidates for the job. The fewer the fully qualified applicants, the more the screener will seriously consider candidates with less than all of the required credentials.

It is important to understand the approach of human resources professionals or recruiters in considering the resumes submitted. Their goal is to screen out as many candidates as they can at each stage: initial review of resumes, screening interview, decision-making interview, and offer. Our clients must remember the principle of "self as product" discussed in chapter 20 and focus on mentioning what is most marketable about them, rather than identifying the flaws that are not pertinent until a later stage of the hiring process. When candidates find an ad – print or online – to which they wish to respond, certain guidelines apply, as described below.

Client Tips: Responding to Job Ads:

- For print ads (e.g., newspaper or magazine), you should wait five to seven days to submit a resume and cover letter. This prevents the application from being rejected simply because the screener is weeding through the initial large stack of responses that typically forms two to three days after the ad runs.

- For Internet-based ads—whether on a job board, company Web site posting, recruiter, or online newspaper listings—you should usually respond immediately, since online ads are sometimes closed once a certain number of responses are received.

- In most cases, the best style of cover letter to use in responding to a newspaper ad is the so-called "T-bar" letter (see fig. 30 as well as chapter 23), which clearly compares the job requirements to the candidate's qualifications. The T-bar letter helps steer those screeners without a great deal of experience or knowledge of the technical nature of the job or equivalent competencies toward a favorable assessment of you—tilting the screening process in your favor. In responding to an online ad, the covering e-mail will not usually accommodate the columnar format of the T-bar letter, but similar information should nevertheless be conveyed to the individual receiving the resume.

- Many ads request a salary history or salary requirements. This is one of the easiest criteria on which to eliminate candidates from further consideration: if you state a salary range that is higher or lower than the salary range authorized for the position, you will not make the cut of those to be interviewed. Most candidates, of course, take the ad's requirements seriously, fearing that they will not be considered if they do not provide salary data.

Figure 30: T-Bar Approach Letter For Ads

Date

Decision Maker, Title
Company Name
Address
City, State Zip

Dear Name of Decision Maker:

Your advertisement for a (insert position title) piqued my interest. It appears you have an exciting opportunity for the right individual - and I believe I am that person.

During my ____ years in the _____ field, I have had a number of accomplishments in which you may be interested. They in fact seem to be a perfect match for your opening:

Your Requirements	My Qualifications
1	1
2	2
3	3

I would welcome the opportunity to meet with you, learn more about the specifics of this position and discuss the ways in which I believe I can meet them. [*Suggested Phrase for Salary Requests:*] I will submit a salary history and other personal information at such time as you indicate serious interest in my qualifications. Please give me a call and we can arrange a time to meet at your convenience.

Sincerely,

Job Seeker
Enclosure (resume)

In a survey of 159 human resource and hiring decision makers nationwide by the Career Management Alliance titled "Revealing Trends in Corporate Hiring Practices," 56 percent of respondents stated that they would consider qualified candidates even when they do not provide salary information as requested; another 31 percent said it depends entirely on candidates' experience. Only 11 percent said they would not consider the application under these conditions. (see www.careermanagementalliance.com)

That survey paralleled another larger study completed earlier by three Vassar graduates in New York City. They reviewed 1,352 ads in the *New York Times* and the *National Business Employment Weekly* over a five-month period. Of these, 272 (20 percent) asked for salary history. The researchers spoke with 200 of these employers, and 94 percent said they considered every letter received. The lesson? Do not provide salary history or requirements until asked about it in the interview. (For more on this topic, see chapters 24 and 26.)

- One thing Jane did right was to try to follow up with the company after she submitted her cover letter and resume. In many cases, the ad will be "blind," meaning that the company name is not listed. But if the company is identified, some attempt to follow up is recommended. However, I recommend that you spend the bulk of your follow-up phone call time on leads from unpublished sources, since following up on advertised openings does not usually accelerate the step-by-step process required to satisfy company standards.

- Even when the job seems perfect for you, if the company name is listed, you will get better results if they use the "dual approach" technique. Besides sending a resume and cover letter to Human Resources, you should simultaneously send a targeted letter (see Fig. 33 for format) to the hiring manager, that is, your prospective boss.

Trade Magazine Ads

One area of advertised openings often overlooked by job seekers is the trade magazines. Published as sources of industry information regarding trends, topics of interest, surveys and the like, many of them also include ads for openings within that field. Some examples include *Ad Week*, HowDesign.com, and Computer Reseller News (www.crn.com). Others are available through such sites as Yahoo and Google by clicking on the subject matter categories ("Business & Economy," "Computers & Internet," etc.) and through trade association sites. Competition for these positions is often lower than those advertised in the newspaper, so job seekers may have more success responding to these than to newspaper ads. Tips for approaching employers through trade magazines are identical to those for newspaper ads.

Recruiters

Executive recruiters will be an important resource for clients who are mid- to upper-level managers and/or executives. To effectively use these recruiters, we must first understand how they work, and counter common misconceptions people have about them. Following are some general insights into how recruiters actually do their work.

- Most recruiters do not place hundreds of people each year, but rather one to two people per month in the executive search firms and a few more among those who focus on other areas (e.g., creative fields, administration and staff support, technology expertise).

- Executive recruiters' first preference is to identify candidates who are working in companies and very successful—the top performers—and recruit them "away" from the company to one of the recruiter's client companies. Approaching these recruiters with an unsolicited resume will usually meet with extreme disinterest, though it can sometimes generate favorable results if the candidate has an exceptional background.

- There are two primary types of recruiters: contingency and retained. Contingency recruiters are paid by the company upon placement; retained recruiters are paid monthly whether any openings are filled or not. Most of your clients will work primarily with contingency recruiters unless they are at the highest levels of management.

- Recruiters are not the same thing as employment agencies, which work with people in generally non-management positions in specific industry areas, placing them in temporary or permanent positions. Employment agencies should be used by nonmanagement-level clients, along with other strategies in their search campaign.

- The typical fee a recruiter earns for one placement is 20 to 30 percent of candidates' first year's salary.

If your clients plan to approach recruiters as part of their search, they should follow the tips below.

Client Tips: Working with Recruiters

- Contact recruiters in the search campaign only if you are seeking a position in an industry in which you have experience. Generally, recruiters only consider candidates seeking the same type of position as the one they are leaving, or the next level up. Recruiters are not an appropriate resource for career changers.

- In your cover letter, clearly state your personal brand (see sample personal brand statements in chapter 23) and your marketable assets. Also, note that cover letters with some recruiters are optional since recruiters know why the resume is being submitted, while others deem them a requirement before they will read your resume.

- Be prepared to document all written and stated facts. About 77 percent of recruiters Google candidates, and 35 percent of recruiters eliminate candidates based on the results of the Google search, according to a 2006 survey by Execunet (www.execunet.com). As misrepresentations of one's credentials on resumes rise, recruiters will be even more diligent in checking references and educational qualifications, so it is critical that they be accurate.

- Clearly indentify in your letter and/or resume the industry and position(s) in which you wish to work. This helps the recruiter better match candidates to existing openings.

- Highlight all relevant accomplishments, briefly and powerfully, in the Work Experience Story format (see chapter 8) or an abbreviated version of it.

- Use a chronological or executive resume format—rather than a functional format—as these are preferred by recruiters (see Chapter 23 for examples).

- Do not become discouraged if you do not hear from the recruiter right away, or if they do not return phone calls—it is nothing personal! If the recruiter does not have an opening on her desk at that moment that matches the your background and targets, she will not call to acknowledge receipt of the resume, but she may still have interest in your qualifications. Feel free to recontact the recruiter in four to six weeks to see if the openings they are working on have changed (and they usually will have by then).

- As a general rule, don't follow up by phone to a letter, e-mail, or fax. "Don't call us, we'll call you" is the mantra of the recruiter. Most recruiters will store resumes submitted to them for a period of weeks or perhaps months, to match to future openings.

To find recruiters to target, see the *Directory of Executive Recruiters* from Kennedy Publications (New Hampshire) and www.kennedyinfo.com.

Internet Job Banks   *< 5% of all jobs filled*

Answering Internet ads via job banks such as www.monster.com and other online resources can put job seekers in competition with even more candidates than other ads. As we saw earlier, as few as 1 percent of non-computer-related job seekers find their new job through a job bank.[64] However, job banks do simplify the search process, especially for those who are open to relocating and can be flexible on the exact responsibilities of the position. Sites such as www.careerbuilder.com streamline the process further by searching multiple job banks simultaneously.

To stand out in a positive way and avoid being lost in the large numbers of applicants to the general job boards listed above, candidates should also target industry-specific job banks. One example is www.biosphere.com for the biotech industry. To find these types of job banks, candidates should consult an industry association office, network with colleagues, or do an Internet keyword search for the job banks that serve the targeted industries.

Even more so than with newspaper ads, job seekers using online job banks should be prepared to contact the targeted company directly or use networking as a supplement to the on-line application. It will also be critical to have an effective electronic resume (e-resume) that meets the requirements of the scanning software many companies are now using. See chapter 23 for tips on composing an e-resume.

One of the critical issues when posting a resume on a job bank is privacy. Once your resume is on the Internet, it can be read and searched by anyone—including one's current employer. Care must be taken to avoid negative consequences—such as being terminated—if and when one's employer finds the employee's resume on the Internet. Increasing numbers of workers and their coaches understand the need for constant networking and scanning of openings for career self-management. However, many employers still see such practices as demonstrating a lack of loyalty to the person's current employer. The benefits of making yourself available to job openings, therefore, must be weighed carefully against the risks of doing so. Many job banks allow individuals to mask their name and employer name to protect confidentiality.

To maximize the number of times a candidate's resume is retrieved by recruiters, job seekers should edit some of the information on their resume or job bank posting at least once every two weeks. This increases the number of "hits" they get because recruiters will search by date posted—if it was not posted, or revised and reposted, in the previous seven days, it will be overlooked by many employer and recruiter searches.

And finally, some job banks offer a "job search agent" technology that pushes opportunities to you. Execunet (www.execunet.com) is one of these, and www.monster.com also offers this feature for qualified executive candidates. This can save considerable time in searching for ads fitting clients' criteria as the software does the work. And it allows clients access to positions when they are posted, eliminating the need to remember to go back and retrieve them. It also precludes being excluded from consideration because the position has been closed to applicants.

Job Fairs

A company – or, more often, an industry in a geographic area – will periodically sponsor a job fair. This is an event where job seekers can go, resume in hand, and supposedly meet in person with hiring managers. These are often done when an industry is having difficulty finding enough suitable candidates to meet a growing need. While these can be useful to some job seekers—particularly those who are staying within their current industry—they can be a waste of time for career changers and others. Job seekers should talk to others who have attended a job fair sponsored by the same entity beforehand if they can, to see what their experience has been.

KEY COACHING CONCEPTS

1. Due to the sheer volume of applicants for published openings, job seekers should not take it personally if the company does not call them right away for an interview.
2. Delaying one's response to a print ad for five to seven days after the ad is published can improve one's chances of favorable consideration, but immediate response is best for online listings.
3. Trade journals and magazines in the target industries also publish job openings and are often overlooked by job seekers.
4. Recruiters should be used by mid- to upper-level management candidates seeking another position in an industry in which they have recent experience.
5. Industry-specific Internet job banks will usually contain more relevant positions than the larger, more general job banks.
6. Job fairs can be a useful search strategy when one's industry target is clear.

22

Accessing the Unpublished Job Market: Using Networking, Search Engines and Proactive Strategies to Reveal Hidden Opportunities

"OPPORTUNITIES ARE USUALLY DISGUISED AS HARD WORK, SO MOST
PEOPLE DON'T RECOGNIZE THEM."
—Ann Landers

The unpublished, or "hidden," job market—where an opening is filled without it ever being advertised—represents approximately 80 percent of the total jobs filled each year.[65] So it is very important to an effective job search campaign. Yet many job seekers do not pursue it — or at least do not realize they are — either because they do not know it exists or they do not know how to access it. It includes opportunities that are revealed through networking with a variety of different kinds of people and targeted direct-mail campaigns to qualified individuals and organizations. And, we have been discussing, an integrated job search campaign must include a carefully chosen mix of job search strategies.

Networking for Unpublished Openings

Networking is a pivotal strategy for tapping into the unpublished market. It can be defined as the process of meeting with appropriate people in a specific industry or career focus area to find out more about what they do and what their current needs are—and thereby developing strategic relationships. This process is also known as "informational interviewing," and the meetings as "information and referral meetings." Networking is not telling everyone you know that you're out of work and need a new job, which is how many uninformed job seekers approach networking—and then bemoan the fact that it does not work for them.

To help your clients maximize the value of their networking, make sure they adhere to the following key principles.

Client Tips: Networking

- **Remember the objective of networking.** The goal of networking is to gain information and referrals, not jobs—at least initially. Your questions should focus on those objectives. Through their personal presence as well as the information you gather, using this approach will eventually reap a job opportunity; but if you focus on that first, you will put their contacts on the defensive and impede your results.

- **Apply the "1:50 Principle."** Everybody knows at least fifty other people from various parts of their life. School, work, church, volunteer activities, sports groups, trade associations, neighbors, friends, family—all of these can become relevant when considering networking. List as many people as you can from these and any other categories. Expand your list by using LinkedIn, Facebook and/or MySpace web sites. Then, realize that each of these people knows at least fifty other people. The likelihood that several of these individuals will know someone who works in one of your target industries is very high. But you should not approach them yet.

- **Use a powerful approach letter.** In most cases, you should mail a letter to the prospective networking contact first, then follow up by phone. Exceptions would include people you already know well, or someone mentioned during a networking meeting whom the contact could call immediately. A sample networking approach letter is provided in fig. 31.

- **Follow up by phone to double the response rate.** Use the phone and e-mail effectively and be politely persistent in reaching the people you want to meet. A letter from someone the person doesn't directly know can easily end up on the low-priority stack of their desk unless a follow-up call is made.

Figure 31: Sample Networking Approach Letter

Date

Decision Maker, Title
Company Name
Address
City, State Zip

Dear Name of Decision Maker:

I am currently seeking a more permanent and diverse management role than my current consulting position provides. As I seek to determine a new direction for my future, my plan is to contact a few professionals within the XXXXXX community to get their insights and to network. That is my purpose in writing to you. If possible, I would like to arrange a time to meet with you for 10 to 15 minutes at your convenience. I am confident that our shared backgrounds in XXXXX will provide a mutually interesting and informative meeting.

As an experienced director of Internet-, software-, and multimedia-based new product development and roll-out, I offer a unique combination of leadership in operations as well as marketing and business development. I have worked with industry leaders such as ABC Company, as well as most recently, Internet start-ups providing cutting-edge on-line services. My Ph.D. in Education, emphasizing Curriculum and Instruction, together with my 10 years of executive level experience, have prepared me to develop, launch and distribute instructionally sound and market targeted products. Among my achievements are managing up to 250 employees, P&L for $18MM, turnarounds, directing 7 highly regarded national technology conferences, and organizing and re-prioritizing 50 simultaneous projects, tripling on-time completion rate.

Because I am aware that many opportunities arise before they are publicly advertised, I realize that getting to know fellow professionals such as you should be an important part of my strategy. The opportunity to exchange ideas and develop contacts with other XXXXXXX professionals would be deeply appreciated.

The opportunity to exchange ideas and develop contacts with other professionals would be deeply appreciated and would be all I ask. I will call your office in a few days to introduce myself and to set a brief meeting. I want to thank you in advance for any assistance and advice you may be able to provide.

Sincerely,

Joe Job Seeker

- **Set a specific time for the meeting—and stick to it.** Ask the networking contact for a fifteen- to twenty-minute meeting, in person if you are within a one-hour drive from the contact and by phone if you are farther away. Incidentally, if you have a specific city to which you would like to move, we recommend that you schedule meetings with two or three key contacts in person and either drive or fly to that city for a few days of networking and interviews. This kind of approach puts you in front of the people you need to meet and creates the possibility of setting up more meetings based on referrals you may get while there.

- **Research the company and networking contact prior to the meeting.** You will create a much more positive impression if prior to the meeting you have visited the company's Web site and otherwise researched the industry and company—even the individual with whom you are meeting, if he/she is reported in industry journals, Who's Who, listed on LinkedIn, Facebook or other social networking web sites, and so on.

- **Take only a list of questions to the meeting; do not take a resume.** If an individual came to a networking meeting with you and started the meeting by laying his resume on the table, what would you think? It changes the tone of the meeting immediately, and puts the focus on jobs instead of information and referrals. You do need to have a verbal summary of your background ready to use (see sample one-minute summary example below), but the resume—if it is requested—can be mailed or e-mailed to the contact after the meeting with a thank-you letter. For some sample questions, see fig. 32.

Sample One-Minute Summary

"I have 15 years of progressively responsible management experience in the graphic arts field, including both internet and print media. Most recently, I was manager of a franchised operation in a major metropolitan market and grew the business from start-up to $40 million in sales. I have an MBA degree and continuing education in various desktop publishing software programs. My strengths include innovative marketing, building rapport with a variety of customers, and building effective teams within a deadline-driven environment."

Figure 32: Suggested Questions To Ask In A Networking Meeting

About the Industry
- How old is the industry?
- How large is it?
- How is it changing now?
- Where do you see growth happening?

About the Company
- When was the company started?
- How large is it?
- What products/services does it produce? (ask only if you were unable to determine through advance research, otherwise ask a follow-on question based on your research)
- What kinds of customers/clients does the company serve?
- Who are the primary competitors to this company?
- How would you describe the organizational culture?
- What is the organizational structure?
- What involvement does the company have with technology? Has technology changed how business is done?

About the Job
- What are the key responsibilities of the job/position?
- What are the biggest challenges?
- What is the profile of a high achiever in this job?
- What type of background (education and work) is typical for people entering this job/field?
- What are the advancement or growth opportunities?
- What salary and compensation range is typical?

About the Networking Contact
- How did you get into this field?
- What do you like best about your job?
- What is your least favorite thing?
- Would you recommend that your son or daughter enter this field and/or job now?
- How has it changed in the past 10 to 20 years?
- What advice would you give to someone in my position?

- **Be sure to ask for referrals to other contacts before closing the meeting.** Whether the meeting has gone very well or not, you should be sure to ask the contact for other people you could talk to (using the contact's name) before ending the meeting. This is how the network grows—if each referral generates two or three other names, your network can expand significantly within a short period of time.

Format of a Networking (or Information and Referral) Meeting

The basic protocol for a networking meeting includes:

- Making introductions and first impressions
- Restating the purpose for meeting
- Briefly summarizing (in one to two minutes) the client's background (remember, no resume)
- Asking the candidate's most important networking questions (see fig. 32 for ideas)
- Asking for referrals ("Who else do you know that I should be talking to?"); candidates should try to schedule the meeting when/where the interviewer is near his or her PalmPilot, Blackberry, Rolodex, Daytimer or other source of contact names and numbers
- Thanking the person for his or her time and closing the meeting
- Sending a thank-you letter within twenty-four hours of the meeting, emphasizing the candidate's assets and reiterating the next step in developing the networking relationship

Help for the Introverted Client

For clients who are particularly introverted, and who resist the idea of networking, here are a few suggestions for how you may help them become more comfortable:

- Role-play a mock networking meeting with them so they know how to conduct a meeting and respond to rejections
- Present the process as a research exercise so that clients see interviews as a means to an end—gathering more information from which to draw conclusions about next steps; many introverted clients respond very well to this approach

- Be sure clients feel very well prepared in all aspects of the meeting format as described above, especially the meeting agenda, questions to ask, and one-minute summary. This will increase their comfort level.

Success Story

As we have discussed, networking can be particularly useful to clients who wish to change careers. It puts them in front of potential hiring managers—the contacts with whom they are networking—in a nonthreatening environment in which they can present their talents and discover the company's needs. Following is one case in which a networking-focused campaign generated multiple offers to facilitate a rather unlikely transition.

> John had become weary of the responsibilities as CEO of a software company. He loved working with people, and matching them to the right job, but disliked the other aspects of his demanding job. He came to a colleague of mine for career coaching to explore what other positions might satisfy him. After a handful of networking interviews, he decided that human resources management was the functional area he wanted to pursue. Obviously, he would have little success approaching published openings since his job change would be viewed as a step down from position of high responsibility he had previously held.

> John conducted a search campaign that relied exclusively on networking. He met with dozens of HR managers and hiring executives over a period of twelve weeks. Due to his diligent research on each company, his positive attitude, attractive personality and his increasing clarity about his goal, he received no less than twelve offers for positions as HR director from companies with whom he had networked.

Targeted Mail Contacts with Companies

Perhaps the most underutilized strategy of all is the mailing of targeted letters. Such letters, addressed to a hiring manager of a target, or potential target company, simply describe the candidate's current situation and background and how the candidate may be able to meet a need of the employer. They can be an excellent way to gain inroads into a firm. The company may or may not have indentified and published its job openings; that is irrelevant to this approach. What clients will be doing is approaching companies within their target industry and geographic range that may have a need that matches their areas of expertise. Once our clients have decided to target a specific industry, and determined the leading firms within the industry they would like to approach, the targeted letter introduces them to the firm and opens the door to further conversation. A targeted letter:

- Is no more than one page in length
- Is addressed to a particular individual in a hiring capacity (two to three levels above where the client would be working)
- Does not focus on jobs, but rather on the potential contribution the candidate could make to the firm
- Highlights the key relevant accomplishments of the candidate in which the firm may be interested
- May (but need not) include the name of a mutual acquaintance who has referred the candidate to the contact
- Should be sent by "snail mail," not e-mail (too easy to erase and may not even be opened)

A sample target letter is provided in fig. 33. Candidates should follow up directly with the hiring manager by telephone or e-mail five to seven days after the letter is sent to pursue a face-to-face meeting, if practical, or, alternatively, for a long-distance search, a telephone appointment for an informational interview.

Figure 33: Sample Direct Targeted Mail Letter

Date

Decision Maker, Title
Company Name
Address
City, State Zip

Dear Name of Decision Maker:

Many high tech companies are coping with these difficult times by hiring the best production and R&D people available. While this may help to "shore up" a company's competitive position, many organizations find that nevertheless their bottom line is slipping. Their usual response? Send in an accountant!

These companies, and perhaps you or some of your subsidiaries, need more than mere accounting help. As VP of Operations for a $100 million hardware manufacturer, I directed the turnaround of a company that was on the verge of closing. As a result, 2007 was the most profitable year they had ever had, and 2008 looks even better.

This experience, and my prior work within the industry, has given me a great deal of insight into how a company can get into trouble - and more importantly, the danger signs to watch out for. Once I enter a firm, I'm able to assist its management team in identifying ways in which they can run their financial systems more efficiently and economically and I have a proven track record of success in improving both revenues and profitability:

* Improved cycle time by 25% within 1 year through re-engineering key processes
* Established a Management Information System that linked management strategy to actual production results, further improving both profitability and internal communications
* Upgraded the hardware and software systems used to manufacture components of the company's key product line, allowing production to triple within 2 years

I have an M.B.A. as well as 15 years of progressively responsible management responsibility in operations, strategic planning, MIS, finance and project management.

I would appreciate the opportunity to meet with you to discuss the contribution I could make to your organization. I will call you in a few days to follow up on this letter and see when a convenient time might be. Or if you prefer, please feel free to call me at (123) 456-7890.

Sincerely,

Job Seeker

News and Company Events As a Vehicle for Job Search Contacts

In addition to referral-based and targeted mailings, tying an approach letter to a recent event in the industry or company can improve its chances of leading to a meeting. New product launches, receipt of venture capital or other investment or grant funds, relocation, expansion, and the like are all appropriate types of events for this purpose. Also key are "people on the move" sections in business publications that announce promotions and new hires. News of such events can be found by perusing the local business journal, the *Wall Street Journal,* the business section of the client's local paper, and trade magazines. The question to keep in mind while reading these articles is, "What job opportunities might this event lead to?"

Example

- If a company announces that it just received venture capital, it may need R&D people to develop or refine a new product, marketing and sales people to sell it, operations people to manage production, and finance people to account for the production and sales.
- If a company announces a merger, some redundant jobs may be lost, but the company may also need people to manage the newly formed staff, to assist with the consolidation of two cultures and sets of processes into one, and to reevaluate the financial aspects of the new company.

A sample news event–generated approach letter is provided in fig. 34.

Keys to Getting a New Job Created

Though it may sound far-fetched, it is not uncommon for a candidate to persuade a company to create a new job—one that did not previously exist—that perfectly meets the candidate's needs. There are several keys to making this happen, as described in the tips that follow.

Client Tips: Getting a New Job Created for You

- Determine what you want to do.
- Find a company/industry who could benefit

Figure 34: Sample News Event Letter

Date

Decision Maker, Title
Company Name
Address
City, State Zip

Dear [Decision Maker:]

I read with interest the article about your firm in the (insert Newspaper or whatever source) regarding with the probability of your expanding your (insert related skill or whatever). (Discuss the parts of the article that you feel particularly well-qualified to address) As I read this article, I found myself particularly interested in [Company Name] and in being part of your new expansion. That is why I am writing to you directly.

As an experienced director of Internet-, software-, and multimedia-based new product development and roll out, I offer a unique combination of leadership in operations as well as marketing and business development. I have worked with industry leaders such as ABC Company, as well as, most recently, Internet start-ups providing cutting-edge online services. My Ph.D. in Education, emphasizing Curriculum and Instruction, together with my 10 years of executive level experience, have prepared me to develop, launch and distribute instructionally sound and market targeted products. Among my achievements are managing up to 250 employees, P&L for $18MM, turnarounds, directing 7 highly regarded national technology conferences, and organizing and re-prioritizing 50 simultaneous projects, tripling on-time completion rate.

I would appreciate having the opportunity to discuss your plans to develop further insight into a possible association. I will call your office early next week to arrange an appointment. I look forward to talking with you.

Sincerely,

Job Seeker

- Conduct one or more informational interviews with one or more hiring managers within target companies to learn more about their needs
- Identify a need they have that you could fill
- Submit a proposal for a job you could do for them
- Persuade them to accept it and start work

Remember: a job is simply a match between a need and someone who can fill it at less cost than the return (or expected return) from the employee's services. As may be apparent from this discussion of the unpublished market, it requires greater initiative, creativity, and "out of the box" thinking than the published market. But it pays high dividends: when a job is found in this way, it can be customized to the individual's needs and will often pay more than a generic published opening would because it is created at the client's behest and based on what he or she brings to the table. It is well worth introducing our clients to this key segment of the job market.

KEY COACHING CONCEPTS

1) Networking is simply the process of meeting with people in a specific industry or career focus area to find out more about what they do and what their current needs are—and to build useful relationships.
2) By following several tips on the networking approach and honoring the typical format for a networking meeting, the process may generate multiple job opportunities.
3) An underutilized strategy to recommend to clients is addressing a direct targeted letter to a hiring manager in a target company outlining what the candidate can offer to the company.
4) News events are another basis for approaching a company to suggest applying the candidate's services to solve problems or leverage opportunities raised by the event.
5) It is possible to have a company create a job for candidates if the client can prove that they will add more value than the cost of the job.

23

Resume Design Secrets: Developing the Client's Personal Brand and Highlighting Their Most Marketable Attributes

"NEVER TRY TO TELL EVERYTHING YOU KNOW. IT MAY TAKE TOO SHORT A TIME."
—*Norman Ford*

In this chapter, we introduce the "do's and don'ts" of resume preparation so that you can help your clients compete successfully for the positions they are seeking. As with any of the other aspects of job search mechanics, you may want to establish a strategic partnership with a specialist, in this case a professional resume writer.

Principles for Powerful Resumes

To prepare an effective resume, your clients (and/or their resume writer) should heed the principles outlined below.

Client Tips: Resume Preparation

- **Remember that a resume is a marketing tool, not a complete chronology of a lifetime of work.** Content should be selectively chosen using the "self as product"/"personal branding" mind-set. If in doubt as to whether to include a hobby, award, accomplishment, or skill description, ask, "Will this make me more marketable for this position if I include it?" If not, leave it out.

- **Realize the primary purpose of a resume: to get an interview, not a job—at least not directly.** Remember that the job search is a two-part process. The first part is marketing oneself sufficiently on paper (or through networking) to get the interview. The second part is selling oneself in person at the interview to ultimately get the job. (More about that in the chapter 24.)

- **Lead with your best tangible skills.** Many job seekers make the mistake of putting their "soft" skills in the first one-third of their resume. This is usually not what screeners are most interested in. And since most recruiters and screeners will only review a resume for ten to twenty seconds before making an initial yes-or-no decision, the critical information must be contained in the first one-third of the first page! Fig. 35 is a roadmap of the selection process and where to emphasize which type of skills. Experience should precede education unless the degree was obtained within the past year.

Figure 35: Three Phases Of Selection Process

PHASE	QUESTION RECRUITER/SCREENER IS ASKING	SKILLS TO EMPHASIZE
1	"Can you do the job?"	Tangible skills
2	"Will you do the job?"	Tangible/intangible skills
3	"Do you fit into the position and company?"	Intangible skills

- **Customize the resume for each job opening applied for.** In the pre-1980s workplace, it was common to prepare one resume and use it for all purposes. That no longer works, since employers need to see the specific ways in which applicants' qualifications meet a particular job's requirements. Aspects of the resume to be customized include the job title (if used), the accomplishments or

Work Experience Stories to highlight and whether or not to include education or recent training.

- **Use a chronological resume (especially with recruiters) unless you fit one of the categories of exceptions.** There are two basic types of resumes: chronological, in which the person's work experience, accomplishments, and education are listed in reverse chronological order (see fig. 36), and functional, in which the person's background is organized in clusters of skills or types of accomplishments drawn from the positions they have held over the course their career, followed by a brief listing of work history (see fig. 37). Fig. 38 provides an alternative format for managers and executives to use, and Fig. 39, an "executive biography," to summarize the qualifications of a C-level executive to a prospective employer. (All resumes courtesy of Michelle Dumas, www.distinctiveweb.com)
- **Use a functional resume** (fig. 37) **when one of these exceptions applies:**
  - You are changing fields or careers
  - Your work history is very long or has gaps in it
  - You have a wide range of skills that can be more effectively showcased in this format
  - Diverse accomplishments from a long career at one company need to be emphasized
  - A record of frequent job changes needs to be deemphasized
  - You lack work experience, e.g., a new worker moving into the workplace for the first time or mother returning to the workforce after years of absence raising children
- **Begin the resume with "Summary of Qualifications" instead of "Job Objective."** In general, job objective statements are out of favor in the U.S. unless the resume is for a recent graduate. An objective can unduly narrow the scope of positions for which the applicant would be considered. The summary of qualifications should include a brief overview of your background and a couple of very short bulleted representative accomplishments.
  - **Continue with applicable sections of the resume, depending on your background.** Another required section is experience, if you have experience relevant to this job. If you are new to the job market, educational degrees and

Figure 36: Sample Chronological Resume

JOHN BATES

935 Colonial Village § Princeton, NJ 50436
Home: (555) 897-0287 • E-mail: johnbates@jbatesemail.com • Cell: (555) 209-7120

SENIOR SALES MANAGER / DIRECTOR

Driving record profitability and revenue gains across diverse industries in global environments

Results-proven sales and marketing manager with track record of success as key management team member with full P&L authority helping lead rapid growth and expansion of several leading global corporations in diverse industries. Grew Acme national accounts sales revenue $767 million in 3 years, turned around sales performance of a last-place branch to #1 out of 98, championed business expansion into global locations, and spearheaded a small manufacturer to record first-year sales and recognition by *Inc. Magazine* as one of the fastest-growing companies in the U.S. Strengths include:

- **Worldwide Sales Management**
- **Market Development & Dominance**
- **Strategic Vision & Growth Planning**
- **Partnerships & Strategic Alliances**
- **New Product Development & Launch**
- **Sales Team Building & Leadership**

PROFESSIONAL EXPERIENCE

Stoufer Corporation, Princeton, NJ
2003-Present

Leader in pharmaceutical, biotech, and microelectronics industries and division of a $5 billion international service provider.

GROUP SALES & MARKETING DIRECTOR

Brought on board to direct worldwide sales and marketing, leading 13 direct reports in growing revenue and profitability through establishment of formal sales processes and expansion into key international markets. Introduced and established Miller Heiman Strategic Sales process, CRM technologies, and improved forecasting process.

Key Results:

- Drove year-over-year sales increases, delivering 24% growth in 2004 and 212% growth in 2005.
- Named corporate-wide *Sales Director of the Year*.
- Opened key markets and accounts in Canada and Central America; currently planning European expansion.

Cabot, Inc., Boston, MA
2001-2003

$ 4.3 billion leader in major global markets of climate control, industrial solutions, infrastructure, health care, and security & safety.

SALES & MARKETING DIRECTOR

Directed sales, marketing, and customer service for 5 company-owned branches, 167 distributors' partners, and key national accounts. Provided leadership for 10 direct reports, 70+ indirect reports, and 1140+ distributor representatives.

Key Results:
- Increased sales significantly, exceeding division sales plan 31% in 2003.

Araby Corporation, Chicago, IL
2000-2001

World premier manufacturer/ distribution division of $86 million automatic door company.

SALES & MARKETING DIRECTOR

Recruited by CEO to lead worldwide sales, marketing, engineering, and customer service. Additionally, charged with full authority for $12 million operations of manufacturing and sales organization in Ireland. Installed new leadership team to energize U.K. organization and provide new direction. Re-engineered field organization to focus on target markets. Led 9 direct, 51 indirect, and 579 distributor representatives.

Key Results:
- Delivered average annual year-over-year sales growth of 11% within a negative growth market.
- Built potential new revenue stream of $20-30 million by establishing several key strategic business alliances.

Grodnick Group, Boston, MA
1998-2000

World's leading manufacturer and distributor of automatic packaging systems.

BUSINESS UNIT MANAGER

Handpicked by President and EVP to take over worldwide sales, marketing, product development, engineering, and manufacturing with full accountability for $39 million business unit with 8 direct, 89 indirect, and 450 agents, distributors, and manufacturers reps. Developed business plans to increase market leadership and profitability. Spearheaded development of next generation products; built niche markets and sales processes.

Key Results:
- Grew sales from $11 million to $39 million in less than 2 years. Increased margins while adding value to product and services for steady improvement in sales revenue averaging 40.5% annually.
- Expanded sales activities into emerging markets throughout Europe and Far East.

Gucciardo, Inc., New York, NY
1995-1997

$81 million global manufacturer/distributor. Recognized by INC. Magazine as one of the fastest growing companies in the U.S.

SALES, MARKETING, PRODUCT DEVELOPMENT SENIOR MANAGER

Joined executive team charged with developing corporate vision, strategic business plans, and pioneering market direction to drive accelerated growth, market leadership, and profitability. Refocused organization on emerging and high-growth sectors. Cultivated strategic alliances and developed acquisition strategies. Managed entire lifecycle of product development. Led 10 direct, 43 indirect, and 1200 distributor representatives.

Key Results:
- Established Gucciardo as true worldwide sales company, generating record revenue growth of $23 million.
- Repositioned outdated product, driving 62.5% increase in sales revenue.

Hannigan's, Inc., Orlando, FL
1991-1994

$1 billion manufacturer/distributor of contract office and medical furniture.

SALES DIRECTOR – SOUTHEASTERN U.S.

Managed P&L for sales of 23-state area. Supervised and delegated activities for 11 direct/93 indirect reports and 470 dealer sales reps. Drove innovative sales, marketing, and management programs with clear goals for fulfilling objectives. Strengthened go-to-market strategies by heading company-wide, President/CEO sponsored task force.

Key Results:
- Exceeded sales plan, overachieving $270 million goal by over 13% in a negative growth industry.
- Re-engineered and enhanced dealer distribution channel through new joint planning process.

Gummel Company, Boston, MA
1988-1991

Leading-edge color copier and printers technology. Joint venture partnership between Gummel and Sayko of Japan.

SALES & MARKETING MANAGER

Led start-up venture between Seiko and Mead, developing sales, marketing, and product development organization and opening worldwide distribution channels.

Key Results:
- Persuaded Board of Directors to approve last-minute, over-budget product enhancement, resulting in immediate ROI and $3 million+ sales growth.
- Gained immediate marketplace credibility by targeting internationally recognized showcase accounts.
- Fostered team environment and achieved turnover rate less than 42% of industry average.

Early career with **Acme Corporation**, *rapidly advancing through the ranks in progressive direct sales, senior sales, marketing, and general management positions. Spearheaded explosive 745% growth of national accounts program to $870 million in just 3 years. Turned around last place branch to #1 largest revenue ranking among 98 branches. Produced $190 million new incremental revenue in 2 years through creation of new contact negotiator group.*

EDUCATION & PROFESSIONAL QUALIFICATIONS

B.S., Business Administration / Marketing - Boston University, 1988

Recent Continuing Education: Certified Miller Heiman Strategic Sales Instructor • Executive Strategic Leadership • Center for Creative Leadership • Executive Leadership Program – Kellogg Northwestern • Executive Sales Leadership Seminar – AMA • Kennedy School of Business Leadership Seminar – Harvard University • Senior Executive General Management, Marketing, & Sales Program – Kellogg Northwestern Graduate School

Board of Directors, American Association of Sales Professionals / Member, Sales Executive Council

Figure 37: Sample Functional Resume

TERESE MACO

89 Thompson Avenue ▪ Boston, MA 98765 ▪ Phone: (555) 555-5555 ▪ E-mail: tmaco@email.com
Relocating to Chicago, IL

QUALIFICATIONS PROFILE

Energetic and enthusiastic sales professional with more than 10 years of cross-industry experience. Accomplished in both territory and retail sales. Positioned as #1 sales producer among peers and delivered 6-figure sales growth. Natural sales abilities with a special talent for building trust and rapport with customers. Proven skill in establishing long-term, profitable customer relationships. Poised and professional demeanor with an articulate and persuasive communication style. Strengths include:

❑ Consultative Selling	❑ Account Management
❑ Prospecting & Business Development	❑ Sales Presentations
❑ Customer Relations & Service	❑ Overcoming Objections & Closing

EXPERIENCE HIGHLIGHTS

Sales & New Business Development

- Increased sales and referrals for flooring products $750k by initiating and cultivating relationships with building inspectors, general contractors, and real estate developers.

- Generated more than $500k in new accounts annually for home-delivered grocery products; maintained an exemplary 80% closing rate, consistently surpassed sales goals, and won multiple honors and awards for top production.

- Selected, based on personal sales achievement as #1 ranked representative in office, to train new sales representatives in successful presentation, needs assessment, and closing techniques. Oriented new reps through sales meetings and on-the-job instruction.

Customer Relations & Account Management

- Built long-term relationships with territory of 175 customers, establishing mutual trust and respect during initial consultative sales presentation. Identified needs and developed customized grocery orders. Overcame cost objections through sales process that emphasized benefits.

- Consulted with 1,000+ homeowners to establish understanding of flooring needs and desires; advised on product solutions, negotiated prices, closed orders, and coordinated installation.

- Handled patient relations, scheduled appointments, prepared medical reports, and assisted with third-party billing in a fast-paced cardiac rehabilitation center. Answered patient inquiries discreetly and sensitively, maintaining strict confidentiality.

Problem Solving & Organization

- Guided all operations, financial affairs, and sales of a flooring center; supervised 2 sales associates. Resolved customer complaints and vendor problems resulting from prior mismanagement.

- Managed the office of a privately owned ambulance company; oversaw scheduling and dispatching of 15 staff members and a fleet of 3 ambulances. Maintained top efficiency through the use of computerized accounting and administrative systems.

- Coordinated third-party billing for a large medical college, serving as primary liaison between physicians and insurance companies to ensure accurate and timely payment.

EDUCATION

A.S., BUSINESS ADMINISTRATION, Webster Community College, 2005
Massachusetts Real Estate License, 2003

EMPLOYMENT HISTORY

SALES MANAGER, *Alexander's Flooring Center*, Boston, MA, 2004 - 2005
SALES REPRESENTATIVE, *Grocery Sales, Corp.*, Rollins, NJ, 1994 - 1999
OFFICE MANAGER, *Ambulance Services*, Rollins, NJ, 1993 - 1994
ADMINISTRATIVE ASSISTANT, *Cardiac Rehab Center*, Timmons, NY, 1992 - 1993
ACCOUNT REPRESENTATIVE, *Consulting Services*, Woodland, NY, 1989 - 1992

Figure 38: Sample Executive Resume

WILLIAM S. RICHARDS
54 High Street • Some Town, WA 00000 • (555) 555-5555 • email@email.net

SENIOR SALES & MARKETING MANAGEMENT EXECUTIVE
Worldwide Semiconductor Equipment & Electronics Component Markets Expertise

Sophisticated global business executive with P&L management experience and 20 years of achievement focused on semiconductor and electronic components industries. Lived and worked in Hong Kong, leading Asia sales team and managing subsidiary operations in Taiwan, Korea, China, and Southeast Asia. Excellent skill recruiting and retaining top-talent leaders and managing cross-functional teams of 135+ employees, distributors, and manufacturer reps.

Proven leader of change, business restructuring, team rationalization, and growth, delivering significant revenue and profit gains in every position for past 10+ years, including dramatic turnaround of failing company in <4 years to produce 100%+ increase in EBITDA. Led multi-cultural team to generate 100%+ increase in revenues, capturing dominant market share in Pacific Rim region during period marked by historic deflation of Asia currencies.

PROFESSIONAL HIGHLIGHTS

XYZ Company, LLC
2001 – Present
Global leader in the design, development, and production of thermal management systems for multinational customers in diverse electronic markets.

SENIOR VICE PRESIDENT, SALES AND MARKETING

Top-ranking sales and marketing leader with P&L responsibility for $100 million annual North America and Asia Pacific sales, $8 million expense budget, and $10 million EBITDA budget. Managed 7 senior-level direct reports, 130+ indirect reports, 13 manufacturer reps, and 26 distributors. Directed global sales, marketing, product management, marcom, customer service, and finance, in addition to managing newly acquired and integrated manufacturing operation in Taiwan.

Member of executive team that steered company from the edge of bankruptcy, returning to solvency and growth following series of problems that had impacted customer satisfaction, market share, and credibility. Served as first central leader for global account management and value creation programs, optimizing and rationalizing teams, bringing together a regionally fragmented organization, and providing leadership for both the North American and Asia Pacific sales and marketing teams.

Developed strategic turnaround plan, translated into action, and executed complete organizational transformation. Reorganized around technical competency and global services, enabling service excellence and competitive advantage worldwide. Turned decline and losses into revenue growth, market share gains, and profitability.

- Increased sales 69%, from $89 million to $150+ million, a rate of growth 2X higher than market.
- Doubled EBITDA from $6 million to $12.7 million in 4 years.
- Raised high-end server market share from <10% in 2001 to >50% in 2006.
- Improved gross margins dramatically, from 3.7% in 2001, to 18% just 2 years later, and 22% by 2005.
- Lowered selling costs from 13% of sales in 2001 to 8.3% in 2005.
- Closed 3 non-profitable Asian production facilities and built 3 sales subsidiaries (Singapore, Shanghai, Taipei).

Rebuilt corporate mission, vision and value proposition. Repaired damaged market image and customer relationships, reversed deterioration of brand equity, and restored customer satisfaction.

- Revived customer satisfaction, improving survey feedback 60%.
- Strengthened new-business win ratio from less than 10% to more than 35%.
- Recruited new impact leaders, 2 in U.S. and 2 in Asia; dramatically reduced employee turnover.
- Rectified troubled relationship and built #1 customer, more than tripling sales to $35+ million.
- Grew major account sales from $0 to $20 million in 4 years and doubled a second account to $10 million in 2 years.

LS Corporation
1988 – 2001

Billion-dollar provider of products that improve productivity in microelectronics, biopharmaceutical and life sciences manufacturing.

VICE PRESIDENT, NORTH AMERICAN SALES – Microelectronics Division (2000 – 2001)

Promoted to take charge of North American sales organization generating $60 million annual revenue and $27 million profit. Headed 5 direct reports and oversaw technical sales force of 50, managing all customer-facing operations for semiconductor manufacturers and OEM equipment. Led team to achieve dominant market share positons in all US based state-of-the-art wafer fabs. Positioned division for eventual spin-off.

Revised and improved sales strategy, hired new sales management talent, simplified sales incentive plan, and established peer review board. Brought new level of focus, direction, and vision to major global account team suffering from low morale and fumbling due to lack of clarity around key priorities.

- ▶ Built overall revenue 16% from $51.8 million to $60 million in a single year.
- ▶ Produced 54% growth rate in global account team sales, increasing to $11.5 million.
- ▶ Drove exponential growth in sales of photo-dispense products, to $18 million annually.
- ▶ Achieved cohesion among fragmented sales team and lowered sales management turnover to 0%.

MARKETING DIRECTOR – Gas Products Division (1998 – 2000)

Fortified newly consolidated gas filtration, purification, and measurement business with marketing leadership. Managed 26 direct/indirect reports in strategic marketing, product management and technical field support. Controlled $10 million budget. Appointed as acting assistant GM with additional R&D responsibility for 3 months. Identified 2 acquisition targets.

Architected strategic growth plan fueled by new products and niche acquisitions. Restructured marketing operation, transforming a chaotic, disorganized group into a cohesive team. Created new field marketing and

applications technical support organizations and integrated with sales organization worldwide.

- ▸ Salvaged high-priority digital product launch, ultimately launching successfully and securing key design win.
- ▸ Orchestrated multiple new product launches – all on time and successful. Increased sales of new products 30%.

DIVISION SALES MANAGER – Microelectronics Asia, Hong Kong (1993 – 1998)

Selected for overseas relocation and tasked with leading the charge to create a dedicated sales and service organization to serve microelectronics customers, replacing existing non-specialized sales network. Managed P&L for Asia Pacific and 3 subsidiaries generating $35 million revenues with 50% contribution margins. Expanded headcount from initial 17 and led team of 40, including 5 direct reports in relationship building, customer service, and account management activities.

Built strong cross-cultural team of Japanese, Taiwanese, Singaporean, Korean, and Chinese managers that served as backbone for market dominance in the Pacific Rim. Executed growth plan and developed new markets.

- ▸ Mobilized more than 2-fold sales growth from $17 million to $35 million in 2 years.
- ▸ Delivered 100%+ of sales plans each year for both revenues and contribution margins.
- ▸ Captured > 70% share of business from 3 major customers.
- ▸ Acted quickly, minimizing margin erosion and achieving sales plan during the 1997 deflation of Asia currencies.
- ▸ Integrated 3 sales forces and service centers during merger.

SENIOR MARKETING MANAGER/PRODUCT MANAGER – Microelectronics (1990 – 1993)

Recruited to join marketing team as product manager, then promoted to duplicate success with larger, more mature gas filtration product line. Led team of 3 in all strategic, product, and field marketing functions, headed development of applications white papers and managed inert and specialty gas labs used for demonstrations.

Reinvigorated product line and launched industry's first integrated product, generating $2 million first-year sales. Defined and launched third-generation product derivative for mature product line that set division record for largest first-year sales.

- ▸ Restarted stalled development and doubled product line growth in 1 year from $4 million to $8 million.
- ▸ Launched new product that met competitive threat and generated $5 million first-year sales.

OPERATIONS PLANNING SUPERVISOR – TM Manufacturing Operations (1989 – 1990)
FORECAST ANALYST II – ABC Manufacturing Operations (1988 – 1989)

EDUCATION

M.B.A., *Summa cum Laude*, Some College (1998)
B.A., Economics, *Summa cum Laude*, Some State College (1988)

Continuing education: Sales Management   Making Mergers Work
Multicultural Management   Product Evaluation and Planning   TQM and
Improvement Process   Managing New Product Development and Teams
Positioning Strategies and New Product Launches   Interpersonal Skills
Negotiation Skills   Project Management

Figure 39: Sample Executive Biography

KATHERINE WHITNEY

7092 Baron Drive ~ Lake City, FL 60923

h (555) 907-2098	kwhitney@email.com	c (555) 290-2654

Executive Biography

Daring, bold, self-reliant, and gutsy. A measured risk-taker who thrives on challenges, is creative in her approach to solving problems, and who always keeps the bottom-line a top priority. These are words and phrases that those who know Katherine (Kathy) Whitney often use to describe her to others. Certainly these traits show in her successful executive career that includes impressive achievements and results year after year. Yet, unlike many leaders with such an intense drive and results-focus, Kathy is also a visionary and a highly effective and influential manager of people known for leading by example and for illustrating a genuine commitment to mentoring and developing her staff.

Having reached the senior vice-president level in a world-leading $10+ billion revenue international financial services firm with a focus on asset management and securities services, Kathy offers exceptionally strong qualifications for leadership of operations, client services, and change management in the financial services or related industries, such as insurance, banking, or investment banking. In such a large corporation, Kathy has had the opportunity to cultivate her leadership strengths in both hierarchical and matrix-management structures, and in various positions she has provided executive guidance for up to 1,200 professionals in locations across North America and Europe. Her oversight has extended to providing client services for 600 institutional and corporate clients with combined portfolios valued at up to $1.5 trillion, as well as leading major business initiatives such as operational transformation, business process reengineering, creation of global utilities, merger integration, consolidations, and offshoring.

Beginning her career with The Federal Bank of America Corporation in an administrative role, Kathy demonstrated her high-potential leadership traits right from the start, quickly earning her promotions to serve in the diverse roles of statistical analyst, senior master trust accountant, and trust officer. In 1987, Kathy was promoted into her first executive role as a vice-president of specialized accounting services in the Institutional Trust Department. This role incorporated a sales and business development aspect unlike any other position she had held. But, of course, Kathy rose to the challenge, adapting the model and expanding product offerings to open a new market and attract a new client base. Before earning her next promotion, she had successfully increased trust revenues 15% while also establishing a completely new system of internal controls and management reporting processes that enabled business growth, with the secondary benefit of lowering operating costs 20%.

In positions since then, Kathy has been even more successful. One of her most important achievements revolves around her commitment to client service excellence. As a senior vice-president for global client service delivery, Kathy was charged with driving the design and implementation of a new operating model to improve the delivery and quality of services to clients. Kathy responded by championing a best-in-class service model that helped propel the asset servicing business from almost last place (#14 of 15) to achieve a #1 service rating industry-wide, a ranking that they have since sustained for the past six years. As a result of Kathy's initiatives in applying a continuous improvement mindset and leading Six Sigma projects to strengthen productivity, efficiency, quality, and performance, she can also claim more than $17 million in cost savings over the past ten years.

Kathy Whitney earned her B.S. degree Magna cum Laude from Anspach University in 1986, with an emphasis on Business Management and Accounting. She was awarded her M.P.M. degree with a focus on Management of Financial Information and Resources from Lorber University in 1988.

Today, Kathy resides with her family in Lake City, Florida. She is seeking her next executive opportunity in the Miami region with companies in the financial services and related industries. Kathy can be reached at her residence at (555) 907-2098, on her mobile phone at (555) 290-2654, or by email at kwhitney@email.com.

accomplishments during school would precede experience. Other optional sections at the end include any publications you have authored, awards received (when relevant to the job), and any professional associations (avoiding political or religious affiliations, as this is legally prohibited information).

- **Follow design protocol.** Use standard-size paper, white or cream in color, as well as standard fonts such as Times Roman, Arial or Helvetica, printed in black ink. This will help convey a professional impression.

- **Consolidate your background into no more than two pages.** Even clients with twenty-five or more years of experience can selectively include information that will position them for the job in one to two pages. This is the standard in virtually all hiring scenarios except academia, government positions, scientific research positions, and executive biographical narrative resumes.

- **Avoid any unnecessary information, but include all that is required.** Resumes in the old workplace included personal information such as health status, race, gender, religion, and age information that is now prohibited – leave it out! (Note: In Europe and some other markets, personal information is still considered relevant. Consult authorities in your country for the latest trends.) On the other hand, be sure that your name and phone number appear on all pages of the resume and on the reference sheet (in case the pages get separated), and double check to be sure that all information is complete.

Personal Branding and Job Search

Throughout the client's marketing campaign, his/her personal brand statement should be communicated. It needs to possess three qualities, according to *Career Distinction: Standing Out by Building Your Brand* by William Arruda and Kirsten Dixson (www.careerdistinction.com):

1. It consists of just one sentence.
2. It can be easily understood by a 12-year-old.
3. You could recite it from memory at gunpoint.

Following are two personal brand statement examples from Arruda and Dixson:

"Sitting at the intersection of technology and business, I use my passion for communication to help IT professionals in Fortune 100 companies express themselves in ways that are understood by business people."

"I inspire and activate high-achieving salespeople in healthcare organizations through my focus on motivation, positivity, empathy, and competition."

For more examples and guidelines on personal branding, see www.careerdistinction.com

Cover Letters

Each time clients submit a resume to a published opening, they should include a cover letter. Its primary role is to get the recipient to read the resume (and in turn, call the applicant for an interview). An effective cover letter must:

- Be letter perfect and free of typographical errors
- Specifically list what job the applicant is applying for and where he/she saw the notice
- Be addressed to a specific person within the company (since personalization will get better results, and this also allows the sender to follow-up)
- Highlight key achievements as they relate to the job, using a "T-Bar" format as in fig. 30 in chapter 21 and fig. 40 below
- Be less than one page in length
- Tell the reader what to do next (call me, wait for my call, read the enclosure, visit my online blog or portfolio, etc.)
- Have current and accurate contact information for the candidate

References

Caution your clients to use references strategically, and to avoid listing them on their resume. Including references' names on a resume is akin to handing a perfect stranger your business plan or financial statement at a cocktail party. You would not do it! In fact, you would have to work up to giving that person your business card, right? Clients should have ready three to six references, listed on a separate sheet with their name and contact information. Ideally, one or two of their former supervisors should be included, as well as subordinates (if they are or seek to be a manager) and peers. Personal references are optional, and they should not be listed on the resume itself either.

Figure 40: Sample Cover Letter

John Bartz
97 Revolutionary Lane, Concord NH 90843
Phone: (603) 709-5555 ⊙ Email: jbartz@email.com

(Date)

(Name of Hiring Authority, Title)
(Name of Company)
(Address)
(City, State Zip)

Dear (Mr. or Ms.) (Last Name):

   With more than a decade of performance-based progression to senior-level executive management in large corporate and international business environments, I offer well-honed, proven abilities as the visionary, creator, and driver of strategies and business plans that have consistently delivered record-setting gains in sales, profits, and market share.

   If you are currently working with a client who would benefit from a management executive and expert marketer with outstanding cross-functional qualifications spanning all aspects of operations and financial management, we should talk. With the sale of my present employer pending, I am exploring new challenges that will allow me to apply the full scope of my business development and management talents to grow and expand a dynamic company. Perhaps you know of such an opportunity. If so, I will welcome the opportunity to explore it further.

   Details of my background and contributions are documented in the enclosed résumé, and it is with complete confidence that I present them as a representative of the value and return on investment I will bring to your client. Perhaps most critical to this success has been my innovation and resourcefulness in solving the diverse challenges and problems that I faced in my career. Whether charged with leading the turnaround of a multimillion-dollar business unit, spearheading start up of a subsidiary operation, or executing major expansion initiatives, I have delivered.

   Please be aware that I am open to relocation throughout the US or internationally, and that I possess excellent business skills in the global arena, particularly in the Latin American markets. Compensation requirements will be negotiable, dependent on geographic location, benefits, and the nature of the position.

   In advance, thank you for your time and attention. I look forward to your response.

Sincerely,

John Bartz
Enclosure

Courtesy of Michelle Dumas, www.distinctiveweb.com

Creating an Electronic Resume

Electronic resumes ("e-resumes") are different from standard (hard copy) resumes in several ways. First, they avoid the use of any bold, italics, bullets, borders, or other formatting that will be lost when pasted into an e-mail. And they must use simple, standard fonts such as Arial, Courier, or Times Roman. They must also be brief and to the point.

Professional resume writer and career coach Michelle Dumas (www.distinctiveweb.com) suggests the following process to convert a standard resume to an e-resume:

1. Use the "Select All" feature in the Edit menu of Word and remove all bold, italics, bullets, and underlining.
2. Change the margins to 1 inch on the top, bottom, and left, and 2 to 2.5 inches on the right. The goal is to have no more than 65 characters across one line.
3. Save the document as a text-only (*.txt) format in Word.
4. Close the document, then reopen in Notepad to make the changes and reformat with keyboard-only document enhancements as all bullets, lines, etc. will be distorted.
5. Test the document by sending it in an e-mail to yourself before sending it to a prospective employer.

To elicit favorable employer consideration from an e-resume, clients should follow the additional guidelines below.

Client Tips: E-resume Preparation

- **Put the most important information at the top of page 1.** Employers search for their most important criteria first—the same way they write job listings. In addition, many search engines base their hits on the top one-third of page 1. Not coincidentally, that represents one screenful of information, and what employers will see when they first access your e-resume. Critical content for this section includes contact information, keywords pertaining to the target job, representative achievements (briefly stated) and a listing of the ten most recent years of your work experience.

- **Include a keyword list at the top.** Include hard skills first, beginning with technical knowledge or training you have. Then, use key action words as required by the job (implemented, created, managed, etc.). Any pertinent soft skills such as communication skills or organizational abilities would go next in the keyword list. See the sample keyword list below. The list can be woven into the summary of qualifications and throughout the document.

Sample keyword list for production manager:
Fortune 500 experience. ISO-9002 implementation. Managed production of hardware components. 500-person production team manager. Organizational skills. Team builder. Budget development and management. Meets or exceeds production deadlines.

- **Use multiple forms of critical terms.** Internet "spiders" (as well as systems relying on scanning) look for both the verb and noun form of a key word. So in addition to "managed" you will want to include "manager" and "management" in the first half of page 1—or somewhere else in the resume if the skill is of secondary importance.

- **Be redundant to get more hits.** Mentioning each critical skill at least three times triples the odds of an employer finding and selecting your resume. But do not overdo it. Some software systems count it against you if you use terms more than a certain number of times.

A sample electronic resume is provided in fig. 41 Courtesy of Michelle Dumas, www. distinctiveweb.com.

Resume-Screening Software

Most large employers use software to scan and/or screen incoming applicants' resumes to streamline the screening process. If a help wanted ad identifies the company, your clients can contact the prospective employer by phone to ask whether they scan incoming resumes. If they do, clients can send one copy for scanning and one for review by a live person (being careful to specify which one is for which purpose). To ensure proper scanning by the software, clients should adhere to the following guidelines.

Figure 41: Sample Electronic Resume

Patricia A. Tagan
209 Wenke Street
Orlando, FL 00000
(555) 555-5555
email@emailaddress.net

===

TARGET: EXECUTIVE ASSISTANT / ADMINISTRATIVE ASSISTANT
Results-proven administrative professional offering 9 years of
progressive experience in manufacturing and financial services
industries, leveraging organizational and analytical skills, customer-
focus, and multi-tasking abilities to contribute in a variety of roles.
Deep interest in applying skills within an administrative support
position within a manufacturing company.

Advocate for new ideas and creative alternatives to increase
organizational efficiency; leader by example, promoting "a place
for everything and everything in its place," helping to streamline
operational and administrative processes. Proven ability to adapt,
change, learn, and grow. Excellent ability to easily, efficiently, and
independently handle complex tasks and multiple, deadline-driven
projects. Strong interpersonal communication skills and highly
professional liaison to both internal and external customers.

===

STRENGTHS & SKILL AREAS
- Administrative Support
- Purchasing Assistance
- Risk & Credit Analysis
- Confidential Document Handling
- Vendor/Supplier/Partner Relations
- Budget & Financial Statement Analysis
- Shipping & Receiving/Inventory Control
- Database/Spreadsheet Applications
- Customer Support & Service
- Data Control & Management
- Process Redesign & Improvement
- Policy/Procedure Implementation

==

EXPERIENCE HIGHLIGHTS

ABC Financial - Orlando, FL, 2002 - Present
~~~~~~
UNDERWRITING PRODUCTION ASSISTANT / ASSISTANT BRANCH MANAGER

Promoted and rotated through various positions and departments,
developing and enhancing analytical, communication,
administrative, and organizational skills. Became relied upon in
company by all levels of staff and management as "go-to person"
for information and "outside-the-box" problem-solving abilities.
Built strong portfolio of transferable qualifications in
financial-risk analysis and decision-making; financial
statements analysis; pricing, margins, overage/shortage, and
budget analysis; detailed documentation and file management;
internal controls/policies and procedures; and customer
communications.

Selected Contributions:

* Process & Efficiency Improvement - Improved overall
departmental workflow and efficiency; applied excellent
organizational skills to streamline paperwork and processes,
frequently recommending new ideas and fresh approaches to clear
bottlenecks. Repeatedly recognized for solution-orientation and
contributions to enhancing efficiency.

* New Systems Implementation - Selected as 1 of 15 in the region
to assist with corporate software rollout project; participated
in conference calls and met on-on-one with programmers to
provide user-level perspective supporting efforts to refine
software functionality/usability and correct bugs.

* Multi-Tasking & Workflow Management - Met challenges and
consistently delivered on time within a fast-paced environment
with changing guidelines, daily deadlines, and monthly
productivity targets. Continuously turned 80-90% of pipeline
monthly, using spreadsheet application and database to
efficiently manage high volume of workflow.

* Operational Effectiveness - Helped build a strong, organized, and effective operational team; created, implemented, and trained employees in enhanced workflow procedures that significantly increased quality/accuracy and efficiency by coordinating tasks to leverage unique strengths of individual team members.

* Customer Service & Support - Recognized by management for customer-focus and consistently achieving high levels of internal and external customer service. Called upon frequently by referral sources to provide assistance in analyzing specific situations and recommending potential product solutions, ultimately resulting in increased sales volume.

Office Team (contracted to Acme Corp) - Orlando, FL, 2002
~~~~~~

PURCHASING ASSISTANT

Temporary position assisting purchasing manager within a manufacturing environment to process purchase orders, maintain database, and coordinate with suppliers, freight lines, and shipping/receiving department. Earned offer for full-time employment.

Selected Contributions:

* Purchasing Department Improvement - Attended meetings and supported purchasing manager in implementing new policies and procedures. Recommended organizational and process changes to increase efficiency.

Best Mortgages - Kissimmee, FL, 2000 - 2002
~~~~~~

ANALYST

Processed customer applications, compiling, verifying, and typing information while ensuring that all data was complete and met established mortgage-loan standards. Checked accuracy of applications with credit bureaus and coordinated scheduling for property abstracts, surveys, and appraisals. Submitted complete applications for underwriting approval and prepared documents for closings. Assisted investors, coordinating transactions from origination to closing.

Selected Contributions:

* Sales Support - Played indirect role in business development through efficiency in handling a large workload, resulting in smooth, timely transactions. Generated high volumes of referral business as result of customer and partner confidence. Consistently met commitment and close dates and maintained excellent monthly turn ratio of 80%+.

* Partner Relationships - Developed and cultivated excellent working relationships with partner companies, including title companies, appraisal firms, and credit bureaus, helping ensure fast, smooth transactions.

National Mortgage - Atlanta, GA, 1999 - 2000
~~~~~~
RECEPTIONIST/OFFICE COORDINATOR

Managed high-volume, multi-line telephone system and provided wide range of administrative support functions. Answered requests for information from employees and managers. Supported management by typing memos, reports, and correspondence. Processed and distributed incoming and outgoing mail.

HW Manufacturing - Atlanta, GA, 1999
~~~~~~
RECEPTIONIST

Screened and directed incoming telephone calls. Supported engineering and purchasing management on special projects as assigned. Managed and maintained inventory and shipping/receiving databases.

==

COMPUTER SKILLS

Advanced computer skills with Microsoft Word, Excel, and
Outlook; Lotus Notes; and AS400.

===
EDUCATION

A.S., Business Administration, 2000
Some Community College, Some City, GA

Client Tips: Making Your Resume Scanner-Friendly

- The first line must contain only your name. Otherwise, the scanner gets confused. So use a separate line for your address, phone number and email address.

- Plain is better: avoid bolding, italics, underlining, fancy borders, and so on.

- Avoid columns and graphics. Since scanners and screening software are programmed for simple alphabetical letters and numbers, fancy features such as columns and graphics tend to get run together or otherwise get distorted when scanned. This is a very unfortunate reason to be rejected from consideration!

- Make sure the image is crystal clear. Print on a high-resolution laser printer if possible, and submit an original, not a photocopy.

- Use a keyword section. Just as with an e-resume, be sure to include a keyword section that will allow the computer to sort you into the "qualified" stack of candidates.

Resume Distribution Services

In addition to submitting a resume in response to a specific opening, candidates can also use a resume distribution service that will send resumes (or targeted letters) to companies meeting certain specifications (set by the user, whether coach or client). The advantage of using such services is that it broadens clients' exposure within the industries they have targeted. Typically, candidates can determine the geographical areas, industries, size of companies, salary levels, and positions toward which their qualifications are directed. One service that we recommend is www.resumespider.com.

When clients decide to use one of these services, two things are critical: (1) be sure that the service provides them with the names of the individuals to whom your materials were sent to facilitate phone follow-up, and (2) they should avoid the services that charge substantial fees ($3,000 to $10,000 or more) for this type of service. They can obtain comparable or superior results by working with a coach and using the suggestions in this book!

Web Portfolios

A new way of letting prospective employers know about a candidate is through the use of a "Web portfolio," which draws from the information in the e-resume and includes multiple web pages such as

- Highlights
- Resume
- Certifications
- Special Projects
- Related Work History

Job seekers can then include the link to their web portfolio in cover letters in lieu of, or in addition to, a resume attachment or enclosure. Candidates who should consider this medium would include those who want to create a more personal or innovative image to their prospective employer, or those who wish to show technological expertise. Certainly, Web site designers should have online samples of their work as well.

Creating a blog using www.blogger.com, www.typepad.com or www.blogspot.com is an easy for a candidate to create an online presence. For a portfolio of online web portfolios and resource to help you and your clients create them, see http://www.brandego.com/samples.php.

Employment Applications

Except for entry-level positions, employment applications tend to be a mere formality (if used at all). However, a note on them is appropriate in case your clients raise questions about completing the application. To successfully complete an employment application, clients should follow the guidelines below.

Client Tips: Employment Applications

- Bring a summary of all the details you will need for the application with you. Dates, employer and reference names, phone numbers, and other information that will be required to complete the application should be on a sheet to which you can refer as needed.

- Be honest; expect that the information you provide will be verified.

- Describe your accomplishments positively and with enough detail. Let the screener have a "snapshot" of your past work experience. Instead of "Fulfilled all job requirements," say, for example, "Successfully completed daily data processing for a 100-item chart of accounts; initiated new system to organize reports for ease of access."

- Do not be afraid to omit salary/wage information. Just as with cover letters, information about your past pay may be used to screen you out before the screener becomes familiar with what you offer.

- Don't answer illegal questions. If the application asks about personal disabilities, gender, sexual preference, race, religion, health issues, marital status, or other legally prohibited information, leave it out and, if necessary, discuss it tactfully in the interview.

For a more complete treatment of the subject of resume preparation, see the resource list in the Career Coach's Toolbox (p. 394).

KEY COACHING CONCEPTS

1. Communicate to your clients the following guidelines concerning the proper use and application of resumes.

   • Remember that a resume is a marketing document, not a complete chronology of a lifetime of work.

   • Realize the primary purpose of a resume: to get an interview, not a job— at least not directly

   • Lead with your best tangible skills

   • Customize your resume for each opening for which you apply

   • Use a chronological resume (especially with recruiters) unless you fit one of the categories of exceptions

   • Begin with a summary of qualifications instead of a job objective

   • Continue with applicable sections of the resume, depending on your background

   • Consolidate your background into no more than two pages

   • Avoid any unnecessary information, but include all that is required

   • For electronic or scannable resumes, include a keyword section, use only plain text, and put the most important information on the first third of page 1

   • Use a resume distribution service to enhance your exposure among target employers

   • Consider a Web portfolio to present more unique qualifications and/or show technological savvy

2. Advise clients to provide references as a separate document, rather than list them on their resume

3. Encourage clients to approach employment applications, if used, as strategically as they would any other part of the job search process.

24

Interviewing Strategies That Get the Job

"DO NOT HIRE A MAN WHO DOES YOUR WORK FOR MONEY, BUT HIM WHO DOES IT FOR THE LOVE OF IT."
—*Henry David Thoreau*

The next step in the job search process is usually a job interview. No matter how favorably clients have presented themselves in writing through a powerful cover letter and a customized resume, the interview can make or break their chances of being hired.

Job interviewing in today's workplace is much more of an art than a mere skill. While certain aspects of it can be learned and practiced, the unique dynamics of interviews also require candidates to observe and respond to the nonverbal cues of the interviewer. That is, listening between the words that are being spoken can often provide invaluable insights into what the interviewer is really looking for and how he or she is evaluating the applicant.

The interview is actually the beginning of a new relationship with the staff of the prospective employer. So both candidate and interviewer want to make a good impression! Company policies and practices regarding interviews vary widely, and interviews also vary at different stages of selection and at different levels of the organization (e.g., an interview for an entry-level employee will be less complex and involved than one for a CEO). So for all these reasons it will be helpful to think of interviewing as an "art"—one in which all parties involved are contributing to create the relationship between, and roles of, applicant and company.

For clients to be successful at interviewing, we need to work with them in several areas:

- Pre-interview strategies that get them past the screener and help get them be prepared for the interview
- The logistics of interviewing, including first impressions, dress, and scheduling
- The two primary types of interviews, screening and decision-making, and how one's approach must be different with each
- How to answer the most commonly asked questions during the interview
- Ways to avoid becoming defensive when shortcomings are raised
- Key follow-up tactics after the interview

Pre-Interview Strategies

When does the interview start? Many people think it is when they walk into the reception area of the hiring organization. Wrong! The interview actually starts when the prospective employer responds to the applicant's letter, resume, or other approach—that is, in the first phone call. If the client mishandles this call, there will be no interview. Following are some helpful hints you can give your clients prior to the interview.

Client Tips: Interview Preparation

- **Handle the phone call professionally.** Have a phone line dedicated to your job search if you can (especially if you have young children or teenagers in the house). The voicemail message should be simple, professional, and in your own voice. For example, "You've reached the voicemail for Sam Smith. I'm sorry I've missed your call, but I will return it as soon as possible if you leave your name, phone number, and message." Consider letting all calls go to voicemail (even if you are right there) to ensure that you have the information you need in front of you when you return the recruiter's call. And if you are conducting your search while employed, you may want to use your cell phone as your job search line so that you can receive (via voicemail) and return calls during breaks in your work day—for example, your lunch hour.

- **Handle the callback strategically.** When you call the company representative back (even if it is just five minutes later), your goal is to set an appointment for a screening interview. To give you some time to prepare for the interview and learn more about the company, avoid getting into a screening interview during the callback. Even scheduling it for the next day gives you more preparation time. And after the day and time for the interview are set, do not forget to ask the following key questions to help you with research, scheduling, and positioning:

  - o "How long do you expect the meeting(s) to last?" (so you allow ample time)
  - o "With whom will I be meeting or talking at this interview?" (so you can check on their background if any information is available)
  - o "What can you tell me about the position in addition to what the advertisement or posting indicates?" (helps you choose Work Experience Stories that are relevant to the full range of requirements)
  - o "Was there anything in particular about my qualifications/background that interested you?" (what they say may surprise you!)

- **Do your homework prior to the interview.** Gather background information on the industry, company, and interviewer through their Web site and other source material referred to in prior chapters.

  [A sample pre-interview company research data sheet that clients can use to summarize their pre-interview research findings is provided in the Career Coach's Toolbox (p. 380)]

- **Know how to answer common interview questions and handle any shortcomings you may have.** Review the list of the ten most commonly asked interview questions—and the best/worst answers—in fig. 42.

  [There are literally hundreds of interview questions that could be asked of a candidate during either a screening or a decision-making interview. However, those listed in fig. 42 are more common than others and, once a client knows how to answer them, the strategy for answering other questions follows suit.]

- ***Prepare questions to ask the interviewer during the interview.*** Choose from the list in fig. 43.

Figure 42: Best and Worst Answers to the Ten Most Commonly Asked Interview Questions

Question	Best Answer	Worst Answer
1. Tell me about yourself.	This is often the first question in an interview. Assume they want a summary of your work-related qualifications; prepare a one-minute "personal commercial" (either consisting of or drawing on your personal brand statement) that includes: • an overview of work done during the past ten years only (not entire career), • your academic degree(s)—but only those related to the position, • a few of your specific skills that relate to the job requirements. (See a sample one-minute summary on p. 234.)	• "What would you like to know?" • Talking about where you were born and raised, how many children you have, personal/non-job-related information

Question	Best Answer	Worst Answer
2. What are your salary requirements?	• *Defer:* "I don't know enough about the job yet to respond; can you tell me about the expectations for the first six months?" • *Turn it around:* "I'm sure you pay a competitive salary, and I'm flexible. What is the range you've budgeted for the position?" • *Give a broad range:* If you have to give a number, state the range of your total compensation package including the value of benefits, bonuses, etc. over past five to ten years. (See chapter 26 for details on negotiating compensation.)	"I wouldn't consider less than $100,000. What do you pay?"
3. What are your greatest strengths?	This question is used in the behavioral interviewing style which is most common today. The answer should include: • concrete/tangible job skills (e.g., increasing sales, managing a turnaround or merger, written communications, teambuilding, software programming) • actual stories or examples of how you used those skills to achieve a specific result.	"I'm really a great person, a team player, and I'm sure I'd fit right into your organization." (The problem: these are subjective or intangible traits, not concrete job skills.)

Question	Best Answer	Worst Answer
4. What are your weaknesses?	Response should cite a trait that may have been a challenge in the past but which you have worked to overcome – e.g., "Early in my career I struggled with impatience due to my high personal standards. With time I have learned to vary my expectations with the situation."	• "I don't really have any." • "Well, I know you want someone who knows the computer, and I really don't have any experience with that." (This is a job search *shortcoming*, not a weakness—and you certainly don't want to volunteer it.) • "I tend to be a perfectionist." (overused)
5. What are your career goals?	"I'd like to become increasingly valuable to your firm by consistently exceeding the performance standards and learning new skills."	• "I'd like to have your job." (intimidating) • "I don't really have any." (Has the candidate thought past the next paycheck?)
6. What did you like most about your last position?	Tie the answer into the company's needs and/or show your initiative or outstanding performance—e.g., if interviewing with a growth firm, you could say "What I liked best was the opportunity to grow the sales in our region by 50 percent over five years."	Answering without thinking about the interviewing company's needs. If you say you liked the independence of your last job and the interviewing company wants people who fit into the established "company-think" and stay within the boundaries of their job, that could disqualify you.

Question	Best Answer	Worst Answer
7. What did you like least about your last position?	"Though I liked most of the aspects of the job and company, the one limitation was lack of growth opportunities." (shows initiative)	• "Well actually, I'm suing my former employer for unethical practices." • "I disliked the bureaucracy." (when interviewing with a large, highly structured firm or agency)
8. How quickly do you think you will be ready to contribute to our firm?	"I believe I can contribute almost immediately. In past positions, I've had to learn a lot of [e.g., terminology] in a short time, and did quite well. For example…" (tell a story)	"Since I don't have experience in your industry, it will probably take three to six months before I am really valuable." (And they are supposed to pay you for this?)
9. Why did you leave your last position?	• "The company reorganized and my position, along with a number of others, was eliminated." • "I had achieved as much as I could within that company and felt the need to seek another job to continue to grow."	• "I was forced out because I didn't get along with my coworkers." • "My boss was out to get me."
10. Why do you want to work here? Or, Why should we hire you?	Strut your stuff! Summarize the answers you've given to their questions as they relate to the job requirements, in a concise one- to two-minute response. (And reiterate this when you do your thank-you letter, within twenty-four hours of the interview.)	• "Well, it seems like a pretty good place to work." • "I understand you pay above market wages, and money is the most important thing to me."

Figure 43: Sample Questions to Ask at an Interview

- "What has led to this position coming available?"
- "Is this a new position?"
- "Why have you gone outside the company to fill this position?"
- "How long did the person I'm replacing hold the job?"
- "How many times has the job been vacant in the last five years?
- "What are the strengths and weaknesses of the person I'm replacing?"
- "Assuming I'm offered the job and take it, what benchmarks does the company expect to be achieved in the first six to twelve months?"
- "How are performance reviews conducted?"
- "What is the number one priority for the person who takes this job?"
- "What do you see as the main strengths a person needs for this job?"
- "What are some of the longer-term objectives you have for this job? For your department?"
- "What is the number one challenge in this position?"
- "How has the company been successful over the last few years?"
- "What is the company's current market share or position in the industry? (if your research didn't answer it)
- "In what areas do you see the company's primary strengths?"
- "What three to five traits would the ideal candidate for this position possess?"
- Closing question (always ask this): "What are the next steps in your selection process?" (Clarify, follow up, and leave with permission for recontact.)

Role-playing the interview with your clients can pay large dividends. One of our Professional Certified Career Coaches™ did interview coaching with a media manager who had been out of work for twelve months. After this role-play session, he successfully interviewed for and got a position as broadcast manager for a national television sports network. Interview coaching can make a difference!

Logistics of Interviewing

There is more to interviewing than preparation and asking and answering questions. We must be sure our clients know how to schedule the interview when they will be most favorably considered and dress appropriately.

Scheduling the Interview

Certainly there are times when clients have no choice as to the day or time of the interview. But in many cases they are given a choice. Research has shown that Monday is the worst day to interview, with Friday a close second.[66] If clients have some options regarding timing of the interview, the most positive impression will be made in a midday time frame. A few other hints: for management/exempt positions, don't be in a hurry to be the first one interviewed—the first person interviewed is three times less likely to be hired than the last one, though the rule is reversed for non-managerial-level positions. Keeping an interview appointment during bad weather bestows a significant advantage—assuming the interviewer is able to make it in, too. It shows eagerness and dedication.

Dress for Interviews

In the old workplace, dressing for interviews was easy: people wore a three-piece suit. Now that casual dress codes have become much more common and dress varies by industry, company, and region of the country, it is more difficult to predict what will be appropriate. As a rule of thumb, applicants should dress just a little nicer than they would for day-to-day work. If unsure, best practice is to err on the side of being conservative. This is another question that clients can ask during the interview scheduling phone call if they are unsure about appropriate dress.

In addition, clients need to be sure their grooming is impeccable. Both men and women should keep jewelry, cologne/perfume, and accessories to a minimum, but pay careful attention to such details as the condition of one's shoes (polished, heels not worn down). Women should carry only a briefcase or purse, not both. Basic hygiene should be observed. For additional information on dress for interviews, see

John T. Molloy's *The New Dress for Success.*[67] Finally, applicants should bring a list of their references to the interview to present if/when it is asked for.

During the Interview

Once the interview day arrives, clients should rehearse their brand statement and answers to frequently asked questions, envision a positive outcome, and enter the building or other facility with confidence. Ensuring that they make a good first impression, understand what type of interview they will be having, and know how to overcome shortcomings will position them well to obtain the result they want.

Optimizing First Impressions

Creating the right first impression is a vital part of success. Often it is not experience or qualifications, but rather personality and personal presentation that make the biggest impression. Researchers tell us that 55 percent of our communication is nonverbal: tone of voice, dress, posture, facial expression, and physical appearance.[68]

In addition, our clients need to:

- Greet receptionists warmly, ask them a few questions about what it is like to work there, and get their name for later follow-up and acknowledgment (they are the ones who will help candidates get through to the hiring manager later on the phone)
- Have some chitchat prepared to use when the interviewer comes out to greet them
- Make direct eye contact with the interviewer
- Shake hands firmly, but not too vigorously, with the interviewer
- Be the first to make a statement or ask a question to position themselves as a proactive participant in the interviewing process

Types of Interviews

There are two primary types of interviews—screening and decision-making—and a few variations on each. The client's role and approach will vary with each type.

Screening interviews are usually done by trained human resources staff who are skilled in interviewing. They will make the interviewee feel comfortable (unless a stress element is part of the criteria of the job, in which they may do just the opposite). They will proceed through a prepared list of questions, logically and systematically. The purpose of the screening interview is to screen out all candidates who do not meet all of the basic job requirements. Therefore, any skill deficiencies or questions not answered to the interviewer's satisfaction will provide a reason to eliminate candidates from further consideration. Job seekers should understand each question that is asked, and provide only the information requested. Volunteering more than is asked for will usually do more harm than good in this type of interview.

Screening interviews are often done over the telephone. The advantage of this method for our clients is that they can have their notes regarding their company research, answers to interview questions, and the like in front of them. However, since the screener does not have the visual input of their appearance and other nonverbal cues, it is critical that clients' verbal presentation be as close to flawless as possible.

The **decision-making interview,** on the other hand, is usually done by the manager or person who will actually make the hiring decision. These people are usually not skilled in interviewing, which may cause job seekers to feel more awkward than in a screening interview. In many cases it will be necessary for job seekers to take a more proactive role in this type of interview and its direction and content, to succeed. For example, the candidate may be the one that asks many of the questions or suggests what needs to be covered.

The primary style of decision-making interview has changed from the old skills question-and-answer style to "behavioral interviewing." This means candidates need to be prepared to not only answer the question asked, but also to illustrate the answer with a story or respond to a hypothetical situation by demonstrating their reasoning process. Clients with well-prepared Work Experience Stories will be well prepared for this common type of interview. Some variations on the decision-making interview are the group interview, the serial interview, the interview that includes a meal, and the so-called blessing interview, as described below.

- **Group interview.** Here, several managers or other company representatives interview a candidate simultaneously, usually around a conference table. Coaching tips for this type of interview include making eye contact with each person in the group while answering a question, candidates' addressing questions to more than one of the interviewers, and following up with each interviewer individually after the interview by letter.

- **Serial interview:** This approach has candidates undergo a series of interviews with various company representatives one after the other, often lasting as long as a full day. It can be grueling! Their challenge is to stay as fresh and spontaneous with the last of five to eight interviews as they were for the first one. From the company's standpoint, this approach allows the interviewers to compare notes about what they observed, and often one will notice something that the others missed.

- **Interviews over a meal.** Another whole set of issues are added to the situation when food is involved: whether or not to order a cocktail, what kind of food to order to create the right impression (and not be too messy), how to balance answering the interview questions with finishing one's food, and learning to follow the cues of the others present to show that the candidate fits in. Common sense goes a long way here: it is generally best to avoid smoking or ordering cocktails (even if others do) so that your mind remains clear to answer the questions, and ordering something simple and easy to eat so that you can concentrate on what's most important – the interview. Clients should avoid telling off-color jokes or otherwise creating a less-than-professional impression.

- **Blessing interview:** At the conclusion of an interviewing sequence in many medium- to large-sized companies, there is a "blessing interview" with the CEO or general manager of the firm. The purpose of this interview is not to review candidates' qualifications; the interviewer assumes they have met the job requirements through the prior interviews (of which there may be two or as many as seven). Here, the CEO generally wants to see if a candidate's style and personality are a good fit with the organization. Some rather informal or casual conversation is characteristic, and if the candidate is successful the CEO puts his "blessing" or stamp of approval on the decision to hire the applicant. The offer would then follow.

Dealing with Shortcomings

A shortcoming is simply a perceived liability or deficiency in the job seeker's qualifi-cations or background. Nearly every candidate has some shortcoming vis-à-vis the job for which they are applying. Whether they lack the specific education or experi-ence the company desires or face such potential issues as age discrimination, fre-quent job changes, or a termination for cause, the one thing candidates must avoid is becoming defensive regarding that issue—or worse, finding themselves spending a significant part of the interview trying to overcome it.

A powerful technique to use in addressing shortcomings in the interview is to use the "acknowledge and redirect" technique. When applicants are asked a question about a shortcoming, they must simply (a) acknowledge it, (b) redirect the conver-sation to a common area, (c) ask a question, and (d) illustrate how that area bridges the perceived shortcoming. For example: an employer asks the candidate whether she has a master's degree. She answers:

> [Acknowledgment:] I appreciate your raising that issue; I know it was one of the qualifications you listed for the job. [Redirect:] From what you've shared with me today, you're looking for someone that can work well with people and knows the terminology of your industry. [Question:] If I could demonstrate how I have used those skills in several previous positions, would that help relieve your concern?" [Follow with story to illustrate]

The job seeker then tells the story of her past accomplishments that illustrate these skills, thus demonstrating equivalent value despite the lack of the stated requirement.

Client Tips: Handling Shortcomings

- **Termination.** Frame it in terms of a business decision; mention that other positions were also eliminated (if they were). If terminated for cause, state that you just did not see eye-to-eye on some issues with someone at work.

- **Long time with one company.** Highlight different positions within the company, different duties, and number of staff to show that it was more like having different jobs (shows you are adaptable despite a long time at one firm).

- **Frequent job changes.** Point to any commonalities (same industry, same-size company, significant amount of tangible results produced, etc.) between past jobs and this one and state why you are committed to a more permanent position now (if you are). Or, use this pattern to highlight your ability to handle frequent change in a business climate that demands it.

- **Age—too old.** Focus on your fitness and vitality, desire to work indefinitely, and the advantages of being a mature worker such as loyalty, stability, and so on—while showing you have an open mind to new ideas. Of course, this usually will not be raised directly due to employment discrimination concerns.

- **Age—too young.** Focus on outstanding accomplishments in school and anything that shows maturity, including clear longer-term goals.

- **No experience in target industry.** Point out accomplishments in similar functional roles, characterizing them generically to show transferability. For example, when interviewing for a position as chief financial officer at an aerospace firm after years in banking, instead of "At XYZ Bank I was responsible for overseeing accounting and financial analysis of commercial and retail accounts and reduced error rates in our FDIC reporting from 5 percent to 1 percent in six months," say, "At a Fortune 500 corporation, I oversaw accounting and financial analysis for business customers in various industries including aerospace, and reduced error rates by 80 percent within six months."

- **No degree.** Highlight any continuing or professional education, and skills learned on the job, and demonstrate openness to lifelong learning; also emphasize job-related experience to offset lack of formal education.

- **Degree not in area of target job.** Focus more on experience as it relates to the job and on any continuing education that has equipped you to do the job, as well as familiarity with technical concepts, customers, or other aspects of the target industry.

Following Up After the Interview

Whew! The interview is over and your client feels like she did well. Perhaps the interviewer even told her she would be called back for a second interview. Now you have the opportunity to acknowledge and congratulate the client for another part of the process well done!

Before the client even leaves the parking lot of the interviewing company, suggest that she spend a few minutes debriefing the interview on a notepad. This is especially important if she avoided note-taking during the interview—as we recommend—so that she could focus on the nonverbal communication and be perceived as more attentive. The debriefing would answer such questions as, What appealed to her about the position? The company? How does she feel she did in the interview? What are the next steps in the hiring process? What were the names of the interviewers, the receptionist, and others she talked to? Any drawbacks to this position compared to others for which she has interviewed?

Upon return to her home or office, the client can further position herself favorably by sending a thank-you letter reiterating the highlights of the interview, her accomplishments as they relate to the company's stated needs, and any follow-up that was agreed to at the interview, such as a next interview (see sample in fig. 44). This letter should be sent within twenty-four hours of the interview. If the client met with several people, she should send a customized letter to each. Sending hard copy letters is preferred to e-mails, which can be deleted or overlooked. If the client has an online portfolio, blog or profile, a reference to that link in the thank-you letter can reinforce their personal brand further and provide more information to the hiring manager that will encourage positive consideration.

Simply sending this letter gives the client an advantage because fewer than 10 percent of applicants bother to send a thank-you letter. We know of situations where between two equally qualified candidates, the one that sent the thank-you letter was hired primarily because the letter showed initiative.

Figure 44: Sample Thank-You Letter

Date

Interviewer, Title
Company Name
Address
City, State Zip

Dear [Name of Interviewer]:

Thank you for your time in discussing the [position of X] on [day]. I am excited about the possibilities of working with you!

Just to recap, we discussed that the following accomplishments lend support to my ability to confidently meet any challenges related to this position:

     1.
     2.
     3.

I am convinced that my proven track record of [summarize skills being emphasized], can provide both the immediate and long term results you desire.

I am sincerely interested in an association with [Company X]. The environment appears to provide the challenges I am seeking and in which I have always been successful. I look forward to speaking with you again on _____.

Sincerely,

Joe Job Seeker

KEY COACHING CONCEPTS

1. Interviewing is an art, not just a skill.
2. The interview begins with the first callback, not when the candidate appears for a face-to-face meeting on the company premises.
3. For pre-interview success, clients need to handle the phone professionally, handle the callback strategically, do research on the company and position prior to the interview, prepare to answer common questions, prepare a list of questions to ask the interviewer, and know how to deal with shortcomings.
4. It is important that job seekers understand how to make the best first impression, that they schedule the interview (if given a choice) at a time when they are most likely to be selected, and that they dress appropriately for the company and position.
5. There are two primary types of interviews, screening and decision-making.
6. A "one-minute summary" as well as carefully thought-out answers to all of the ten most commonly asked interview questions are a critical part of interview preparation.
7. The "acknowledge and redirect" strategy will help candidates overcome shortcomings and avoid becoming defensive when shortcomings are raised.
8. After the interview, candidates should debrief what has happened and send a thank-you letter within twenty-four hours of the interview to everyone with whom they have spoken.

25

Evaluating Job Offers: Wants Versus Needs

"LIFE IS A PROGRESS FROM WANT TO WANT, NOT FROM ENJOYMENT TO ENJOYMENT."
—*Samuel Johnson*

If clients' search has been successful, they will begin getting offers anywhere from one week to six months after they started their search. Three common mistakes, however, are typically made at this stage:

- Accepting the first offer received,
- Failing to adequately evaluate the offer
- Neglecting to seek improvement of the offer

Coaching suggestions for the first two situations are discussed below; improving the offer is covered in chapter 26.

Accepting the First Offer Received

Clients are often tempted to accept the first offer received, either because they are afraid there will be no other offers, because they have been in the search a long time and need to get back to work, or because they doubt their own abilities and marketable .

To help them avoid making this mistake, you should first let them know that multiple offers are quite common, particularly when they use the suggestions given here regarding a diversified marketing approach. If their lack of an income has put them in bind, it may in fact be unwise to wait for other offers. But for clients who have reached a similar stage in the interview process with several companies and expect other offers soon, it is best to use those multiple offers as leverage to optimize the compensation package of the job they really want. For those clients who are ready to jump at the first offer due to lack of confidence in their own abilities and skills, then coaching regarding that issue will help them overcome it.

Failing to Adequately Evaluate the Offer

Often clients do not know what to do when they have received an offer. For example, clients who failed to adequately consider what their ideal job should include will find it especially difficult to choose once they receive an offer. Some clients make decisions about accepting or rejecting job offers based solely on an intuitive hunch; others overanalyze the offer.

The best guide for clients in considering job offers is to pay attention to their initial intuitive reaction to the offer—but to not let that be entirely determinative. They can turn to "Authentic Vocation Worksheet 10" in the Career Coach's Toolbox (p. 382) for a comprehensive list of criteria that can be analyzed and evaluated. Several offers can also be compared against each other and the client's Authentic Vocation criteria, either to validate an intuitive "yes" to the offer or to reveal shortcomings in it that were not immediately apparent. The categories of criteria to evaluate include the following:

1. **The compensation package.** Here, clients will be analyzing not only whether the salary falls within a desired range, but also whether the benefits include those that are critical to them (i.e., needs versus mere wants). Also, if benefits such as computer allowance, flexible scheduling, child care allowance or facilities, or other nonstandard offerings are desirable to clients, they may need to specifically request them.

2. **Authentic Vocation factors.** Next, clients can ask themselves (or you can ask them) questions to determine whether the job offered satisfies all eight factors of their Authentic Vocation as they have defined it in the first part of the coaching process.

3. **Career development considerations.** To be a career self-manager and to remain challenged, most people also need to know that there are growth opportunities in the position they take and in the company for which they work. Clients who feel this is important may be looking for training or tuition reimbursement to be provided by the company or for a comprehensive organization-wide commitment to employee development.

4. **Work/life balance issues.** As individuals' lives become more complex and stress loads increase, there is a virtual outcry for balance between work and personal life. For employees with young children or ailing parents—or just an unwillingness to continue working unhealthily long hours in a demanding environment—this factor will be very important. Does the job require significant commuting time? Travel as part of the job? Are there policies that encourage flexibility to deal with family issues? These are a few of the considerations in this regard.

5. **Company soundness and position:** Finally, even when candidates find the "perfect" position, it can soon become anything but perfect if the company goes out of business, is acquired soon after hire, or has a poor reputation in its industry. These final factors investigate the risk involved in the company itself (e.g., is it a startup or a well-established company?) as well as its reputation, turnover rate, competitive pressures in the industry, and the like.

Using this combination of intuition and analysis, clients can make a much more well-rounded and better-informed decision whether to accept one offer versus another.

Finalizing the Employment Arrangement in Writing

Offers are often made verbally, and, unfortunately, candidates often accept verbally too. Later, if there are misunderstandings, candidates have no basis on which to enforce what they understood to be the terms of the job. Therefore, it is highly recommended to get the offer reduced to writing. That way both parties are clear on its terms. Some of the items to be included in the written offer are:

- Starting date
- Job title
- Responsibilities/job description
- Benefits (in detail—not a vague "as stated in employee manual"), including company holidays, vacation policy, insurance, retirement benefits, if any, and other relevant topics
- Relocation package, including all aspects (real estate commission, moving expense limits, procedure for reimbursement, whether tax on relocation package is included, temporary lodging, if any; house hunting trips, if any; storage, if any; transportation of any special items such as boats; etc.)
- Transition of 401(k) and medical insurance benefits (e.g., reimbursement for COBRA if there is a waiting period for company medical insurance)
- Stock options or bonuses (check for detail here: is it clear enough so that reasonable minds would interpret the language the same way?)
- Severance benefits, if any

Some executive clients may want a formal employment contract to memorialize the terms of their employment arrangement. Others (including many executives) will be adequately served by a letter of offer, signed by the new employee upon acceptance to acknowledge its terms. This written document should be signed before the client moves to the new location or begins work so that there are no misunderstandings.

KEY COACHING CONCEPTS

1. Three common mistakes at the offer stage are: (a) accepting the first offer received, (b) failing to adequately evaluate the offer, and (c) neglecting to seek improvement of the offer.

2. The categories of criteria to evaluate in reviewing offers include:
   - The compensation package
   - Authentic Vocation factors
   - Career development considerations
   - Work/life balance issues
   - Company soundness and position

3. Verbal offers need to be reduced to writing for clients to adequately consider them.

26

Negotiating the Optimum Compensation Package

"WHEN I WAS YOUNG I THOUGHT THAT MONEY WAS THE MOST IMPORTANT THING IN LIFE; NOW THAT I AM OLD I KNOW THAT IT IS."
—*Oscar Wilde*

At this point clients may have one offer or ten, but they will benefit in any case from coaching to strategize the negotiation stage of the job search. Clients' common misconceptions about negotiating in the context of a job include those listed in fig. 45.

Figure 45: Common Negotiation Misconceptions

Misconception	Truth
The offer as stated is the "best they can do," i.e., there is no room to improve the compensation.	There is usually *at least* 20 percent more compensation available; we have seen packages be increased by as much as 100 percent in rare cases.
This is an "arms-length" negotiation, just like selling a house or car.	It is a unique kind of negotiation because the candidate will be working with these people for some years and this is the beginning of the relationship. It is more like negotiating a prenuptial agreement.

Misconception	Truth
It is best for candidates to maintain a policy of full disclosure when asked what your salary history or requirements are.	Salary is not a relevant issue until the offer stage; until then, candidates should use one of the three strategies discussed below to postpone the discussion until it is pertinent.
When candidates have a long list of items to be negotiated in the offer (and which you want changed), it is best to just raise a few first and see how the employer responds.	Wrong! This can alienate the employer and, in some cases, result in the offer being withdrawn. Instead, candidates should raise all of their "discussion points" at once so that both parties know what is on the table.
The most appropriate term for the document outlining the changes candidates want made to the offer is a "counteroffer."	No, this sets up an adversarial dynamic that will not further a win-win outcome. Instead, candidates should call it a "responsive memo" to preserve the cooperative spirit of the discussion.

Compensation Negotiation Tactics in Three Key Stages

The three key stages of negotiation are pre-interview, interview, and post-interview. The post-interview stage is referred to here as the offer stage. Throughout the process, savvy negotiators will operate with the tenet that they can ask for anything (the worst the person the company say is no, right?), but they can demand nothing. "He who becomes demanding loses" in the negotiating game.

Negotiating During the Pre-Interview Stage

Thorough preparation prior to the interview is essential not only for getting the job offer, but also for negotiating compensation. Not only do candidates need to research the company, but they also want to do some preliminary research into what market salaries are for similar positions. The resources listed below provide free salary data for this purpose.

- http://online.wsj.com/careers
- www.jobsmart.org
- www.abbott-langer.com
- www.wageweb.com
- www.salary.com
- http://www.bls.gov/OES/
- www.rileyguide.com
- http://www.bls.gov/oco/
- http://blogs.payscale.com/ask_dr_salary/

A fee-based service to which you can subscribe, or ask for a per-client report regarding salary data, is Pay Scale, www.payscale.com.

In addition, clients seeking employment in a specific geographic location may want to consult a salary calculator program to make any regional cost-of-living adjustments to the industry averages. (See, for example, http://www.homefair.com/calc/salcalc.html.)

In a stable economy, clients will be well within market standards to seek to improve their prior compensation by 10 to 20 percent. That amount will go down during economic downturns and up when the economy is booming.

Negotiating During the Interview Stage

The topic of compensation can come up anywhere in the interview process. The first rule is to let the interviewer raise the issue. When candidates bring it up before the interviewer does, it makes them look overanxious and more concerned about money than about achieving the right fit between themselves and the job/company.

The second rule of negotiating is that the applicant's goal is to defer the discussion of salary and compensation until the offer stage. Why? Because the only reason an interviewer will raise it earlier is to find a reason to screen out the applicant, and until an offer is made there is nothing to which the applicant can respond (other than market salary ranges, which are just general information). The following three techniques will help defer the compensation discussion until an appropriate time:

1. **Deferral.** Here, whether the issue is raised for screening purposes early on or because the company has a custom of asking about salary in the first interview, candidates can defer discussion of compensation by a response such as, "I don't really know enough about the job yet to say what a reasonable salary would be. Can we discuss the job requirements a bit more and come back to this question?"

2. **Turnaround.** This tactic turns the question around to the interviewer by asking, "What salary range did you have budgeted for the job?" Often, they will tell you.

3. **Broad range.** If the interviewer won't disclose the range, says that it is "negotiable, depending on the qualifications of the candidate," or demands a specific answer, the broad range is an alternative tactic. If prior to the interview the candidate can total the full compensation package as it has ranged over the past three to five years, the response can be something like, "My compensation packages over the past five years have ranged from the low $60s to around $80,000, depending on bonuses, benefits, industry, responsibilities, and other variables." This approach doesn't say that any specific range is acceptable, but avoids the candidate getting locked into a number that's too high or too low.

Recruiters and hiring managers will use an applicant's prior income, if they know it, as a basis for an offer in the new position. They may ask applicants to divulge their current or prior salary. This is not in your clients' best interest if they are trying to better their situation! So a response like this may be appropriate: "My [function/role/industry] was different there than here, though I know the skills I used will transfer easily to this position. Therefore, my prior salary is not really representative of my value to you in this role." Or, "My compensation focused a significant amount of [e.g., stock options/equity, etc.] and not as much on base salary, so I'd like to explore with you my value in this role regardless of how we structure our package."

Negotiating During the Offer Stage: Improving the Offer

As mentioned earlier, most offers have the potential of at least 20 percent more salary as well as additional benefits if they are important to the candidate—but the candidate must ask for them! At the offer stage, remember our key principle: ask for anything, demand nothing. Following are some strategies you can suggest to clients requesting an improved package.

Client Tips: Negotiating the Offer

- Get the offer in writing (as explained in chapter 25). Ask for some time to consider and respond to the offer. Anywhere from two days to a week is reasonable, depending on the level of the position, whether relocation is involved, and the like.

- Review the offer carefully, analyzing it against your wants and needs (as indicated in Authentic Vocation Worksheet 10 in the Career Coach's Toolbox, p. 382). Also compare it with market salary rates (e.g., in the salary data web sites listed on page 299), through trade association data, and any other resources available to you.

- Rather than making a counteroffer, develop a list of "discussion points" to discuss with the hiring manager. All points you want to raise or improve should be included in this list, instead of "piecemealing" the negotiations. Also include the points with which you are in agreement.

- Work with your coach, if desired, to write a response letter or memo in which you again acknowledge the offer, state the terms with which you agree, and list the discussion points together with reasons you want those aspects of the offer to be improved.

- Then call the hiring manager (with whom you will hopefully working directly), rather than Human Resources. You should essentially tell the manager that you appreciate the offer and agree with much of it but you have a few points to discuss, and offer to e-mail or fax the list to the manager for later discussion. Fax or e-mail the list and call back at an agreed time to discuss (let the manager review the list first).

- Have a phone conversation about the items you want to discuss. Help the hiring manager find a mutually acceptable compromise if he or she will not accept the initial proposal.

- If salary is too low, consider expanding job responsibilities or adding a bonus element to justify a higher compensation amount.

- Keep in mind that this process may go on for several rounds before final agreement is reached!

- Memorialize the final agreement in writing, signed by both parties.

Post–Job Search Coaching Opportunities

Just because the client has accepted a position does not necessarily mean that your coaching is over! Whether the client has made a career change, a shift from an office- to a home-based environment, obtained a promotion, or has moved to some other situation, there is a need for further career coaching in many cases. The first three months in a new position are often a "trial period" in which both employee and employer are verifying that the employee is a good fit for the job and the organization. In addition, there is the process of learning the written and unwritten rules of the company culture; coaching can increase the client's awareness and effectiveness in navigating these rules.

In one case I coached a woman following her move from a large corporate environment to a home-based executive position in a smaller company. Part of her goal in taking the position was to have more time with her two young children, but learning to actually take that time—as well as taking more time for herself—took some shifts in her thinking. Coaching helped to implement these shifts. And of course, after a client has been in a job for a few months or years, he or she will often begin thinking about another job change, so you want to maintain contact via a newsletter or periodic email so that you are her "coach of choice" when that time comes.

As we discussed in chapter 19, "Ending the Coaching Relationship," you have future opportunities to assist clients in other job or career changes as well as preparation for performance review or promotion.

KEY COACHING CONCEPTS

1. The compensation negotiation process begins in the pre-interview stage and continues through the offer stage. Clients can ask for anything, but demand nothing.

2. The first rule of negotiating is to let the employer raise the issue.

3. The second rule of negotiating is to defer compensation discussion to the offer stage.

4. Pre-interview research into the company as well as on market salary rates is key.

5. During the interview, three tactics can be used to defer the discussion of compensation: deferral, turnaround, and broad range.

6. In the offer stage, the offer should be put in writing, analyzed against the client's wants and needs as indicated in Authentic Vocation Worksheet 10 (Career Coaches' Toolbox pp. 382) and compared with market rates, and a list of "discussion points" developed. Often, there is at least 20 percent additional compensation available—if the client asks for it! The client should then discuss the list of discussion points with the hiring manager and a mutually acceptable arrangement reached, which in turn must be put in writing.

7. Coaching can continue after clients have taken their new position to help them with the adjustment to the new job and environment.

Conclusion

"THE BEST WAY IS TO UNDERSTAND YOURSELF, AND THEN YOU WILL UNDERSTAND EVERYTHING."
—*Shunryu Suzuki, Zen Mind, Beginner's Mind*

We have said throughout our discussion of career coaching that the process is all about the client. And it is! But as with any helping profession, we must also ensure that we take good care of ourselves, "recharging our battery" regularly so that we can give from a state of overflow and not become drained. So in this final section we explore strategies that will help keep us fresh and prepared to give our clients what they need. We also look at the traits of masterful career coaches to which we can all aspire.

Career Coach Self-Care

Caring for ourselves requires that we take a proactive approach toward our physical, mental, emotional, social, professional, and spiritual health. Engaging in regular meditation, establishing our intention for each day, taking quarterly or semiannual personal retreats, reevaluating our roles, activities, and progress toward our goals—and setting new goals for the future—will help us stay focused and fresh for our work. Here are a few specific daily practices that may also be useful toward this end:

- Focus on maintaining a positive outlook

- Be kind, courteous, and generous to everyone (i.e., follow the Golden Rule)

- Eat lots of fresh vegetables and fruit each day, as part of a varied, balanced diet; avoid excessive alcohol, drugs, and tobacco

- Surround yourself with positive, supportive people with whom you feel mutual support and respect

- Exercise daily, as often as possible outdoors

- Love what you do for your livelihood, but do not mistake it for your identity

- Take time to cultivate meaningful friendships

- Stay in regular contact with God as you understand Him/Her/It to be

- Forgive yourself for past mistakes; refuse to feel guilty—you did the best you could

- Forgive others who have "wronged" you, and refuse to hold resentments, knowing that they did the best they could at the time. Live fully in the here and now!

- Keep growing and trying new things – have a "learning hour" every day!

- Let love rule all your dealings

- Acknowledge others for their specialness. When you feel badly, give of yourself to someone else. Don't be afraid to ask for help and support when you need it.

- Handle money joyfully and wisely.

- Let your true self shine—express your ideas and your creativity in all you do

- Continually challenge yourself to see the new, to live a higher quality of life today than in the past, and to rise to ever- increasing awareness of yourself, God, and others

- Realize that the circumstances in your life are your "laboratory," and that they reflect your beliefs and thoughts. Be open to learning the lessons they present and to accepting your part in creating what happens to you.

The Ongoing Practice of Coaching

Perhaps no other field outside of coaching—and particularly career coaching—requires the same level of personal involvement. As career coaches, our own life becomes a practice venue for choosing to living authentically, selecting work that expresses our passions and purpose, and continuing to engage in self-improvement so that we can be increasingly effective with our clients.

But there is a trap here: we may think we have to be "perfect" to be a good coach—which of course is not true! Instead, we need to continually increase our openness to growth, addressing our issues as they arise but knowing that perfection is an elusive state. Jack Kornfield captures this idea well in *A Path with Heart*:

> In the beginning we may erroneously imagine spiritual growth [like learning coaching] to be a linear journey, traveling over a certain landscape to a faraway destination of enlightenment. But it is better described as a widening circle or spiral that opens our hearts and gradually infuses our consciousness to include all of life as a spiritual whole.[69]

I encourage you to see your work in this way as you develop your practice or begin coaching within your organization. Masterful coaches never stop learning and growing—they know they need to do so to stay ahead of their clients!

Summary of Coaching Skills

This also seems an appropriate juncture to review the coaching skills you have learned. The "Coaching Competencies Self-Assessment" provided in the Career Coach's Toolbox (p. 390) is an excellent tool for determining how many of the seventy ICF coaching skills, or core competencies, you feel comfortable with at this point. Each of these skills can be used mechanically or artfully, by rote or strategically. Which will you choose? Remember our analogy of the musician in chapter 19, and how apparent it is when the musician has a natural gift and "flow" (as described in the book *Flow: The Psychology of Optimum Experience*, by Mihaly Csikszentmihalyi) in their performance,[70] versus a musician who is simply executing the notes from the page in a mechanical way? By setting your goal to be a masterful coach, your clients will gain the added benefit of the "flow" in working with you, and their results will demonstrate it! And that opens the door for enhanced development for both you and your clients.

Characteristics of Masterful Coaches

Like any form of excellence, mastery is often judged subjectively. But we suggest that there are at least a few shared traits (a "baker's dozen") to which we can all aspire in our quest for mastery in this profession:

1. Masterful coaches never stop learning and growing, and engage in Continuous Self-Improvement™.
2. Masterful coaches listen between the lines of what their clients say.
3. Masterful coaches engage their intuition and/or Higher Self in their coaching.
4. Masterful coaches see both the smaller and the larger perspective.
5. Masterful coaches hold a supportive, safe coaching space for their clients.
6. Masterful coaches know how to simply *be* without the need to *do* anything.
7. Masterful coaches use their coaching skills as an artist uses her paintbrush and paints: an appropriate mix, applied artfully, to co-create a beautiful piece of art— the coaching interaction and its results.
8. Masterful coaches know how to balance work and play.
9. Masterful coaches are not afraid to "tell it like it is."
10. Masterful coaches focus on clients and their agenda and embody the principle "It's all about them."
11. Masterful coaches know who their clients are, and who they are not—and are experts on the coaching process.
12. Masterful coaches are confident in delivering their service.
13. Masterful coaches can be effective with a wide range of people.

So now, it is your choice! Will you aspire to mastery in using QuantumShift! coaching skills to facilitate discovery of clients' Authentic Vocation? I hope you will join the rising tide of career coaches doing just that.

Part Five

The Career Coach's Toolbox

Toolbox Contents

Strategic Job Search

COACH TOOLS
Marketing

Skills Development

Usage Notes and Instructions

The following forms, worksheets, checklists, and other tools are designed for the use of career coaches working with individual clients. You may photocopy these copyrighted documents, or you can download them from the Internet at www.careercoachinstitute.com by joining CCI's Virtual Learning Community. A membership fee is required.

Job Satisfaction Inventory

Please circle the appropriate response after each item. 1 = strongly disagree; 2 = no opinion; 3 = strongly agree.

1. I like my current job.	1	2	3
2. I am clear about my career direction.	1	2	3
3. It is easy for me to set goals for myself.	1	2	3
4. I usually attain the goals I set.	1	2	3
5. I have no fears about changing jobs.	1	2	3
6. I think of myself as a successful person.	1	2	3
7. I have high self-esteem.	1	2	3
8. Once I decide to make a change in my life, I usually move ahead and do so without making excuses or procrastinating.	1	2	3
9. I view change as a healthy occurrence.	1	2	3
10. The work environment in my current job meets all of my needs.	1	2	3
11. I know exactly which career field I want to enter (or in which I want to stay).	1	2	3
12. I understand what motivates me to work, and I make job choices based on those factors.	1	2	3
13. I understand the inner needs that I feel a job should fulfill.	1	2	3
14. My inner needs are fulfilled through my work.	1	2	3
15. I know the signs that tell me when it is time for me to change jobs or careers.	1	2	3
16. I enjoy nearly all the tasks performed in my job.	1	2	3
17. My job allows me to satisfy my personal values and fulfill my personal goals as I do the work.	1	2	3

To determine your score, add the total of all numbers you have circled. The highest possible score is 51; the lowest is 17.

Scoring:

40–51 High level of satisfaction

27–39 Medium level of satisfaction

<27   Low level of satisfaction

Authentic Vocation™ Worksheet 1: Life Purpose

The Authentic Vocation process is designed to provide a focus in your work, from concept to implementation. Please work through it thoughtfully; take your time and allow your unique gifts and your true self to emerge as you do.

We begin by exploring the first factor of your Authentic Vocation, life purpose. Find a quiet place and about an hour of undisturbed time, and respond to each of the following questions on a separate piece of paper (or on your computer).

1. What do you love to do when you have spare time?

2. What aspects of your current job or life activities do you thoroughly enjoy?

3. What do you naturally do well?

4. What do you feel have been your ten greatest successes to date?

1	
2	
3	
4	
5	
6	
7	
8	
9	
10	

5. Is there a cause, value, or quality that you feel passionate about?

6. What are the ten most important lessons you have learned in your life?

1	
2	
3	
4	
5	
6	
7	
8	
9	
10	

7. Think back over your life. Are there some issues or perceived problems that have occurred over and over again?

8. What do you daydream (or dream) about doing?

9. Imagine you are writing your epitaph. What things would you want to be remembered for? What things would your life be incomplete without?

10. What would you do if you knew you could not fail?

Now, narrow down your responses to the ten most important aspects of your life purpose and write any themes you notice in the box below.

1	
2	
3	
4	
5	
6	
7	
8	
9	
10	

To compose your life purpose statement, synthesizing your responses to the questions above, use the following format:

"My life purpose is to _____ [essence] _____ through _____ [expression] _____."

The "essence" stays relatively unchanged over your lifetime, and might be something like "enhance peace in the world" or "make the world a beautiful place" or "help women find their own voice." The "expression" is the ways in which the essence is expressing (or can express) in your life right now, and it will change as life circumstances change. An example might be "working in a company that values authentic communication, dedicating myself to conscious parenting, and volunteering at the local library once a month."

Now write your life purpose statement here:

"My life purpose is to _____

through _____."

Symbol Meditation

Instructions: This guided meditation may be used to help you clarify your life purpose. It is a more "right brain" process than answering the ten questions in Authentic Vocation™ Worksheet 1 and draws on your inner wisdom. It can be read to you by your coach or a friend, or tape recorded for playback.

Sit in a chair with a straight back, or on the floor with your spine erect. If you are on a chair, your legs should be uncrossed, feet flat on the floor. Your hands should be lying loosely in your lap in a receptive position.

Relax your body completely. Begin with your feet, and move up through your legs, thighs, stomach, chest, arms, hands, shoulders, neck, head, and face. Take a few minutes to do this.

Now close your eyes and take a deep, slow breath. Count to 4 as you inhale, hold just for a moment, and then release to the count of 2. Now again, slowly, breathe in, hold, and release.

When you are relaxed and breathing slowly, imagine a beautiful meadow. Everything is green and bright, the sun is shining, and there are beautiful flowers everywhere. You hear the sound of a brook babbling joyfully nearby. You have never felt so peaceful.

As you are sitting in this meadow, enjoying the tranquility and beauty of it, you notice a wise being coming toward you. You recognize it as your "Wise Self," even if you have not seen it before. The being comes over to you and sits down near you. You realize that it is making itself available to you to provide whatever information you need for your growth and development.

You then ask this being to give you a symbol of your life's purpose, a symbol that represents your purpose in all of its aspects. Your Wise Self gives you this symbol now. Notice what it is. Do not judge or question it; simply accept it. Decide to remember this symbol. Hold it in your hands and examine it. Does it have a color? A shape? Is it large or small? Does it remind you of an object in the physical world? How does it make you feel?

Thank your Wise Self for this symbol. Now take the symbol and place it inside the center of your chest. This is your energy center of love, the highest love there is. Allow your symbol to energize you, to radiate light throughout every cell of your body. Feel it penetrate your being, allowing you to embody its essence. Allow yourself to experience what it is like to take the essence of this symbol, your essential life purpose, into every aspect of your life. Your work, your relationships, your body, your possessions—all reflect your life purpose as if in a prism.

You look across the meadow and see that your Wise Self is beckoning you to a bridge. The bridge is surrounded by other beings, all very joyful and happy. There is a mood of celebration. You walk slowly toward the bridge, feeling the presence of your symbol within you. You realize that the beings are celebrating you and your newfound awareness of your life purpose.

Your Wise Self explains that the bridge is there to provide a connection between your life purpose and the physical world in which you live. If you are now ready to begin to fulfill your life purpose, as embodied in the symbol, walk across the bridge. Your Wise Self meets you at the center of the bridge and accompanies you to the other side, where the other beings are celebrating and supporting you. You and the other beings rejoice together that you have discovered your life purpose and that you are now allowing it to manifest in physical form. Everything that is necessary for the unfoldment of your life purpose will now come to you, easily, in perfect time, exactly when you need it.

You pause now to savor the moment. You congratulate yourself on this experience of awakening, and on your dedication to your growth. You know that whenever you wish to remind yourself of your purpose and of the support you have for the fulfillment of that purpose, or when you have questions about how to proceed on your path, you can simply return in your mind's eye to this bridge, this special place of celebration.

Then, when you are ready, you become aware of your physical body once more. You return to the present moment, and gently open your eyes.

Authentic Vocation™ Worksheet 2:
Values at Work

You are now ready to explore the second element of your Authentic Vocation, values at work. You will experience job fulfillment when values that are important to you are expressed in your work. The company for which you work should share at least the most important of those values. Otherwise you will experience constant turmoil and conflict, as well as a feeling that you "can't be yourself."

Values at work can be identified most easily by asking yourself, "Why do I work?" or, "What do I want out of my work?" Begin by asking yourself these questions now, and write down your responses.

I work because:
1.
2.
3.
4.

I want to obtain the following things from my work:
1.
2.
3.
4.
5.

Some commonly expressed values are listed below. Rank each of the listed values as (1) not important, (2) moderately important, or (3) very important to you in your choice of career.

Values at Work:

___ Enjoyment (having fun at what you do)

___ Helping other people (in a direct way)

___ Friendships (developing close relationships with co-workers)

___ Helping society (contributing to the betterment of the world)

___ Freedom (flexible schedule, independence)

___ Recognition (being recognized for your work in a tangible way)

___ Creativity (having the opportunity to express your ideas and yourself in your work; innovation)

___ Location (being able to live where you choose)

___ Competition (matching your abilities with others')

___ Power and authority (being in a managerial or leadership position; supervising others; having decision-making authority)

___ Achievement (accomplishing desired objective; mastery)

___ Compensation (receiving money and other benefits commensurate with services rendered)

___ Variety (a mix of tasks to perform and people to interact with during each day)

___ Security (feeling of stability, no worry; certainty)

___ Prestige (being seen as successful; obtaining recognition and status)

___ Aesthetics (attractiveness of work environment; contributing to beauty of the world)

___ Morality and ethics (working according to a code or set of rules; enhancing world ethics)

___ Intellectual stimulation (working in an environment that encourages and stimulates thinking)

___ Public contact (working with customers or clients, as opposed to working alone or working with objects only)

___ Pace (busy versus relaxed working atmosphere)

___ Risk (monetary or other types of risks—e.g., new product development or startup enterprise)

List your top five values:
1.
2.
3.
4.
5.

Now, think about your current job. How many of the values for which you marked "3" ("very important") are being fulfilled through that job? Your answer gives you a very important insight as to why you may feel dissatisfied with that job.

Your Values

This exercise will help you to clarify your values. You will notice that the checklist is divided into six sections with similar values clusters. Review your Work Experience Stories from Authentic Vocation Worksheet 5 and scan the checklist. Put a check to show each value that applies to you. Add to the list other values that describe you. This exercise will take 15-30 minutes.

Values Clarification	Story #							Total #
Section R	1	2	3	4	5	6	7	
Be able to move around in my work								
Do hands-on work								
Meet clear standards								
See the results of my work								
Work outdoors								
Section R Totals								

Section I	1	2	3	4	5	6	7	#
Be able to structure my own work								
Be recognized for my knowledge								
Contribute new learning to a field								
Demonstrate high degrees of skill								
Engage in complex questions & demanding tasks								
Section I Totals								

Section A	1	2	3	4	5	6	7	#
Be able to write or present ideas								
Be free to express my uniqueness								
Be involved in studying or creating beauty								
Create new ideas, programs or structures								
Have personal control over my life & lifestyle								
Section A Totals								

Section S	1	2	3	4	5	6	7	#
Be involved in helping others directly								
Contribute to the betterment of the world								
Feel that my work is making a difference								
Have opportunities for self-development								
Work with others toward common goals								
Section S Totals								

Section E	1	2	3	4	5	6	7	#
Be able to get ahead rapidly								
Be in a position to change opinions								
Have a high standard of living								
Have the power to influence others' activities								
Impress others, have respect & status								
Section E Totals								

Section C	1	2	3	4	5	6	7	#
Carry out responsibilities and meet requirements								
Complete work where attention to detail is required								
Do work where employment is secure								
Do work where tasks are clear								
Have regular hours and predictable work								
Section C Totals								

Insert additional values	1	2	3	4	5	6	7	#

Congratulations on clarifying your values! Circle or highlight the top 5 values that are most important for you.

Authentic Vocation™ Worksheet 3: Motivators and Interests

It is important to understand what motivates you to do something so that you can include those considerations in your job design. Many believe that making more money or getting better benefits will keep them motivated. However, psychologists have found that increasing amounts of money, benefits, and status are only temporarily satisfying. What motivates most of us in the long run are challenging, interesting work; the opportunity to be creative; a chance to make a contribution; a sense of achievement; and recognition for our achievements. What is it that motivates you? The following exercise will help you answer this important question.

My Motivators

Think of at least four instances in which you felt highly motivated to do an activity, whether in a job, school, a hobby, or some other type of situation. List them below, on a separate sheet of paper, or on your computer. Now, consider what each of these activities had in common. Were you in a similar setting? With similar types of people? Doing a particular kind of task you genuinely enjoy? Did you feel a certain way (e.g., challenged, proud, etc.)? List those common threads. These are some of the things that will motivate you to do your best in your job. Can you think of others? Add those to your list. Finally, list the five most important motivators for getting you excited and/or dedicated to doing your best at work.

Interests

Often, but not always, doing what interests us keeps us motivated. Rank the following ten functional areas found within an organization in terms of interest, from 1 to 10. You may want to ask your coach to administer the Strong Interest Inventory™, and/or the Career Transition Report it generates, to confirm your choices.

1 = most interested; 10 = least interested

_____	Administration	_____	Information Systems
_____	Customer Service	_____	Manufacturing & Production
_____	Finance & Accounting	_____	Marketing
_____	General Management	_____	Sales
_____	Human Resources	_____	Research & Development

Authentic Vocation™ Worksheet 4: Knowledge, Skills and Abilities

You are now ready to explore the fourth factor of your Authentic Vocation, skills and abilities. During your career thus far, you have developed some skills through schooling, further honed your natural aptitudes, and developed other aptitudes on the job. On this worksheet you can assess how your skills fit into the most commonly sought skill areas, simply by indicating whether you have used that skill in a "hands-on" way, managed or supervised that function, trained in that skill, or obtained education in that skill.

Knowledge
What formal education have you had (degrees, high school diploma, etc.)?

_____

_____

_____

_____

_____

_____

What continuing education, seminars, workshops or trade school training have you completed in the past 10 years?

_____

_____

_____

_____

_____

_____

What other areas of knowledge do you have that were acquired through "on the job" training?

_____

_____

_____

_____

_____

Functional Skill Sets

Jobs consist of a combination of functional or technical skill sets, with management required in many areas/jobs. You have probably used, with varying degrees, some of the skills from each of the following skill sets:

- Management
- Operations—Manufacturing—Distribution
- Research and Development
- Sales and Marketing
- Corporate Communications
- Human Resources
- Finance
- Administration
- Legal
- Information Systems—Information Technology—Internet
- Graphic Design—Desktop Publishing
- Creative—Artistic—Musical
- Other

In the table below, review each skill set and check each box that applies in each area:

- **Management:** supervising others in that function
- **Hands-on experience:** performing the task directly
- **Training:** trained others in how to do it
- **Education:** learned about it in school, whether or not used at work

Remember to read each section because your expertise overlaps from one Skill Set to another. The skills related to each of these functional skill areas are explained in detail in the next few pages. But first, we look at management generically, since those skills are used in conjunction with other functional areas by those in management roles.

M = Management ; H = Hands-on Experience; T = Training; E = Education

Management Skill Set

Management encompasses supervising others or getting tasks done through others. Following are general skills used in management. Please check the areas in which you have managed (M), have specific hands-on experience (H), have trained managers (T), or have education (E).

M   H   T   E

M	H	T	E		M	H	T	E	
__	__	__	__	Budgeting	__	__	__	__	Joint Ventures
__	__	__	__	Business Planning	__	__	__	__	Labor Relations
__	__	__	__	Business Reengineering	__	__	__	__	Manager Development
__	__	__	__	Change Management	__	__	__	__	Mergers & Acquisitions
__	__	__	__	Consolidations	__	__	__	__	Methods & Measures
__	__	__	__	Corporate Finance	__	__	__	__	Multi-Site Management
__	__	__	__	Cost Control	__	__	__	__	Negotiations
__	__	__	__	Cross-Functional Teams	__	__	__	__	Officer/Board Member
__	__	__	__	Decision Making	__	__	__	__	Organizational Development
__	__	__	__	Developing Policies	__	__	__	__	P&L
__	__	__	__	Diversification	__	__	__	__	Project Management
__	__	__	__	Divestitures	__	__	__	__	Resource Management
__	__	__	__	Employee Evaluations	__	__	__	__	Restructuring
__	__	__	__	Financing—Public/Private	__	__	__	__	Staff Development
__	__	__	__	Government Relations	__	__	__	__	(Business) Startups
__	__	__	__	Growth Strategies	__	__	__	__	Strategic Partnerships
__	__	__	__	Hiring/Firing	__	__	__	__	Strategic Planning
__	__	__	__	International Management	__	__	__	__	Supervision
__	__	__	__	Investor Relations	__	__	__	__	Turnarounds
__	__	__	__	IPO Strategy/Positioning	__	__	__	__	_____

Operations—Manufacturing—Distribution Skill Set

These are the day-to-day operations that enable the company to produce its daily goals in making a product, getting the product to the wholesaler and/or customer, or performing a service.

M H T E

M H T E		M H T E	
_ _ _ _	Assembly	_ _ _ _	Methods & Standards
_ _ _ _	Automation Engineering	_ _ _ _	Multishift Management
_ _ _ _	Bidding	_ _ _ _	New Product Development
_ _ _ _	Call Center Operations	_ _ _ _	Operations Research
_ _ _ _	Configuration	_ _ _ _	Operations Supervision
_ _ _ _	Construction	_ _ _ _	Order Processing
_ _ _ _	Continuous Process Improvements	_ _ _ _	Outsourcing
_ _ _ _	Contract Management	_ _ _ _	Plant Design & Layout
_ _ _ _	Control Systems	_ _ _ _	Policies & Procedures
_ _ _ _	Distribution/Transportation	_ _ _ _	Process Control Supervision
_ _ _ _	Document Control Management	_ _ _ _	Process Engineering
_ _ _ _	Environmental Issues	_ _ _ _	Production Planning
_ _ _ _	Equipment Design	_ _ _ _	Project Coordination
_ _ _ _	Equipment Maintenance & Repair	_ _ _ _	Project Management
_ _ _ _	Equipment Management	_ _ _ _	Prototype Operations
_ _ _ _	Facility Management/Leases	_ _ _ _	Purchasing/Procurement
_ _ _ _	Fleet Management	_ _ _ _	Quality Assurance/Control
_ _ _ _	Installation	_ _ _ _	Safety Engineering
_ _ _ _	Inventory Control	_ _ _ _	Service Support
_ _ _ _	ISO 9000 series	_ _ _ _	Scheduling
_ _ _ _	JIT / WIP / MRP	_ _ _ _	Shipping & Receiving
_ _ _ _	Labor Control	_ _ _ _	Startup Operations
_ _ _ _	Lean Manufacturing	_ _ _ _	Supply Chain Management
_ _ _ _	Logistics	_ _ _ _	Theory of Constraints Manufacturing
_ _ _ _	Maintenance	_ _ _ _	TQM
_ _ _ _	Manpower Planning/ Budgeting	_ _ _ _	Traffic Management
_ _ _ _	Manufacturing Engineering	_ _ _ _	Troubleshooting
_ _ _ _	Materials Handling/ Management	_ _ _ _	Vendor Coordination
		_ _ _ _	Warehousing
		_ _ _ _	_____
		_ _ _ _	_____

Research & Development Skill Set

R&D applies the processes, operations, and techniques of science and technology to create and improve products, processes, and services that may benefit an enterprise, an institution, or a society.

M   H   T   E

M	H	T	E		M	H	T	E	
_	_	_	_	Applied Research	_	_	_	_	Product Applications
_	_	_	_	Basic Research	_	_	_	_	Product Development
_	_	_	_	Chemical Engineering	_	_	_	_	Product Engineering
_	_	_	_	Contract Administration	_	_	_	_	Product Re-engineering
_	_	_	_	Design and Specifications	_	_	_	_	Product Testing
_	_	_	_	Diagnostics	_	_	_	_	Program Development
_	_	_	_	Electrical Engineering	_	_	_	_	Project Management
_	_	_	_	Engineering Support	_	_	_	_	Prototype Development
_	_	_	_	Environmental, Health & Safety	_	_	_	_	Quality Control
					_	_	_	_	R&D Management
_	_	_	_	Feasibility Studies	_	_	_	_	Regulatory Compliance
_	_	_	_	Field Studies	_	_	_	_	Research Publications
_	_	_	_	Lab Management	_	_	_	_	Security
_	_	_	_	Lab/Facility Design & Construction	_	_	_	_	Service Development
					_	_	_	_	Simulation Development
_	_	_	_	Manufacturing/Engineering Liaison	_	_	_	_	Software Tools
					_	_	_	_	Statistical Analysis
_	_	_	_	Mechanical Engineering	_	_	_	_	Synthesizing
_	_	_	_	Modeling	_	_	_	_	Technical Writing
_	_	_	_	New Equipment Design	_	_	_	_	Technology Evaluation
_	_	_	_	Patent Holder	_	_	_	_	_____
_	_	_	_	Process Engineering	_	_	_	_	_____

Sales & Marketing Skill Set

Marketing determines strategies/opportunities to sell profitably and directs the flow of goods from producer to domestic or international consumers or users. The sales function must then achieve the targeted objectives and complete the transaction with the end user.

M H T E

____ Account Management
____ Advertising
____ Brand Management
____ Budgeting/Expense Control
____ Business Development
____ Channel Marketing
____ Collateral Development
____ Compensation Plans
____ Competitive Analysis
____ Contract Negotiations
____ Convention Planning
____ Corporate Identity
____ Customer Relations/Service
____ Direct Sales
____ Distribution Channels
____ Distributor Relations
____ Ecommerce/B2B
____ Field Liaison
____ Field Sales (Outside Sales)
____ Forecasting
____ Goal Setting
____ Image Development
____ Import / Export
____ Incentive Programs
____ Inside Sales
____ International Business Development
____ International Expansion
____ Logo Development
____ Market Research & Analysis
____ Market Rollout
____ Marketing Communications
____ Marketing Plans
____ Marketing Promotions

____ Media Buying/Evaluation
____ Media Relations
____ Merchandising
____ Multimedia Presentations
____ New Account Sales
____ New Product Development
____ Online Marketing & Advertising
____ Packaging
____ Pricing
____ Product Demonstrations
____ Product Introduction/Launch
____ Product Line Development
____ Product Management
____ Product Publishing/Sales
____ Product Sourcing
____ Product Specifications
____ Proposal Writing
____ Radio Media
____ Sales Administration
____ Sales Analysis
____ Sales Forecasting
____ Sales Kits
____ Sales Management
____ Sales Presentations
____ Sales Promotions
____ Sales Recruiting
____ Sales Support
____ Sales Training
____ Showrooms
____ Strategic Alliances/ Partnerships
____ Strategic Planning

— — — — Supply Chain Analysis   — — — — Territory Development
— — — — Supply Chain Management   — — — — Tradeshows
— — — — Survey Design   — — — — Trend Analysis
— — — — Technical Sales Support   — — — — Video Productions
— — — — Telemarketing   — — — — _____
— — — — Television Media   — — — — _____

Corporate Communications Skill Set

The corporate communications function is responsible for planning, executing, and coordinating relationships of the company and its representatives with the company's various publics to achieve acceptance of the company, its objectives, and its conduct. It also involves acquiring knowledge of the business environment required for review and attaining of the company's objectives.

M   H   T   E

— — — — Business-to-Business   — — — — Investor Collateral
         Communication   — — — — Media Presentations
— — — — Community Affairs/Relations   — — — — Press Releases
— — — — Corporate Image   — — — — Proposal Writing
— — — — Corporate Philanthropy   — — — — Public Relations
— — — — Corporate Publications   — — — — Public Speaking
— — — — Corporate Relations   — — — — Risk Management
— — — — Educational Programs   Communication
— — — — Employee Communications   — — — — Shareholder Relations
— — — — Employee Newsletters   — — — — Speech Writing
— — — — Event Planning   — — — — Trade Relations
— — — — Fund Raising   — — — — Web Site Development—html
— — — — Government Affairs/Relations   — — — — _____
— — — — Industry/Association Relations   — — — — _____
— — — — Internet Communications

Human Resources Skill Set

Broadly stated, human resources, or HR, refers to selection, staffing, development, and utilization of an organization's human resources. Organizations design HR programs to develop their staff to their fullest capacities and to maintain ongoing worker commitment.

M   H   T   E

__ __ __ __   Affirmative Action
__ __ __ __   Arbitration/Mediation
__ __ __ __   Benefits Vendor Management
__ __ __ __   Career Counseling
__ __ __ __   Career Development
__ __ __ __   Classified Advertisements
__ __ __ __   Company Orientation
__ __ __ __   Compensation & Benefits
__ __ __ __   Computer-Based Training
__ __ __ __   Corporate Culture & Change
__ __ __ __   Cost-Benefit Analysis
__ __ __ __   Course Development
__ __ __ __   Diversity
__ __ __ __   Downsizing
__ __ __ __   EEOC Compliance
__ __ __ __   Employee Coaching
__ __ __ __   Employee Communications
__ __ __ __   Employee Discipline
__ __ __ __   Employee Relations
__ __ __ __   Employee Selection
__ __ __ __   Executive Recruiting
__ __ __ __   Grievances
__ __ __ __   HR Generalist
__ __ __ __   HRIS
__ __ __ __   Human Resources
                    Management
__ __ __ __   Industrial Relations

__ __ __ __   Interactive Training (Internet)
__ __ __ __   International Employees
__ __ __ __   Job Analysis
__ __ __ __   Job Competencies
__ __ __ __   Labor Negotiations
__ __ __ __   Network Operations
__ __ __ __   Organizational Development
__ __ __ __   Outplacement
__ __ __ __   Performance Measurement
__ __ __ __   Policies & Procedures
__ __ __ __   Psychological Assessment
__ __ __ __   Records Management
__ __ __ __   Recruiting
__ __ __ __   Relocation
__ __ __ __   Salary Administration
__ __ __ __   Succession Planning
__ __ __ __   Team Building
__ __ __ __   Training
__ __ __ __   Training Administration
__ __ __ __   Union Coordination
__ __ __ __   Wage / Rate Analysis
__ __ __ __   Workers' Compensation
__ __ __ __   Workforce Forecasting/
                    Planning
__ __ __ __   Workforce Security
__ __ __ __   _____
__ __ __ __   _____

Finance Skill Set

The finance function plans, directs, controls, and measures the results of a company's monetary operations. In addition, it strives to secure adequate operating funds at minimum cost, invest surplus funds to the best advantage, and maintain a strong financial reputation for the company. It also involves maintaining records and preparing reports to meet corporate legal and tax requirements as well as measuring the results of the company operations.

M	H	T	E		M	H	T	E	
__	__	__	__	Accounting Management	__	__	__	__	General Ledger
__	__	__	__	Accounts Payable	__	__	__	__	Insurance
__	__	__	__	Accounts Receivable	__	__	__	__	Internal Controls
__	__	__	__	Acquisitions & Mergers	__	__	__	__	Investor Relations
__	__	__	__	Actuarial / Rating Analysis	__	__	__	__	IPOs
__	__	__	__	Angel Funding	__	__	__	__	Lending
__	__	__	__	Auditing	__	__	__	__	Lines of Credit
__	__	__	__	Banking Relations	__	__	__	__	Management Reporting
__	__	__	__	Budget Control	__	__	__	__	New Business Development
__	__	__	__	Budgeting	__	__	__	__	Operations Research/Analysis
__	__	__	__	Capital Budgeting	__	__	__	__	Payroll
__	__	__	__	Capital Investment	__	__	__	__	Pension & Fund Management
__	__	__	__	Cash Management	__	__	__	__	Pricing / Forecast Modeling
__	__	__	__	Cost Accounting	__	__	__	__	Private Placements
__	__	__	__	Cost Control	__	__	__	__	Profit Planning
__	__	__	__	Credit / Collections	__	__	__	__	Risk Management
__	__	__	__	Debt Negotiations	__	__	__	__	Road Shows
__	__	__	__	Economic Studies	__	__	__	__	SEC Reporting
__	__	__	__	Equity/Debt Management	__	__	__	__	Special Reports
__	__	__	__	Feasibility Studies	__	__	__	__	Stockholder Relations
__	__	__	__	Financial Analysis	__	__	__	__	Systems Installation/Training
__	__	__	__	Financial Planning	__	__	__	__	Taxes
__	__	__	__	Financial Reporting	__	__	__	__	Treasury
__	__	__	__	Financial Software Packages	__	__	__	__	VC/Investor Presentations
__	__	__	__	Financing	__	__	__	__	Venture Capital Relations
__	__	__	__	Forecasting	__	__	__	__	_____
__	__	__	__	Foreign Exchange	__	__	__	__	_____

Administration Skill Set

Administration deals with support services, primarily focused on the facility and related matters. It oversees all aspects of logistics and the physical plant.

M   H   T   E

M H T E		M H T E	
__ __ __ __	Concierge	__ __ __ __	Office Management
__ __ __ __	Construction	__ __ __ __	Office Relocations
__ __ __ __	Contract Negotiation	__ __ __ __	Mailroom
__ __ __ __	Office Staff Training/	__ __ __ __	Office Equipment
	Supervision	__ __ __ __	Parking
__ __ __ __	Credit Transactions	__ __ __ __	Policies & Procedures
__ __ __ __	Customer Service	__ __ __ __	Project Management
__ __ __ __	Equipment Purchasing	__ __ __ __	Real Estate
__ __ __ __	Facility Management	__ __ __ __	Reception
__ __ __ __	Forms and Methods	__ __ __ __	Records Management
__ __ __ __	HVAC	__ __ __ __	Security
__ __ __ __	Leases	__ __ __ __	Space Planning
__ __ __ __	Library	__ __ __ __	Utilities
__ __ __ __	Logistics	__ __ __ __	_____
__ __ __ __	Telecommunications	__ __ __ __	_____

Legal Skill Set

Those in the legal function perform tasks and responsibilities required by law or by-laws of the corporation. Appraises and advises the company of all phases of its operations and relations from a legal viewpoint. Counsels on, prepares documents required by, and represents the company in connection with governmental controls, requirements, and statutory obligations. This function is not restricted to attorneys; many managers, HR staff, and others perform these tasks.

M	H	T	E		M	H	T	E	
—	—	—	—	Anti-Piracy Investigation	—	—	—	—	Labor Issues
—	—	—	—	Antitrust	—	—	—	—	Leases & Records
—	—	—	—	Board of Director Affairs	—	—	—	—	Legislative Affairs
—	—	—	—	Case Management	—	—	—	—	Licensing
—	—	—	—	City, County, State Issues	—	—	—	—	Litigation
—	—	—	—	Contract Administration/	—	—	—	—	Lobbying
				Mgmt	—	—	—	—	Mergers & Acquisitions
—	—	—	—	Copyrights & Trademarks	—	—	—	—	Patents
—	—	—	—	Corporate Secretary	—	—	—	—	Political Relations
—	—	—	—	Documentation	—	—	—	—	Purchase Agreements
—	—	—	—	EEO, OSHA, EPA, FDA, etc.	—	—	—	—	Real Estate Law
—	—	—	—	Employment Law	—	—	—	—	Regulatory Compliance
—	—	—	—	Federal Issues	—	—	—	—	Safety Regulations
—	—	—	—	Financial Regulations	—	—	—	—	Securities Registration
—	—	—	—	Government Contracts	—	—	—	—	Shareholder Proxies
—	—	—	—	Government/Legislative	—	—	—	—	Stock Administration
				Affairs	—	—	—	—	Taxes
—	—	—	—	Incorporation	—	—	—	—	Transactions
—	—	—	—	Intellectual Property	—	—	—	—	_____
—	—	—	—	International Agreements	—	—	—	—	_____

Information Systems—Information Technology—Internet Skill Set

Works with hardware, software, networks, data, and personnel supporting business objectives in high-tech areas.

M   H   T   E

__ __ __ __ Analog Design

__ __ __ __ Algorithm Development

__ __ __ __ Applications Database Admin.

__ __ __ __ Applications Development

__ __ __ __ ASP Applications Systems
             Provider

__ __ __ __ Broadband Networks

__ __ __ __ Business Systems Planning

__ __ __ __ Cabling

__ __ __ __ Capacity Planning

__ __ __ __ Chip Design

__ __ __ __ CRM-Client Relationship
             Mgmt

__ __ __ __ Computer Aided Design

__ __ __ __ Computer Architecture

__ __ __ __ Computer Configuration

__ __ __ __ Computer Interface

__ __ __ __ Computer Operations

__ __ __ __ Computer Selection

__ __ __ __ Computer Systems Conversion

__ __ __ __ Data Center Operations

__ __ __ __ Data Mining

__ __ __ __ Data Processing Management

__ __ __ __ Data Security

__ __ __ __ Database Administration

__ __ __ __ Database Development

__ __ __ __ Desktop Publishing

__ __ __ __ Desktop Video Publishing

__ __ __ __ Diagnostics

__ __ __ __ Digital Design

__ __ __ __ Digital Signal Processing

__ __ __ __ Distributed Processing

__ __ __ __ Ecommerce/B2B

__ __ __ __ Electronic Data Interface (EDI)

__ __ __ __ Enterprise Asset Management
             (EAP)

__ __ __ __ Enterprise Level Applications

__ __ __ __ Enterprise Resource Planning
             (ERP)

__ __ __ __ Equipment Selection

__ __ __ __ Field Support Engineering

__ __ __ __ Game Design

__ __ __ __ Graphics

__ __ __ __ Hardware Management

__ __ __ __ HTML/XML

__ __ __ __ Information Management

__ __ __ __ Information Technology
             Admin.

__ __ __ __ Integration Software

__ __ __ __ Intranet Development

__ __ __ __ Languages—Java, C+++, etc.

__ __ __ __ Linear Programming

__ __ __ __ Linux Operating System

__ __ __ __ Methodology Engineering

__ __ __ __ Microprocessors

__ __ __ __ Modeling

__ __ __ __ Multiplexors

__ __ __ __ Network Engineering

__ __ __ __ Network Operations
             Management

__ __ __ __ Object Oriented Development

__ __ __ __ Office Automation

__ __ __ __ Performance Monitoring

__ __ __ __ Peripheral Equipment

— — — — Portal Design/Development   — — — — Telecommunications
— — — — Process Development   — — — — Test Engineering
— — — — Programming / Coding   — — — — Tracking Systems
— — — — Project Management   — — — — UNIX
— — — — Release Management   — — — — Usability Engineering
— — — — Software Customization   — — — — User Education/
— — — — Software Development   Documentation
— — — — Software Engineering   — — — — User Interface
— — — — Spreadsheets   — — — — Vendor Relations
— — — — Supplier Integration   — — — — Vendor Sourcing
— — — — Systems Analysis   — — — — Voice & Data Communications
— — — — Systems Applications   — — — — Web Development/Graphic
— — — — Systems Development   Design
— — — — Systems Design   — — — — Website Content Writer
— — — — Systems Testing   — — — — Website Editor
— — — — Systems/Software Installation   — — — — Wireless Systems
— — — — Systems/Software Training   — — — — Word Processing
— — — — Technical Evangelism   — — — — _____
— — — — Technical Support/Help Desk   — — — — _____
— — — — Technical Writing

Graphic Design/Desktop Publishing Skill Set

This function involves using the visual arts to create marketing and advertising materials, web content, and similar collateral pieces for use in promotion.

M H T E

M	H	T	E		M	H	T	E	
__	__	__	__	Action Scripting	__	__	__	__	Organizing Work Flow
__	__	__	__	Adobe Acrobat	__	__	__	__	Photo Scanning
__	__	__	__	Color Correction	__	__	__	__	Photoshop
__	__	__	__	Color Theory	__	__	__	__	Preparing Presentations
__	__	__	__	Converting from Mac to PC/	__	__	__	__	Pre-Press, Production
				PC to Mac	__	__	__	__	Process colorColor
__	__	__	__	Creating Client Mock-ups	__	__	__	__	Project Management
__	__	__	__	Creative Copywriting	__	__	__	__	QuarkXPress
__	__	__	__	Dreamweaver	__	__	__	__	Spot Color
__	__	__	__	Emailing Files, Attachments	__	__	__	__	Troubleshooting, Problem
__	__	__	__	Flash					Solving
__	__	__	__	FreeHand	__	__	__	__	Typography
__	__	__	__	FTP'ing on Internet	__	__	__	__	Understanding Print Bids
__	__	__	__	HTML Coding	__	__	__	__	Uploading Files to Internet
__	__	__	__	Illustrator	__	__	__	__	_____
__	__	__	__	InDesign	__	__	__	__	_____
__	__	__	__	Mounting Artwork					

Creative/Artistic/Musical Skill Set

People with creative, artistic, or musical skills use these abilities in creative expression, often outside the context of the corporate environment.

M H T E

— — — — Ability to Improvise   — — — — Manual Dexterity
— — — — Attention to Detail   — — — — Musical Composition
— — — — Character Development   — — — — Musical Ear
— — — — Computer Design   — — — — Sense of Rhythm
— — — — Creative Writing   — — — — Story Line Development
— — — — Drawing   — — — — Visual Composition (Balance,
— — — — Eye-Hand Coordination   Form, Color)
— — — — Fine Motor Control
— — — — Imagination, Creativity   — — — — _____
— — — — Intuition, Silencing Inner   — — — — _____
     Critic

Other

What other skills can you identify below that you possess which may be useful in your work?

— — — — _____

— — — — _____

— — — — _____

— — — — _____

Open List Approach to Skills
(an alternative to Authentic Vocation™ Worksheet 4)

You have developed some skills that you can use in your ideal job. Examples might be typing, setting up and maintaining a bookkeeping system, using a table saw or similar tools, selling, and a host of others, depending on your field(s) of expertise.

List as many of these work skills as you can think of below.

1.
2.
3.
4.
5.
6.
7.
8.
9.
10.
11.
12.

You may be highly competent in some of the skills you have listed, but you may not enjoy using those skills. Part of our objective in designing your ideal job is to create a job you *enjoy*, not just one you are good at doing. To help you in this process, place an "E" next to each skill you enjoy using. These are the skills you will want to focus on using in your ideal job. Finally, put an "A" next to those skills you consider to be natural abilities – things that come easily to you and that you enjoy.

Authentic Vocation™ Worksheet 5: Work and Other Experience

You are now ready to explore the fifth factor of your Authentic Vocation™, work and other experience. List your work and other experience by position and industry in the table below.

Position	Industry

For each position listed, write one or more Work Experience Stories. The three elements of a Work Experience Story are:

- **Challenge** or circumstance when you began the project or task
- **Action** you took to create a result or solve a problem
- **Result** that followed, quantified whenever possible

Here is an example of a Work Experience story:

Challenge. When I was promoted to sales and marketing director for Region 5, we were the lowest-performing region of the thirty regional territories. My challenge was to bring the sales and overall performance numbers up as quickly as possible.

Action. To do so, I met with the twenty-person sales staff, jointly established ten aggressive goals for the next six to twelve months, and developed a promotional strategy to increase customer awareness of our products which included incentives for new purchases within a stated length of time.

Result. Within ninety days, sales were up by 15 percent, and by year-end we were second in the nation with $1.2 million in sales.

Now, write at least three Work Experience Stories, on a separate sheet or on your computer, or each of your positions. They will also be integrated into your resumes, interview preparation, and so on. You should have at least eight to ten stories in all, one per skill, and at least one per job. If you wish, you can use the keywords in Authentic Vocation Worksheet 4 to help trigger ideas for stories.

Authentic Vocation™ Worksheet 6:
Job/Career Targets

You are now ready to explore the sixth factor of your Authentic Vocation, job/career targets. Now it is time to do some homework. (Did you think you were done with that?) Use your responses to life purpose questions 1–3 in Authentic Vocation Worksheet 1, as well as Authentic Vocation Worksheets 2–5, as the basis for some possible targets. You need to do some research on each to help you design a new job or career. Your local library and the Internet have a wide selection of resources to assist you.

Begin by spending some time browsing through the O*Net web site at http://online. onetcenter.org/, which will give you all the job classifications in various major career fields, as well as the Occupational Outlook handbook at http://www.bls.gov/oco/. As you browse through this resource, jot down the Standard Occupational Classification (SOC) numbers and descriptions of up to twenty job or career classifications that sound like you would enjoy doing and feel you could do well—even if you might need additional training or education to do so. The site also helps you match your skills to specific job requirements. Don't choose a code only because it fits your training or is in the line of work you are comfortable in. Be open to new ideas. Ignore for now considerations about money, location, education, experience, licenses, and so on—we will return to them in Authentic Vocation Worksheet 8. Do not rule something out because you do not think you can make enough money doing it.

Now, narrow your choices down to your top ten favorites. Consider first the choices that sound like the most fun, and second, those that are consistent with your leisure activities, favorite job tasks, and enjoyable natural skills. In this part of the exercise, you may take into account such things as education, location, and other "practical" considerations to some extent—but don't limit yourself too much. Mark those that sound fun as well as are within the realm of practicality with a star.

You should now have a list of ten career areas and/or job descriptions that sound like fun to you and are at least within the realm of possibility. Now, let's return to your list of values from Authentic Vocation Worksheet 2. Can you narrow your list of job types further by comparing your important values with each of your ten choices? If you can see at the outset that your important values cannot be fulfilled in one of your chosen careers or jobs, consider eliminating it from your list, since it will not result in the satisfaction you are seeking. Note, however, that you may not be able to determine that until you have a particular company in mind or have talked to people working in that industry. Cross off any of your ten favorites that are inconsistent with your important values and/or life purpose.

Be careful not to eliminate areas before you are fully informed. If some of the items on your list are areas you have not considered before, you may want to do some networking with others in the field, or do some additional research on that career area before deciding whether you can fulfill your value(s) in that job.

If you want to continue this research in more detail, you may want to consult directories such as Dun and Bradstreet, Standard and Poor's, Thomas Registry, Moody's, local and state directories, as well as individual industry reference books.

Authentic Vocation™ Worksheet 7: Work Environment

You are now ready to explore the seventh factor of your Authentic Vocation, work environment. Your work environment can either enhance or detract from your enjoyment of the work. The items listed below will help you evaluate each aspect of your work environment so that you can design it just the way you want. Jot down your answers on paper or with your computer.

1. **Geographical location.** Where would you like to work? In the state and city where you live—or somewhere else altogether? Perhaps this is a perfect time to explore that possibility realistically. Would you like to work in an office or outdoors? In an urban or rural setting? Do you want to travel as part of your job?

2. **Pace.** A second aspect of your work environment is the pace of the business or office. Do you enjoy an environment that is bustling and busy, or do you prefer a peaceful, slower pace? How many hours do you want to work each week?

3. **Support.** One way to avoid burnout is to surround yourself with a supportive environment—one in which you have a sense of significance, autonomy, challenge and support, and in which there are relatively few unmodifiable work stress factors. Mentoring programs, new employee orientation and similar programs can also build support. Conversely, some people like a lot of independence. Indicate whether you prefer to have a low, moderate, or high degree of support.

4. **Compensation.** How much money do you want to earn in your ideal job? What benefits do you require? List these on a separate sheet or your computer screen. You can also want to use Authentic Vocation Worksheet 10, "Wants/Needs Analysis," in this regard. Do you prefer the predictability of a salary or the benefits of commission- or contract-based work?

5. **Size.** It is important to evaluate whether you work best alone, with one or two co-owners, or in a large company setting. To help you evaluate your optimal work setting, consider the following profiles of the solo worker, the partner, and the team personality.

The Solo Worker

- Is independent
- Prefers working alone; likes privacy
- Is highly creative and contemplative
- Has a few carefully chosen friends
- Resists authority
- Is motivated by opportunity to create and to get credit for creation
- Likes to take risks
- Fears loss of control

The Partner

- Enjoys (and needs) give and take feedback when making decisions and in conversation
- Is most creative in context of a close relationship
- Has a few long-term friends
- Needs equal amounts of time alone and with others
- Is an excellent listener
- Feels power comes from shared resources
- Shares risk-taking with partner
- Fears rejection by partner

The Team Personality

- Enjoys esprit de corps of large organization, including process of gaining consensus
- Wants to be alone about 20 percent of the time
- Is motivated by competition
- Forms many friendships easily
- Comfortable with authority figures
- Is most creative in context of praise from team members and from leader
- Enjoys belonging to clubs
- Shares risks with team members and leader
- Fears loneliness

You may find you have aspects of two of these profiles, or maybe even all three—but you probably share more qualities from one than from any of the others. Which one most closely describes you: solo worker, partner, or team personality?

If you are a team personality type, also consider how large a company you wish to work for. Though the team dynamic is present in a ten-employee company and a thousand-employee company, your day-to-day experience in those two companies will be quite different. What size is your ideal company/ employer?

6. **Primary function.** Next, consider whether you prefer to work primarily with people, with data, or with things. Think about your hobbies and past jobs. What activities have given you the most joy—those involving interaction with people, working with data or information, or working on things with your hands?

7. **Corporate culture.** This is expressed in the company's vision, values, and mission. Culture, or "how we do things around here," is another important factor in work environment. Do you prefer a company that is conservative or radical, socially conscious or not, employee-oriented or bottom-line/results-oriented? Do you prefer that the company has a clear vision and mission, or that it "go with the flow"? Describe your ideal employer's culture.

Summary: What would your ideal day at work be like? Where would you be doing it? What other aspects of the work environment are important to you? Write down your thoughts for future reference.

Entrepreneurial Quiz

Do you have the entrepreneurial personality?

Question	Yes	No
Is it important to you to accomplish something meaningful with your life?		
Do you typically set both short- and long-term goals for yourself?		
Do you usually achieve your goals?		
Do you enjoy working on your own?		
Do you like to perform a variety of tasks in your job?		
Are you self-disciplined?		
Do you like to be in control of your working environment?		
Do you take full responsibility for your successes *and* failures?		
Can you place the needs of your business above your family when necessary?		
Are you in excellent physical, mental, and emotional health?		
Do you have the drive and energy to achieve your goals?		
Do you have work experience in the type of business you wish to start?		
Have you ever been so engrossed in your work that time passed unnoticed?		
Do you consider "failures" as opportunities to learn and grow?		
Can you hold to your ideas and goals even when others disagree with you?		
Are you willing to take moderate risks to achieve your goals?		
Can you afford to lose the money you invest in your business?		
When the need arises, are you willing to do a job that may not interest you?		
Are you willing to work hard to acquire new skills?		
Do you usually stick with a project until it is completed?		
TOTAL		

Give yourself 1 point for each "yes" answer. You should have a score of at least 15 if you are to be successful as a business owner. While it is not necessary to answer yes to all of these questions to be successful, if you answer no to some of them you will want to evaluate what that means to you and how significantly it may impact your ability to run your own business.

Ideal Job Template

1. My life's purpose is to _____
   through _____

2. My top five work values are:
   a._____
   b._____
   c._____
   d._____
   e._____

3. The factors and situations that motivate me are: _____
   _____ .

4. The skills that I enjoy using and want to use in my next job are: _____
   _____ .

5. The things that I have enjoyed about my past jobs that I wish to recreate in my next job are:

   _____

6. •   My chosen career areas are: _____
   •   My ideal job titles are: _____

7. My ideal work environment is described by the following:
   Geographic area:

   _____

   Pace:

   _____

   Degree of support: ____ Low ____ Medium ____ High

Compensation range: $_____to $_____

Benefits desired: _____

_____

Company size: _____

Preferred work style (solo, as a partner, or on a team): _____

Primary focus (people, data, or things):_____

Company culture:_____

Following is a description of my ideal job:

_____

_____

_____

_____

_____

_____

_____

_____

_____

_____

_____

Authentic Vocation™ Worksheet 8: Business Reality

Now that you have explored your life purpose and the other seven factors of your ideal job, you should have a fairly accurate picture of the next job/career you wish to pursue. In the space below, describe your ideal job as accurately and completely as you can, stating it as though you already have the job. For example,

> I am working in a high-tech company of approximately thirty-five people, in San Jose, California, doing computer assisted design. I make a salary of $85,000 and have the following benefits: 401(k) plan, three weeks' vacation annually, and medical and disability insurance. I feel wonderfully satisfied in my work, since I work primarily with computers (my passion) and have two floating days off each month (in addition to weekends) to pursue my main hobby, hiking.

Describe your ideal job using the following Authentic Vocation factors:

My life purpose (AV Worksheet 1): _____

My values at work (AV Worksheet 2): _____

My motivators and interests (AV Worksheet 3): _____

My skills and abilities (AV worksheet 4): _____

My work and other experience (AV worksheet 5): _____

My job/career targets (AV worksheet 6): _____

My work environment (AV worksheet 7): _____

Note: Alternatively, you can use the Ideal Job Template on page 352.

Then, incorporate these elements into a narrative summary on a separate screen or piece of paper describing the ideal job as though you already had it.

Business Reality

Your next step will be to filter your vision for your ideal job through the lens of "business reality."

1. **Determining market need**

   Does your job target meet a need in the business world or workplace? Or do you need to make some changes for that to occur? For many traditional job roles there is always a market need. This includes salespeople, operations managers, and support staff. Other positions may require research into sources such as the Occupational Outlook Handbook (http://bls.gov/oco/) to determine whether the occupation you have chosen is projected to be growing, stable, or declining over the coming years.

2. **Evaluating Financial Feasability**

   Using one or more of the Internet salary sites listed below, determine what the average salary range is for the type of work you have described:

   - http://online.wsj.com/careers
   - www.jobsmart.org
   - www.abbott-langer.com
   - www.wageweb.com
   - www.salary.com
   - http://www.bls.gov/OES/
   - www.rileyguide.com
   - http://www.bls.gov/oco/
   - http://blogs.payscale.com/ask_dr_salary/

My minimum: $_____ per year
My maximum: $_____ per year
Average for this occupation: $_____ per year

3. Measuring Job Targets for Viability

For each target, determine:

Desired company size:_____

Desired position/job/function/role: _____

Desired geographic area: _____

Size of target market:

a. Total number of organizations:_____

b. Number of probable positions fitting
    desired criteria in each organization: _____

a x b = Total number of probable and suitable positions: _____

---

4. Understanding the Job Search Timeframe

Do you know how long your job search should take? The typical search takes three to six months, or one month for every $10,000 of salary. What plans have you made to support yourself financially during your search? Consider the following factors, each of which may extend or reduce your search time:

- Clarity about your job target(s)
- Geographic scope you will consider
- Whether you are making a career change
- Size of your network of contacts
- How marketable your skills are
- Market/economic conditions
- Your attitude, self-confidence and personality style
- Financial reserves (including severance)
- Support from family and friends
- Amount of effort/commitment you invest

Authentic Vocation Profile

Client	Date

ASSESSMENT RESULTS

Strengths My top five talents are...	Assessment Highlights

AUTHENTIC WORK

Life Purpose

Values My top 5 work values are...	Motivators / Interests The factors and situations that motivate me are...

Knowledge, Skills & Abilities My key skills that I enjoy using and want to use in my next job are...	Work Experience The things that I have enjoyed about my past jobs that I wish to recreate in my next job are...

Environment	Ideal Job Description *The following is a description of my ideal job...*
Geographic Area:	
Pace:	
Degree of support around me:	
Compensation Range $___ to $___	
Company size:	
Solo/Partner/Team Setting:	
People/Data/Things as Primary Focus:	
Company Culture:	

JOB TARGETS

My chosen career area is:	My ideal job titles are:
The outlook for each of my ideal jobs is:	

ASSESSMENT RESULTS

Results of assessments I have taken that should be factored into my Authentic Vocation are:	

Ideal Day Exercise

A powerful tool to help clients break through barriers is to ask them to describe their "ideal day." Even the instructions for the exercise are a stretch for many people. They must go beyond "I see myself as a sales representative for a consumer products company working with Fortune 500 customers." That's a start! But for it to penetrate to the subconscious level—which is critical for activating the powers of individual creativity—clients must use both their intellect and emotions in the exercise.

Instructions to client:

Imagine that you are writing a movie script depicting a day in your ideal life. You must describe every detail of the scenery, your feelings, and your activities, as well as the people with whom you are interacting. Describe it in such vivid form that a movie director (someone besides you) could read your description and instruct others in building the props, casting the characters, bringing the right personality and style to the acting, and sequence the activities the actors are doing! Include your work, your home, your family life, your leisure activities, any special aspects in your environment, the pace, and each activity you do from dawn until bedtime. Imagine there are no restrictions on time, money, or any other aspect. Ready? Write that description in the space below, on a separate sheet, or on your computer. Take 10 to 20 minutes.

Professional Balance Wheel

1. Within each of the eight areas depicted, circle the number that best represents your level of satisfaction in that area of your career.

    7 = completely satisfied; 1 = completely dissatisfied

2. Connect the numbers around the circle to form a wheel.

    The rounder the wheel, the more balanced your life is. Imagine how your car would travel if all the wheels were in this shape!

Are You Coachable?

Please circle the appropriate number next to each of the statements below. You should then review the results of this quiz with your coach so that together you can determine whether coaching is the right option for you at this time.

1 = not at all true; 2 = somewhat true; 3 = true; 4 = very true

NT ST T   VT

1   2   3   4   I am prepared to be on time for all coaching appointments as scheduled, and to give at least 24 hours' notice if I cannot.

1   2   3   4   I am willing to take an active role in the coaching process and to follow through on action steps as agreed with my coach.

1   2   3   4   I am at a point in my life when I will try out new ideas and ways of doing things, as agreed with my coach.

1   2   3   4   I am willing to allow my coach to facilitate my process of discovery, and to freely share the insights I experience.

1   2   3   4   I am ready to willingly enter into a partnership with my coach to create a life that is even better than I have imagined.

1   2   3   4   I am willing to be open, honest, and authentic with my coach.

1   2   3   4   I am willing to recognize my own limiting issues and beliefs and to take responsibility for changing when it is in my best interest.

1   2   3   4   If at any time I feel the coaching relationship is not working for me, I will share this with my coach and work toward a mutually acceptable solution.

1   2   3   4   I have sufficient funds to invest in the coaching—I see coaching as an investment in my personal and/or professional future.

1   2   3   4   I do not have any depression, anxiety, other mental illness, or any other issue that would interfere with my ability to be coached.

_____ Add total score of all numbers circled

Scoring key:

10–16 Coaching may not benefit you now

17–25 You may be coachable, but will need to adhere to all agreements carefully

26–32 You are coachable

33–40 You are very coachable and should be a delightful client!

Coaching Agreements

COACHING AGREEMENT "A"

This agreement, between _____ (referred to as "Coach") and _____ (referred to as "Client") will begin on _____ _____, 200_, and will continue for a minimum of three months. At the conclusion of three months, this agreement will convert to a month-to-month renewable contract.

Coaching Relationship. Client understands that coaching is an ongoing, interactive, professional relationship designed to help Client achieve his/her desired results in work and in life. Coaching is not therapy; if Client desires therapy, he/she should seek the services of a trained therapist.

Dates and Times. Coaching sessions shall take place each _____ (day of the week), beginning on _____, at _____ a.m./p.m. Unless otherwise agreed, coaching shall be done by telephone, and each session shall be approximately 30 minutes in length (except for the initial intake session, which shall run _____ minutes). Client shall call Coach at the agreed time; if the line is busy or goes to voicemail or Coach does not answer, Client shall call again in five minutes. If Coach again does not answer, the session shall be deemed to be postponed.

Fees. The fee for the initial intake session is $_____ ,and for the initial three months of coaching is $_____ per month [or, alternatively, $_____ for the XYZ Coaching Package, which shall include: insert description]. Fees are payable (check one) _____ in advance, in exchange for a ___% discount off the full fee; or ___at the beginning of each month at or before the first session of each month. An average of four sessions per month is used in calculating the monthly fee (if any). The monthly fee is not waived for periods when Coach or Client may be on vacation. Assessments to be administered during the coaching interaction shall be billed in addition to the monthly coaching fees unless otherwise agreed in advance.

Cancellation. Client is required to give Coach at least 24 hours' notice of intended cancellation of a weekly session, or the session is forfeited. A $25.00 fee will be assessed for each missed appointment. This fee is in addition to the monthly fee. If a session is missed due to Coach unavailability as described in the previous paragraph, the session shall not be forfeited, but shall be rescheduled at the Client's and Coach's mutual convenience.

Client's Responsibilities. Client agrees to:

- Arrive at each session on time

- Bring an issue or agenda to the session

- Turn off cellular phone, call waiting, pager, and other distractions during the session

- Let the Coach know if at any time the coaching is not working as desired and use his/her best efforts to resolve any issues that may arise with Coach.

Coach's Responsibilities. Coach agrees to:

- Hold all of the information disclosed in the coaching sessions in confidence

- Facilitate Client's progress toward his or her goals

- Use his or her best efforts within the guidelines of the coaching relationship

Termination. This agreement may be terminated by either party upon at least thirty (30) days' written notice to the other.

Entire Agreement. This written agreement constitutes the entire agreement between the parties. It shall be governed by the laws of the state of _____. If any provision of this agreement shall be deemed invalid, the remaining provisions shall remain intact. If any dispute should arise from this agreement, it shall be resolved according to rules of the American Arbitration Association.

So agreed this ____ day of _____, 200__.

_____   _____
Client   Coach

Coaching Agreement "B"

Date

Dear _____,

I am pleased to have the opportunity to work with you in the capacity of Coach, with the intention of facilitating your achievement of personal and professional goals and desired outcomes. These goals and outcomes will be of your own design. In the course of this process, I will not provide expert advice, but rather will facilitate your strategies for discovering and achieving what you choose. The purpose of our inter-action is to keep you on-purpose and aligned with your intentions and to support your success.

Coaching services will be provided at mutually agreeable times and places. Coaching services will consist of one half-hour in-person or telephone session per week for a period of three months, renewable month-to-month thereafter. The fees for the coaching services shall be $_____ per month, due and payable at the beginning of each month. If you desire to pay your three months of services in advance, you will be entitled to a ____% discount off the full fee.

The services to be provided by the Coach to you, the Client, are designed jointly with you. Client acknowledges that coaching is not expert advice, therapy, or counseling but is a professional service designed to facilitate your forward progress on the is-sues of your choice.

All matters discussed in our sessions will be held in strictest confidence. The Coach will be honest and straightforward, asking clarifying questions and making requests, among other techniques. As the Client, you will also be honest and straightforward, will appear for your sessions on time, will give at least 24 hours' notice if you must cancel a session, and will bring an agenda or issue to be discussed to each session.

If these terms are agreeable to you, please so indicate by signing in the appropriate space below. I look forward to working with you.

_____   _____

Client   Date   Coach   Date

Coaching Agreement "C"

Coach Name
Address
Phone
E-mail

1. I agree to be on time for each phone or in-person appointment. If the session is conducted over the phone, I agree to call the Coach at the agreed time.
2. I agree to an initial series of twelve sessions within a three-month period.
3. I understand I can terminate the relationship at any time, and that if I decide to do so it will be in the context of a scheduled session for that purpose. I understand that I can seek a second opinion from another consultant/coach at any time.
4. Sessions are approximately thirty minutes in length.
5. I agree to pay $_____ each _____, starting_____.
6. I agree to have the payment in the Coach's office by the 1st of the month.
7. I agree to make session cancellations by calling at least 24 hours before the scheduled appointment. I understand that if I fail to do so I will be charged.
8. I agree to take an active role in the consulting process by being absolutely honest with Coach and myself. I especially agree to be absolutely honest about my feelings or issues I have about the coaching process or about the Coach.
9. I understand that the Coach is not a licensed psychotherapist and will not diagnose or treat mental or emotional disorders for a fee.
10. I understand that the Coach uses coaching techniques such as assessments, questioning, feedback, ideas, and challenges, and I agree to participate in the use of these techniques.
11. I agree to complete all agreed-upon assignments and requests for information.
12. I agree to fax or send assignments so that they arrive at Coach's office three days before a scheduled session.
13. I understand that I am absolutely responsible for my own business, life, and actions, and that I initiate the consulting/coaching process with this in mind.
14. I understand that the Coach does not work with Clients who are actively in

the grip of a chemical addiction (drugs or alcohol). I agree to report any use of such substances immediately to my Coach. I understand that at least 14 days' substance-free must be attained before beginning the consulting/coaching process.

15. I understand that the Coach actively markets his/her practice based on a formalized referral system. If I am satisfied with the results of this work, I will refer two other individuals for a risk-free, explorative consultation.

16. My most important consulting/coaching goals are:

_____

_____

_____

_____

_____

17.   My coaching/consulting history:

Experience	Outcome	Reason Terminated

18. I agree to take 100 percent responsibility for my complete understanding of, and agreement with all the information above. I understand that by honoring these agreements I greatly enhance the effectiveness of the coaching process.

Name _____

Date _____

Coaching Intake Form

Name: _____

Address: _____

City/state/ZIP: _____

Telephone: Day_____Evening_____Cell_____

Fax: _____

E-mail address: _____

Web site (if any): _____

Name of employer (if any): _____

Employer's address:_____

City/state/ZIP:_____

My position/title: _____

How long? _____

Duties: _____

_____

_____

Previous position/title: _____

How Long? _____

Duties: _____

_____

_____

Summary of prior work experience:

_____

_____

Previous assessments completed: [comp: make a table]

Assessment	MBTI	DISC	PVQ	ECI	Proscan
Date					
Result (if known)					

What degree(s) and certifications do you have?

Degree/ Certification	College/ University	Major	Year Obtained

In the past, have you worked with:

A coach?   Y/N   How long/what years?

A therapist?   Y/N   How long/what years?

Major issues addressed: _____

_____

What is the primary reason(s) you are entering into a coaching experience at this time?_____

_____

_____

Marital status:

Married	Divorced	Single	Widowed	Other

Note: Our coaching relationship is confidential. Unless you disclose issues that your coach is required to disclose to the authorities (e.g., intent to harm yourself or others), all of the content of our conversations will be held in confidence.

Is this confidentiality policy acceptable to you? Y/N

[handwritten: What would it take to move you to more satisfied?]

How would you rank your current level of satisfaction with each of the following areas of your life?

Life Area	Very Satisfied	Satisfied	Dissatisfied
Work			
Emotional health			
Physical health/well-being			
Mental health			
Finances			
Spirituality/religion			
Relationship with spouse/significant other			
Relationship with children			
Relationships with boss or co-workers			
Social network/friendships			
Self-confidence/self-esteem			

[handwritten: What has been your process up to now in finding your careers & figuring out your career direction?]

What was your greatest success in the past year? _____

_____

_____

In your lifetime? _____ *What made this successful for you?*

_____

_____

What is your biggest challenge right now? Or put another way, what factors are holding you back from having everything you want? _____

_____

_____

Describe below your ideal life, assuming you could create your life exactly as you want it to be: _____

_____

_____

_____

_____

_____

What are your most important goals for the next six months? *Which goal is most imp't? Is there one you'd like to focus on first?*

1	
2	
3	
4	
5	
6	

In next session, we'll want to come up w/ a coaching plan. + I'll email you form. 6-8 goals for next 90 dys + develop some action steps.

What are you like when you are at your best? _____

_____

_____

_____

How would you like me to be as your coach? (e.g., demanding, gentle, challenging, etc.) _____

_____

_____

_____

_____

What else would you like me to know about you and your current life situation?

_____

_____

_____

_____

Thanks for completing this form! Please e-mail the completed form to me at: [coach's e-mail address] prior to our intake session.

Coaching Plan Worksheet

Use the following worksheet to design your Coaching Plan. Please complete each column, working together with your coach, to outline the main goals you will work on during your coaching.

Goal (with timeline)	Action Steps	Result

Remember:

"Goals" are what you want to accomplish and should be specific, realistic, and measurable (including a timeline), and should depend solely on your efforts. They should answer these questions:

- "What do I want to change in my life in the next three to six months?"
- "What do I want to improve?"
- "What is in my way that I need to overcome?"

"Action Steps" are the steps you take to achieve your goals. They should answer these questions:

- "What specific actions will I take to achieve my goal(s)?"
- "What action steps are most urgent (i.e., must be done first) and which are less urgent?"
- "If I need more resources, information, or contacts to achieve my goal, where will I find it?"

"Results" are the ultimate outcome of achieving your goals. For example, if your goal were to get your Web site designed and uploaded to the Web, the result would be providing a source of information through which to attract clients and in turn build your business. These should answer these questions:

- "What is the payoff for completing the action steps?"
- "How will achieving this goal help me fulfill my long-term or lifetime goals?"
- "What will I have after completing this goal that I do not have now?"

Coaching Call Preparation Form

E-mail this form to [Coach] 24 hours **before** your call.

E-mail address:

Name: _____   Date: _____

My greatest wins since our last call: _____
_____
_____
_____

The commitments I made to myself on our last call: _____
_____
_____
_____

What I was able to do around those commitments: _____
_____
_____
_____

Challenges I am facing:_____
_____
_____
_____

Opportunities that I am facing: _____

_____

_____

_____

What I want to focus on with my coach today is: _____

_____

_____

_____

After Coaching Call Reflection Form

E-mail this form to [Coach] within 12 hours **after** your call.

E-mail address: _____

Name: _____ Date: _____

The ways I benefited as a result of our call: _____
_____
_____
_____

Commitments I am making to myself for this week: _____
_____
_____
_____

Systems, habits, practices, or programs I am working on to help support my
efforts: _____
_____
_____
_____

Questions, ideas, or issues that I am still thinking about that we did not discuss:
_____
_____
_____

What I would like you, [Coach], to do more or less of to coach me optimally:

_____

_____

_____

What you can do for me that I would like most is: _____

_____

_____

_____

Authentic Vocation™ Worksheet 9:
Job Search Marketing Plan Template

This worksheet is designed to be both a format for a coach/client co-designed job search plan (columns A–H) and a weekly client activity summary (columns I–L).

Designed for:					Date:			Actual Activity			
(A)	(B)	(C)	(D)	(E)	(F)	(G)	(H)	(I)	(J)	(K)	(L)
Action	Total	Week 1	Week 2	Week 3	Week 4	Week 5	Week 6	Ltr Sent	Calls	Interviews	Offers
Unpublished (60%)											
Networking											
Associations											
Alumni											
Influentials											
Friends/associations											
Follow-up calls											
plus new contacts											
Direct targeted											
to Employers											
News events											
Published (40%)											
Recruiters											
Ads											
Job Board Postings											
TOTALS											

Company Research Data Sheet

Use this data sheet to summarize your research on companies you are considering targeting or with whom you have interviews scheduled. Make as many copies of this sheet as needed, one per company.

Company overview: _____

_____

_____

_____

_____

History, size, growth: _____

_____

_____

_____

_____

Products and/or services:_____

_____

_____

_____

_____

Clientele/customer base: _____

_____

_____

_____

_____

Key management people: _____

_____

_____

_____

_____

Company culture: _____

_____

_____

_____

_____

Possible needs/areas of expansion: _____

_____

_____

_____

_____

Other notes:_____

_____

_____

_____

_____

_____

_____

_____

_____

_____

Authentic Vocation™ Worksheet 10: Wants/Needs Analysis

Fill in the "Wants" and "Needs" columns on the worksheet as part of your Authentic Vocation discovery process, especially during your exploration of Authentic Vocation factor 7, "Work Environment." Then, when different job offers come in, you can compare them in detail.

Item	Wants (yes or no, or amount as appropriate)	Needs (yes or no, or amount as appropriate)	Job Offer 1 (yes or no, or amount as appropriate)	Job Offer 2 (yes or no, or amount as appropriate)
Compensation				
Salary				
Bonuses/commission				
Stock options				
Relocation package				
401(k) plan, match				
Medical insurance				
Holidays/vacation				
Life insurance				
Disability insurance				
Sick/personal leave				
Travel expense reimbursement and/or company car or allowance				
Severance package				
Health club membership				
Computer allowance				
Tuition reimbursement				
Other benefits desired				

Item	Wants	Needs	Job Offer 1	Job Offer 2
Authentic Vocation™ Fit:				
Expresses my life purpose				
Job/company in alignment with my key values				
Motivates me				
Fits my desired job/industry target				
Uses my favorite skills				
Leverages my past experience				
Embodies desired work environment				
Conforms to business reality and meets my financial needs				
Career Development:				
Training provided/required for skills development				
Future career growth				
Cross-training encouraged				
Career development plans used in performance evaluation and planning				
Work–Life Balance:				
% travel required				
Flexible work options				
Hours expected/required				
Family-friendly policies (e.g. time off for children's needs allowed/encouraged)				
Commuting time/distance from home				

Item	Wants	Needs	Job Offer 1	Job Offer 2
Company Analysis:				
Risk factor (e.g., startup vs. well-established company)				
Turnover levels				
Revenues expanding, static, or declining				
Competitive pressures in industry				
Expected job stability				
Merger/acquisition potential				
Reputation (consult Better Business Bureau, customers of company, and other staff)				

What Is Authentic Vocation™?

Have you been feeling restless or discontented in your job? Like something is missing, but you don't know what? The key may be a whole new approach to career development: Authentic Vocation.

Authentic Vocation is different than other skills-based approaches used to identify your calling or ideal work. It starts with your life purpose and builds a template for your ideal work from that critical base. The eight basic factors of Authentic Vocation are as follows:

1. **Life purpose.** What is the purpose or mission of your life that must be expressed through your work?
2. **Values at work.** What values must be expressed in your work for optimal satisfaction?
3. **Motivators and interests.** What motivates you to do your best?
4. **Skills and abilities.** What skills do you have that you want to continue using?
5. **Work and other experience.** What experience can you leverage in your next position?
6. **Job/career targets.** What job positions and/or industries would suit your goals?
7. **Work environment.** What location, culture, and other workplace factors would be critical in your total work environment?
8. **Business reality.** Is your target occupation financially viable? Can you make a living at it? If not, what needs to be adjusted so you can?

The diagram below illustrates how the first seven factors form the work template, which must be filtered through the eighth factor, business reality, to give you a true Authentic Vocation.

If you are seeking greater fulfillment at a job that also meets your financial needs and allows you to "have a life," then Authentic Vocation coaching may be for you.

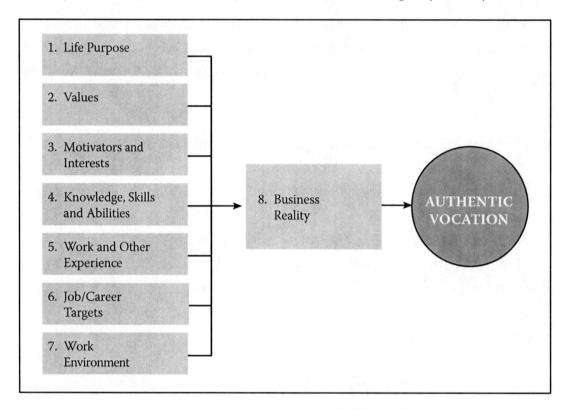

For more information, call us at [coach phone number and e-mail].

What Do Career Coaches Do?

Career coaching is an interactive process of exploring work-related issues—leading to effective action—in which the coach acts as both a catalyst and facilitator of individual and, in turn, organizational development and transformation. Career coaches connect people with their passion, purpose, values, and other critical aspects of their ideal work. They equip their clients with career management skills that can be used in future transitions in addition to enhancing their current work. They also facilitate their clients' process of developing and implementing a job search or business startup plan to activate their Authentic Vocation™. The desired outcomes of career coaching for clients include enhanced self-awareness, clarity about life purpose and goals, increased self-management, and improved quality of life.

What career coaches do:

- Connect clients with a deeper level of motivation than "just a job"—clients discover their passion and purpose to guide their decisions, empowering them to choose work they love, make a good living, and still have a balanced life
- Distinguish themselves from career counselors and consultants by building career management skills, which enable the client to navigate future transitions
- Probe for deeper levels of motivation that, when addressed, can cause a lasting QuantumShift!™ rather than providing just a "quick fix"
- Create effective coaching interactions by listening, providing feedback, asking powerful questions, observing, and modeling
- Remove blocks to career progress, such as self-limiting beliefs, incomplete awareness of marketable skills, lack of purpose, and more
- Improve clients' ability to market and sell themselves in the job market regardless of economic conditions
- Increase individual potential for career growth and future earning power
- Assist clients in becoming "career self-reliant," taking control and ownership of their own career development

- Enhance clients' job satisfaction through the discovery of their Authentic Vocation

What internal career coaches do (inside their organizations):

- Increase employees' awareness of career paths and enhance fit to achieve "right person/right job"

- Improve the capability of both employees and the client organization to manage constant change and transition

- Provide and model communication styles that enhance internal problem-solving skills, appreciate differences, and lead to long-term progress, rather than creating dependency on the coach

- Promote a win-win balance of work/life priorities, using the desired states of both employees and organization as benchmarks

- Guide organizational systems to evolve their culture by increasingly valuing their employees, implementing career development as a priority, and optimizing human capital

- Blend training, organizational development, career/employee development, and coaching at every level in the organization

To get results and to learn more about how to enhance your personal and/or organizational capability, please call for more information. Your initial telephone consultation is free.

[Coach name, e-mail address]

Evaluating Communication Clarity

QUESTION	YES	NO
Did the client understand what I said/asked? (How do you know?)		
Did the client answer easily or pause before answering?		
If the client (e.g., an introvert) paused after my question, were they processing or were they confused? (Again, how do you know?)		
Did I use the client's processing style in formulating my question (e.g., visual, auditory, kinesthetic, auditory-digital; thinking vs. feeling; sensing vs. intuitive)?		
Did my question further the client's understanding of their issue, or cause further confusion?		
Did I mirror back what the client said? Summarize/bottom-line?		
Did I go deeper and probe to Level 2 or 3 aspects of the issue?		
Did the client's perspective on the issue shift as a result of my coaching?		
Did I use as few words as possible?		
Did I avoid asking more than one question at once or combining two issues into one question?		
Is the client more aware of his or her beliefs, systems of meaning-making, and/or self-concept because of my coaching and/or choice of language?		
Did I avoid getting caught up in the client's "story" or "script" and focus on the facts in my language?		
Did I avoid using language that conveyed my own prejudices or biases, but instead use gender- and race-neutral language?		
Did my questions and/or feedback help the client distinguish facts from interpretation?		
Was I direct, saying what I meant, and avoiding "beating around the bush"?		
Did I take time to prepare for the call, both mentally and by reviewing any notes from last time or coaching call prep forms prior to the appointment?		

Coaching Competencies Self-Assessment Checklist

From time to time as a career coach you can measure your competencies on this self-assessment. Check "NC" for not competent, "C" for competent, or "VC" for very competent.

NC	C	VC	Competency
___	___	___	1. Understands and exhibits the ICF standards of conduct
___	___	___	2. Understands and follows ICF ethical guidelines
___	___	___	3. Clearly communicates the distinction between coaching and other related professions
___	___	___	4. Refers clients to other professionals as needed
___	___	___	5. Understands and effectively discusses with client the guidelines and parameters of the coaching relationship (e.g., logistics, fees, scheduling, inclusion of others)
___	___	___	6. Reaches agreement about what is appropriate in the relationship and what is not
___	___	___	7. Determines whether there is an effective match between coaching style and client needs
___	___	___	8. Shows concern for client's welfare and future
___	___	___	9. Demonstrates personal integrity
___	___	___	10. Establishes clear agreements, keeps promises
___	___	___	11. Demonstrates respect for client
___	___	___	12. Provides ongoing support for and champions new behaviors (including those involving risk taking and fear of failure)
___	___	___	13. Asks permission to coach in sensitive areas
___	___	___	14. Is present and flexible during the coaching process; "dances in the moment"
___	___	___	15. Accesses his or her own intuition, trusts his or her own inner knowing
___	___	___	16. Is open to not knowing, takes risks

—   —   —   17. Sees many ways to work with the client, chooses in the moment what is most effective

—   —   —   18. Uses humor effectively

—   —   —   19. Confidently shifts perspectives, experiments with new possibilities for own action

—   —   —   20. Demonstrates confidence in working with strong emotions

—   —   —   21. Attends to client and client's agenda

—   —   —   22. Hears client's concerns, goals, values, and beliefs concerning what's possible

—   —   —   23. Distinguishes words, tone of voice, and body language

—   —   —   24. Summarizes, paraphrases, reiterates, mirrors back

—   —   —   25. Encourages, accepts, explores, and reinforces client's expressions

—   —   —   26. Integrates, builds on client ideas and suggestions

—   —   —   27. Bottom-lines

—   —   —   28. Allows client to vent, or "clear" a situation

—   —   —   29. Asks questions reflecting active listening, understanding of client perspective

—   —   —   30. Asks questions that evoke discovery, insight, etc.

—   —   —   31. Asks open-ended questions

—   —   —   32. Asks questions that move client toward what they desire

—   —   —   33. Is clear, articulate, and direct in giving feedback

—   —   —   34. Reframes, articulates to enhance client understanding

—   —   —   35. Clearly states coaching objectives

—   —   —   36. Uses appropriate language

—   —   —   37. Uses metaphor and analogy

—   —   —   38. Goes beyond what is said

—   —   —   39. Invokes inquiry

—   —   —   40. Identifies client's underlying concerns

—   —   —   41. Helps client discover new thoughts, beliefs, perceptions, emotions, moods, etc. to assist them achieve what is important to them

__ __ __   42. Communicates broader perspectives to client, inspires commitment to shift viewpoint and find new possibilities

__ __ __   43. Helps client see different, interrelated factors affecting them

__ __ __   44. Expresses insights in useful, meaningful ways

__ __ __   45. Identifies major strengths vs. areas for learning and growth

__ __ __   46. Asks client to distinguish between trivial and significant issues

__ __ __   47. Brainstorms and assists client to define actions to deepen new learning

__ __ __   48. Helps client focus on and explore concerns and opportunities central to coaching goals

__ __ __   49. Engages client to explore alternative ideas and solutions and evaluate options

__ __ __   50. Promotes active experimentation and self-discovery

__ __ __   51. Celebrates client successes

__ __ __   52. Challenges client's assumptions and perspectives to provoke new ideas, possibilities

__ __ __   53. Advocates points of view aligned with client goals and, without attachment, engages client to consider them

__ __ __   54. Helps client "do it now"

__ __ __   55. Encourages stretches and challenges as well as a comfortable learning pace

__ __ __   56. Consolidates collected information, establishes coaching plan

__ __ __   57. Creates plan with results that are attainable, measurable, specific, and with target dates

__ __ __   58. Makes plan adjustments as warranted

__ __ __   59. Helps client identify and access resources for learning

__ __ __   60. Identifies and targets early successes

___ ___ ___ 61. Clearly requests actions to move client toward his or her goals

___ ___ ___ 62. Demonstrates follow-through by asking client about actions committed to during prior session

___ ___ ___ 63. Acknowledges client for actions taken, learnings since last session

___ ___ ___ 64. Effectively prepares, organizes, and reviews with client information obtained during sessions

___ ___ ___ 65. Keeps client on track between sessions, holds attention on coaching plan

___ ___ ___ 66. Focuses on coaching plan but remains open to adjusting it

___ ___ ___ 67. Can move back and forth between big picture and current situation

___ ___ ___ 68. Promotes client's self-discipline, holds client accountable (including specific plan and time frames)

___ ___ ___ 69. Develops client's ability to make decisions, address key concerns, develop self

___ ___ ___ 70. Positively confronts client when they do not take agreed-upon actions

___ ___ ___ **TOTALS**

Calculate your total in each column. Retake this self-assessment periodically to measure your progress. Is your "very competent" score increasing?

Professional Resources for Career Coaches

Professional Associations:
Coaching:
- International Coach Federation: www.coachfederation.org
- Coachville: www.coachville.com
- Professional Coaches and Mentors Association: www.pcmaonline.com

Career Development:
- Association of Career Professionals International (ACP): www.acpinternational.org
- Institute of Career Certification International: www.careercertification.org
- International Career Development Conference: www.careerccc.com
- National Career Development Association: www.ncda.org
- State Career Development Associations: www.ncda.org (some)

Books

Career Coaching and Career Development

Baber, Anne, and Lynne Waymon, *How to Fireproof Your Career*. Berkley, 1995.

Beck, Martha. *Finding Your Own North Star*. Crown, 2002.

Bench, Marcia. *Career Infopreneur's Success Roadmap*. High Flight Press, 2007.

Bench, Marcia. *Discovering Your Authentic Vocation*. High Flight Press, 2003.

Berman-Fortgang, Laura. *Take Yourself to the Top*. Warner, 1998.

———. *Live Your Best Life*. Warner, 2001.

Bolles, Richard, and Howard Figler. *The Career Counselor's Handbook*. Ten Speed Press, 2000.

Buckingham, Marcus, Curt Coffman. *First Break All the Rules*. Simon and Schuster 1999.

———. *Now Discover Your Strengths*. Simon and Schuster, 2001.

Enelow, Wendy. *101 Ways to Recession-Proof Your Career.* McGraw-Hill, 2002.

Gallwey, W. Timothy. *The Inner Game of Work.* Random House, 2000.

Levoy, Gregg. *Callings.* Three Rivers Press, 1997.

Lore, Nicholas. *The Pathfinder: How to Choose or Change Your Career for a Lifetime of Satisfaction and Success.* Fireside, 1998.

Change and Transition

Bench, Marcia. *Don't Just Survive, Thrive During Transition.* High Flight Press, 2003.

Bridges, William. *Transitions.* Perseus 1980.

———. *Managing Transitions.* Perseus, 1991.

Changing Workplace

Bridges, William. *Creating You & Co: Learn to Think Like the CEO of Your Own Career.* Perseus, 1998.

———. *Jobshift: How to Prosper in a Workplace Without Jobs.* Perseus, 1995.

Goleman, Daniel. *Working with Emotional Intelligence.* Bantam, 2000.

Handy, Charles. *The Hungry Spirit: Beyond Capitalism—A Quest for Purpose in the Modern World.* Broadway, 1999.

Handy, Charles, and Warren Bennis. *The Age of Unreason.* Harvard Business School Press, 1998.

Johnson, Spencer, and Ken Blanchard. *Who Moved My Cheese?* Putnam, 1998.

Naisbitt, Nana, et al. *High Tech, High Touch.* Nicholas Brealey, 2001.

Rifkin, Jeremy. *The End of Work.* Tarcher, 1996.

Coaching Techniques

Bench, Marcia. *Quantum Shift Coaching.* High Flight Press, 2004.

Crane, Thomas. *The Heart of Coaching.* FTA Press, 2002.

Hargrove, Robert. *Masterful Coaching.* Pfeiffer and Co., 1995.

Richardson, Cheryl. *Take Time for Your Life* (Broadway, 1999.

Whitworth, Laura, et al. *Co-Active Coaching.* Davies-Black Publishing, 1998.

Corporate Career Development

Bridges, William. *The Character of Organizations: Using Personality Type in Organization Development.* Davies-Black Publishing, 2000.

Hendricks, Gay, and Kate Ludeman. *The Corporate Mystic.* Bantam, 1996.

Knowdell, Richard. *Building a Career Development Program.* Davies-Black Publishing, 1996.

Niemela, Cynder, and Rachael Lewis. *Leading High Impact Teams.* High Impact Publishing, 2001.

Senge, Peter, et al. *The Dance of Change: The Challenges to Sustaining Momentum in Learning Organizations.* Doubleday, 1999.

Whyte, David. *The Heart Aroused.* Currency/Doubleday, 1996.

Creativity and Motivation

Cameron, Julia. *The Artist's Way.* Tarcher/Putnam, 1992)

Csikszentmihalyi, Mihaly. *Flow: The Psychology of Optimal Experience.* Harper Collins, 1991.

Executive Coaching and Leadership Development

Bolman, Lee G., and Terrence Deal. *Leading with Soul.* Wiley, 2001.

Fitzgerald, Catherine, and Jennifer Garvey Berger. Executive Coaching: Practices and Perspectives. Davies-Black Publishing, 2002.

Goldsmith, Marshall, ed. *Coaching for Leadership: How the World's Greatest Coaches Help Leaders Learn.* Jossey-Bass, 2000.

Goleman, Daniel, et al. *Primal Leadership: Realizing the Power of Emotional Intelligence.* Harvard Business School Press, 2002.

Job Search Techniques

Baber, Anne, and Lynne Waymon. *How to Fireproof Your Career.* Berkley, 1995.

Bench, Marcia, *Turbo-Charge Your Job Search.* High Flight Press, 2003.

Wendleton, Kate. *Building a Great Resume.* Five O'Clock Club, 1999.

———. *Interviewing and Salary Negotiation.* Five O'Clock Club, 1999.

———. *Getting Interviews.* Five O'Clock Club, 2000.

———. *Targeting the Job You Want.* Five O'Clock Club, 2000.

Ladder of Inference

Argyris, Chris. *Increasing Leadership Effectiveness.* Wiley, 1976.

———. *Reasoning, Learning and Action. Individual and Organizational.* Jossey-Bass, 1982.

———. *Knowledge for Action.* Jossey-Bass, 1993.

———. *On Organizational Learning.* Blackwell, 1993.

Argyris, Chris, R. Putnam, and D. Smith. *Action Science.* Jossey-Bass, 1985.

Argyris, Chris, and David Schon. *Theory in Practice.* Jossey-Bass, 1974.

Senge, Peter. The Fifth Discipline Fieldbook. Currency Doubleday, 1994.

Life Purpose and Work

Adrienne, Carol, and James Redfield. *The Purpose of Your Life.* Eagle Brook, 1999.

Leider, Richard. *The Power of Purpose.* Berrett-Koehler, 1997.

———. *Whistle While You Work.* Berrett-Koehler, 2001.

MBTI® Assessment

Hirsh, Sandra Krebs. *Introduction to Type and Career.* CPP, Inc., 1993.

———. *Introduction to Type and Coaching.* CPP, Inc., 2000.

Tieger, Paul, and Barbara Barron-Tieger. *Do What You Are.* Little Brown, 2001.

Personal Branding

Arruda, William and Dixson, Kirsten, *Career Distinction: Stand Out by Building Your Brand* (Wiley 2007)

Recruiters

Gurney, Darrell. *Headhunters Revealed!* Hunter Arts Publishing, 2000.

Resumes

Criscito, Pat. *Designing the Perfect Resume.* Barrons, 2000.

———. *Resumes in Cyberspace.* Barrons, 2001.

Crispin, Gerry, and Mark Mehler. *CareerXroads.* 2002.

Enelow, Wendy. *Best Resumes for $100,000+ Jobs.* Impact, 2002.

Farr, Michael, and Louise Kursmark. *America's Top Resumes for America's Top Jobs.*

Yate, Martin. Resumes That Knock 'Em Dead. Adams Media, 2001.

Sabbaticals

Dlugozima, Hope, et al. *Six Months Off.* Holt, 1996.

Rogak, Lisa Angowski. *Time Off From Work.* Wiley, 1994.

Self-Employment

Edwards, Paul, and Sarah Edwards. *Working From Home: Everything You Need to Know about Living and Working Under the Same Roof.* Tarcher, 1999.

Gerber, Michael. *The E-Myth Revisited.* Harper Business, 1995.

All Business. http://www.all-biz.com/

CCH Business Owners. http://www.toolkit.cch.com

Entrepreneur Magazine. http://www.entrepreneur.com

Information for Small Businesses. http://www.sec.gov/smbus1.htm

National Foundation for Women Business Owners. http://www.nfwbo.org

SBA: Small Business Administration Home Page. http://www.sba.gov/

Small Business Development Centers. http://sbinformation.about.com/smallbusiness/sbinformation/library/reference/blstate.htm

http://smallbizmanager.com/

Spirituality and Work

Barrett, Richard. *Liberating the Corporate Soul.* Butterworth-Heinemann, 1998.

Belf, Teri-E. *Coaching with Spirit.* Jossey-Bass/Pfeiffer, 2002.

Bench, Marcia and Ann Ronan. *Work as a Spiritual Path.* High Flight Press, 2004.

Briskin, Alan. *The Stirring of Soul in the Workplace.* Berrett-Koehler, 1998.

Casto, Michelle. *Get Smart! About Modern Career Development.* Get Smart! Publishing, 2000.

Coombs, Ann. *The Living Workplace.* Warwick, 2002.

Fox, Matthew. *The Reinvention of Work.* Harper Collins, 1994.

Guillory, William. The Living Organization: Spirituality in the Workplace. Innovations International, 2001.

Heider, John. *The Tao of Leadership.* Bantam, 1988.

Jaworski, Joseph. *Synchronicity: The Inner Path of Leadership.* Berrett-Kohler, 1996.

Jones, Tom. *A Career Devotional Journal.* Career Life Publishing, 2002.

Klein, Eric, and John Izzo. *Awakening Corporate Soul: Four Paths to Unleash the Power of People at Work.* Fair Winds Press, 1999.

Mitroff, Ian. *A Spiritual Audit of Corporate America.* Jossey-Bass Business, 1999.

Peppers, Cheryl. *Bringing Your Soul to Work: An Everyday Practice.* Berrett-Koehler 2000.

Renesch, John. *Getting to the Better Future: How Business Can Lead the Way to New Possibilities.* NewBusinessBooks, 2000.

Richmond, Lewis. *Work As a Spiritual Practice.* Broadway, 1999.

Sisk, Dorothy, and E. Paul Torrance. *Spiritual Intelligence: Developing Higher Consciousness.* Creative Education Foundation, 2001.

Williams, Nick. *The Work We Were Born to Do.* Element Books, 1999.

Teleclasses

www.teleseminarsforcoaches.com

www.teleclass.com

www.teleclass4u.com

www.teleclassinternational.com

Appendix 1: Frequently Asked Questions About Career Coaching

In our discussions with prospective students over the past several years, some questions arise frequently and can be answered in a relatively straightforward way. Our answers to these questions are listed below. If you have more questions about career coaching or the CCI training, please visit the FAQ section on our web site at www. careercoachinstitute.com or e-mail us (contact information is provided at the end of this book).

Q: I'm thinking about career coaching but don't want to go back to school. Don't career coaches have to have a master's degree in counseling?

Career *counselors* are usually required to have a master's degree; coaches are not. Currently, there are no educational requirements in most states in the U.S. for coaches. However, some states subject some coaches to state regulations; check with your state's employment or labor department to see what the requirements are where you live. Career coaching is not the same as career counseling, as we will see below. If one were going to be a counselor, they should certainly get a degree in that field! But career coaching is a discrete skill, the primary prerequisite for which is specific coaching training and a knowledge of career development principles. Whether practicing in the U.S. or abroad, degrees in counseling or psychology are not required to be a highly effective coach.

Q: If I can talk to people about their job-related issues, then can't I call myself a career coach?

The short answer? No. While there are no specific requirements for career coaches, career coaching does require specific training in coaching knowledge, skills, and abilities. A coaching interaction is much more than a mere conversation; it has a strategic component and a transformational impact that puts it at a much higher level than a mere conversation. And clients' professional future is at stake; are you willing to risk giving uninformed "advice" versus becoming, through training and experience, a trained professional—or referring the client to one?

Q: Since I've been doing career counseling or career consulting for years, can't I just use the "career coach" label since it seems to be the latest thing in career development?

Again, the answer is no. Coaching is much more than simply a repackaging of career counseling; rather, it is a discrete approach and skill set that must be learned. Career counselors often have a structured approach to their work with clients, usually work in person, and are frequently expected to give the client advice about which career path or job opportunity they should pursue. Career coaches, on the other hand, are charged with asking questions and using other coaching skills to elicit clients' own answers, drawing on their inner wisdom. And their services are usually provided by phone and/or the Internet. If someone is giving advice, they are not coaching.

Q: I'm already a coach, so when people come to me about a job-related issues, can't I call myself a career coach?

Maybe, if you meet certain conditions. Remember, there are no legal requirements in most states in the U.S. for coaches to get specific training or register with a government agency to call themselves coaches. If you have received formal coach training and have an effective coaching model that you are using, your coaching skills may be transferable. However, to coach individuals in career issues also requires knowledge of career development theories and principles as well as the science/art of resume writing, helping clients capitalize on their strengths and minimize weaknesses in an interview, components of an effective job search campaign, and the like. Specific training in these areas is needed to supplement coaching skills for individuals to truly call themselves a career coach; our Authentic Vocation model and the chapters on job search mechanics in this book will help fill that gap.

Q: Aren't other kinds of coaching, such as business and executive coaching, more "advanced" and specialized than career coaching? It seems like career coaching is just a place to begin one's practice; career coaching by itself isn't a substantial enough specialty area on which to build a practice. Or is it?

To put it simply, career coaching is not as easy as it looks! But it is a viable practice specialty. The best career coaches make six-figure incomes. Some of them choose to supplement their actual 1:1 coaching with writing books, e-zines, and articles; teaching; training; conducting teleclasses; or speaking because they enjoy the variety of activities around the career development theme. But far from being a "basic beginning" for a coaching practice, it is a very viable ongoing business, with continuous opportunities to learn, grow, and refine our skills.

Q: I don't think career coaching would be right for me because I don't enjoy writing resumes, practicing interviewing, and helping clients with negotiations; do I have to do those things?

This is one of the best things about career coaching: you can do it in whatever way fits your personality and preferences! Some career coaches prefer to focus on the direction-setting or personal exploration part of the process, helping clients figure out "what they want to be when they grow up," as we like to put it. Others prefer the tangible, immediate-results work involved in designing a job search strategy, writing (or critiquing) resumes, role-playing interviews and negotiation sessions, and the like. And still other independent practitioners do all of this! Internal career coaches (those employed by an organization) may have additional responsibilities. So career coaching is a field that can be tailored to the individual coach's preferences.

Q: I notice that your Authentic Vocation™ model explores several areas before it gets to skills and work experience. Isn't it best to focus on what I'm good at in determining my next job?

This is a premise of many career development theories. It can be effective with new graduates or new entrants to the workplace, or to those wishing to find a new job within the same industry and/or position they have held in the past. However, for the majority of people who will seek out career coaching (having exhausted their own resources and ideas about what would most fulfill them), a skills-based model will not achieve their desired result. Instead, the process must begin at a deeper level with their overall life purpose or mission, values, and the like in order to match what they do with what they love and what has meaning for the client. CCI's Authentic Vocation model does this.

Q: Isn't it tough to make money at career coaching, especially during tough economic times?

On the contrary! Career coaching is the one specialty in the coaching field that is recession-proof and actually expands during economic downturns. Why? When the economy turns down, companies lay off more workers, requiring outplacement services (which have added coaching as one of their services to such companies) as well as career centers (which can be set up and/or staffed by career coaches). In addition, there are more individuals in job or career transition at these times, and those who are not are overworked and worried about whether they will be the next to be laid off. So while independent practitioners may find that they need to offer fee incentives and/or affiliate with an outplacement firm or other organization to serve the clients who have needs during economic lows—if we assume individual clients have less disposable income to invest in coaching—they will find a lot of work to be done!

Q: Why should I pay for career coaching when I can get helpful advice about my career from my family and friends?

Remember the old saying, "You get what you pay for"? There are several reasons family and friends' advice may not be in your best interest regarding your career. First, they lack the objectivity and training that a coach has. And second, even if the change you're considering is good for you, it may make them uncomfortable if they prefer you to stay as you are, causing them to discourage or sabotage you. And finally, they may be unwilling to provide the unconditional support (even "cheerleading") that a coach will do as you pursue your dreams.

Q: Isn't career coaching usually be done in person?

One thing that is fascinating to most people when they first discover coaching (as a prospective coach or a client) is that most coaching is done by telephone. This is appealing to coaches because it allows them a flexible lifestyle. But it is also appealing to the client because of its convenience! In fact, if you receive training via teleclass—a kind of conference-call format used by Career Coach Institute along with its training program where class members gather "virtually" over the phone for the weekly sessions—you are receiving the very best preparation to be a highly effective coach, over the phone. Coaches learn to hone their listening abilities to listen "between the lines" to the client's energy shifts, hesitations, excitement, style, and other cues that lead to deeply thought-provoking questions from the coach. A minority of coaches coach in person, but between the logistics required to physically get together the need for professional office space, and the sometimes distracting visual cues that are added with in-person coaching, telephone coaching can be the superior medium.

Appendix 2: International Coach Federation Coaching Core Competencies

Author's note: This appendix contains a summary of the International Coach Federation Coaching Core Competencies. A fuller explanation listing all seventy coaching skills embodied in the competencies is available on the ICF web site, www.coachfederation.org.

The following eleven core coaching competencies and their subcompetencies (70 in all) were developed to support greater understanding about the skills and approaches used within today's coaching profession as defined by the ICF. They will also support you in calibrating the level of alignment between the coach-specific training expected and the training you have experienced.

These competencies were used as the foundation for the ICF credentialing process examination. The core competencies are grouped into four clusters according to those that fit together logically based on common ways of looking at the competencies in each group. The groupings and individual competencies are not weighted - they do not represent any kind of priority in that they are all core or critical for any competent coach to demonstrate.

A. Setting the Foundation
      1. Meeting Ethical Guidelines and Professional Standards
      2. Establishing the Coaching Agreement

B. Co-Creating the Relationship
      3. Establishing Trust and Intimacy with the Client
      4. Coaching Presence

C. Communicating Effectively

  5. Active Listening

  6. Powerful Questioning

  7. Direct Communication

D. Facilitating Learning And Results

  8. Creating Awareness

  9. Designing Actions

  10. Planning and Goal Setting

  11. Managing Progress and Accountability

Note: These competencies are current as of 2008. For the expanded and updated version, see www.tinyurl.com/3vbuab.

Appendix 3: Starting a Career Development Initiative at Your Company

This appendix is provided for those readers who work within an organization that does not currently have a career development program—and could benefit from one. The following guidelines should help get the program established. The reader should feel free to contact the author with specific or more detailed questions.

Phase 1: Identify apparent needs. In this phase, the coach or chief coaching officer must determine the nature of the company's needs for career development. For a career development initiative to work, buy-in must exist at all levels of the organization, ideally with the firm commitment of the executive team. The first step in determining whether this commitment exists is to conduct interviews of key stakeholders to determine

- Consequences of not offering career development (lack of succession planning, low morale, etc.)
- Opportunities/benefits that could come from career development program
- Definition of terms: What is career development for *this* firm? Does it apply throughout the organization or just to top management or entry-level workers?

These interviews can be conducted with management as well as human resource and organizational development professionals and team leaders of key functional areas. If desired, a set of uniform questions can be asked of each individual to gather initial data.

Phase 2: Establish task force to confirm needs and strategize approach. The second step in both ensuring commitment at multiple levels and setting the foundation for organization-wide success of the program is to establish a cross-functional task force. Representatives from each functional area including the executive team, HR, OD, Finance, Operations, Marketing, IT, and other key business areas—especially including any departments that have a keen interest in developing their staff—should be invited to participate. The task force should meet regularly (weekly or biweekly) with the chief coaching officer (if any) or senior OD or HR professional chairing the meetings. Their charge is to:

- Determine the best approach to confirm actual company needs for career development services. For example, would an onsite or virtual career center work better? Do the employees need mentors, or opportunities to shadow workers in other areas, or to simply have more training options to build their skills? Will individual coaching be provided by managers or by outside coaches? What kind of career development planning process would be most beneficial? What philosophies/models will be employed? (The Authentic Vocation™ and QuantumShift!™ approaches can be very appropriate and powerful for this use.)

- If an employee survey is commissioned, the task force can decide how to administer it (e.g., paper or online?) and tabulate the results. (This may be a function of the size of the company and how many different locations it has.)

- Once the survey or other mechanism for gathering data to confirm needs is complete, how will the initial program be launched? Will a pilot program be offered in one division or location (our recommendation)? If so, which one and when will it begin? What will it include? Will all positions need to be analyzed and competency models created? Do those already exist, or will another system be used to help match employees with suitable opportunities?

- This task force will also be charged with locating/identifying best practices in internal career development programs in companies within its industry and/or of comparable size and structure.

Phase 3: Initiate preliminary/pilot program. Within several weeks or months after the task force is convened and the approach has been decided upon, it is time to launch the initial program. A strategy to evaluate successes or "failures" (i.e., areas to be improved before full-fledged rollout) must be established before services begin to be offered. All feedback from both participants and service providers must be tallied and needed changes integrated following the pilot or preliminary program.

Phase 4: Ensure confidentiality and clear standards for execution. One of the issues that can make or break an internal career development program is breach of confidentiality. Balancing management's "need to know" what is happening within the coaching or other career development activities against the employees' need for assurance of confidentiality leads, not infrequently, to misunderstandings. The best time to head off such issues is at the beginning, with clear principles for operation that assure confidentiality—usually absent disclosure of criminal, illegal, or other information that must be disclosed to appropriate company or legal authorities.

Phase 5: Encourage participation company-wide. Ready, set, coach! But what if no one wants to participate? It is the job of the task force and all people in leadership roles to encourage people to avail themselves of the career development services and, if necessary, provide initial incentives or require at least one session with a coach or in the career center. Information sessions for each department, brown bag sessions, notices on the company intranet, newsletter, and/or bulletin boards, and the like can help spread the word. Each participant should then complete a feedback form (anonymously if desired) on the services they received so that the program can be continually improved. Especially glowing reviews can be published, either anonymously or with the employee's permission, for the information of others who have not yet joined the program.

Individual employees will in turn need to address various needs depending on where they are in their own career development. Some who are still in the competency-demonstration stage will want to find the best matches of opportunities in the organization that will lead to increases in income and responsibility. Authentic Vocation™ factors 4–8 along with competency modeling and skill/interest assessments, all under the facilitation of a skilled coach, can be very useful for these employees. Others who have entered the quality-of-life phase and/or are approaching retirement will have different needs. For these people, Authentic Vocation™ factors 1–3 and developmental assessments such as the Myers-Briggs Type Indicator® and others, again with the guidance of a competent and sensitive coach, can provide the help these employees need. Still others will be transitioning from manager to leader, struggling to communicate with different personalities or learning styles within the team or company, or feeling stifled or overextended in their current position. Coaching—particularly using the QuantumShift!™ approach—an also assist with these issues. Some employees will simply not be able to meet their needs within the firm, or the company may find it necessary to scale down operations and staff. Career development services can soften the blow and ease the transition out of the company for people in either of these situations.

Phase 6. Evaluate results and continue to improve the program. Whatever the ultimate format and range of services the company implements, it will need to track results. Evaluation forms should be completed by the users of the service—anonymously if desired. At least once a year a broader survey should be administered. It should evaluate not only the employees' satisfaction with the services and ideas for improvement, but also return on investment in the form of business results stemming from the career development work.

NOTES

1. Gallup Organization Poll, "American Workers Generally Satisfied, but Indicate their Jobs Leave Much to Be Desired," September 3, 1999.
2. U.S. Bureau of Labor Statistics, *Number of Jobs Held, Labor Market Activity and Earnings Growth Among Younger Baby Boomers: Results from More Than Two Decades of a Longitudinal Survey* (Washington, D.C., 2002).
3. Daniel H. Pink, "The Future of Free Agency: Changing the Economics of Work," keynote speech delivered as Association of Career Professionals International Conference June 6, 2003, San Juan, Puerto Rico. See also Daniel H. Pink, *Free Agent Nation: The Future of Working for Yourself* (Warner Books, 2002).
4. Laura Tiffany, "Hottest Business Ideas for 2002," *Home Office* (June 2002).
5. See International Coach Federation press release 9/26/07, "Final Report for ICF Global Coaching Study Released."
6. James K. Harter, "Taking Feedback to the Bottom Line," Gallup Management Journal, March 15, 2001, http://gmj.gallup.com/content/814/Taking-Feedback-Bottom-Line.aspx .
7. Gerald Olivero, Denise Bane and Richard Kopelman, "Executive Coaching As a Transfer of Training Tool: Effects on Productivity in a Public Agency," *Public Personnel Management* (winter 1997).
8. Manchester, Inc., "Executive Coaching Yields Return on Investment of Almost Six Times Its Cost," www.mpsgroup.com/news/viewarticle.asp?art=20010104_1&type=pr .
9. Cecilia Capuzzi Simon, "A Coach for 'Team You': Many Who Want a Winning Record in the Game of Life Are Skipping the Shrink and Hiring a Life Coach Instead," *Washington Post,* June 10, 2003.
10. John Naisbitt, Patricia Aburdene, and Pat Burdene, *Megatrends 2000: New Directions for Tomorrow* (Avon, 1991). See also Nana Naisbitt, Douglas Philips, and John Naisbitt, *High Tech/High Touch: Technology and Our Accelerated Search for Meaning* (Nicholas Brealey, 2001).
11. As of this writing, there are no pending legislative measures to regulate coaching, though there have been past attempts. Contact the ICF or your government authority for current requirements.

12. Great Circle Learning, "Mentoring for Performance Improvement," www. gclearning.com, 1998.

13. Thomas Crane, *The Heart of Coaching* (San Diego, CA: FTA Press, 2002).

14. Daniel Goleman, "Leadership That Gets Results," *Harvard Business Review* (March 2000).

15. Families and Work Institute, "Feeling Overworked: When Work Becomes Too Much," May 16, 2001.

16. Charles Garfield, *Peak Performers: The New Heroes of American Business* (New York: Avon, 1986), 85–87.

17. Abraham Maslow, *Motivation and Personality*, 3d ed. (New York: Harper and Row, 1983).

18. Mihaly Csikszentmihalyi, *Flow: The Psychology of Optimal Experience* (Harper Collins, 1991).

19. James K. Harter, "Taking Feedback to the Bottom Line," *Gallup Management Journal* March 2001), 35 http://gmj.gallup.com/content/814/Taking-Feedback-Bottom-Line.aspx .

20. Laura Day, *Practical Intuition: How to Harness the Power of Your Instinct and Make It Work for You* (New York: Broadway, 1997).

21. Viktor E. Frankl, *Man's Search for Meaning* (Washington Square Press, 1997).

22. This tool is also available to members of the CCI Virtual Learning Community. See www.careercoachinstitute.com.

23. For further details, see Marcus Buckingham and Curt Coffman, *First, Break All the Rules* (Simon and Schuster, 1999) or "Taking Feedback to the Bottom Line," *Gallup Management Journal* (March 2001), available at http://gmj.gallup.com/content/814/Taking-Feedback-Bottom-Line.aspx .

24. Frederick Herzberg, et al., *The Motivation to Work* (John Wiley, 1959; reprint, Transaction Publishing, 1993).

25. See Hay Resources Group at www.hayresourcesdirect.haygroup.com/Values/Assessments_surveys/Personal_Values_Questionnaire/FAWs.asp

26. Daniel Goleman, *Working with Emotional Intelligence* (New York: Bantam, 1998), 12.

27. Ibid.

28. U.S. Department of Labor Employment and Training Administration, "Workplace Basics: The Skills Employers Want," 1989, updated 1996.

29. See the author's book *Thriving in Transition* (Simon and Schuster 1996) or the workbook version, *Don't Just Survive, Thrive During Transition* (High Flight press 2002) at www.careercoachinstitute.com

30. Families and Work Institute, "Feeling Overworked: When Work Becomes Too Much," May 16, 2001.

31. Daniel Goleman, *Working with Emotional Intelligence* (New York: Bantam, 1998).
32. Telework Trendlines for 2006, http://www.workingfromanywhere.org/.
33. Ibid.
34. Ibid.
35. Julia Cameron, *The Artist's Way* (New York: Tarcher/Putnam, 1992).
36. Kate Wendleton, *Targeting the Job You Want* (Career Press, 2000), 107.
37. See Danah Zohar, *Quantum Self* (Quill/William Morrow, 1990), 31–32.
38. Manchester, Inc., "Maximizing the Impact of Executive Coaching," (survey), 2000.
39. Marcus Buckingham and Donald O. Clifton, *Now Discover Your Strengths* (: Simon and Schuster, 2001).
40. Gerald Olivero, Denise Bane and Richard Kopelman, "Executive Coaching As a Transfer of Training Tool: Effects on Productivity in a Public Agency," *Public Personnel Management* (winter 1997).
41. John Byrne, "How to Lead Now," *Fast Company* (August 2003)
42. Shunryu Suzuki, *Zen Mind, Beginner's Mind* (New York and Tokyo: Weatherhill, 1980).
43. Gregg LeVoy, *Callings: Finding and Following an Authentic Life* (Three Rivers Press, 1998)
44. See Fred A. Wolf, *Taking the Quantum Leap* (Perennial, 1989).
45. Joseph Jaworski, *Synchronicity: The Inner Path of Leadership* (San Francisco: Bennett-Koehler, 1998), 124.
46. International Coach Federation Coaching Core Competencies – see www.coachfederation.org
47. Ibid.
48. Chris Argyris and Donald Schon, *Theory in Practice* (San Francisco: Jossey-Bass, 1974).
49. Chris Argyris and Donald Schon, *Theory in Practice* (San Francisco: Jossey-Bass, 1974).
50. Ibid.
51. Napoleon Hill, *Think and Grow Rich,* reissue (Random House, 1990).
52. Julia Cameron, *The Artist's Way* (New York: Tarcher/Putnam, 1992).
53. Laura Day, *Practical Intuition: How to Harness the Power of Your Instinct and Make It Work for You* (New York: Broadway Books, 1997).
54. International Coach Federation, www.coachfederation.org
55. Ibid.
56. Diane Fassel, *Working Ourselves to Death* (San Francisco: Harper, 1990).
57. Susan Jeffers, *Feel the Fear and Do It Anyway* (Fawcett, 1988)

58. Bob Nelson and Kenneth Blanchard, *1001 Ways to Reward Employees* (Workman, 1994).

59. See, e.g., CCI's Job/Career Design series of books at www.careercoachinstitute. com

60. See Richard Bolles, *What Color Is Your Parachute?* (Ten Speed Press, 2002); and www.jobstar.org/hidden/hidden.cfm.

61. C. G. Jung, *Synchronicity* (Princeton University Press, 1973).

62. Mary Guindon and Fred Hanna, "Coincidence, Happenstance, Serendipity, Fate, or the Hand of God: Case Studies in Synchronicity," *Career Development Quarterly* (March 2002).

63. See www.jobstar.org/hidden/hidden.cfm.

64. See Richard Bolles, *What Color Is Your Parachute?* (Ten Speed Press, 2002) and www.jobstar.org/hidden/hidden.cfm .

65. See www.jobstar.org/hidden/hidden.cfm.

66. See "Job Interview Tips: Best times," Pagewise 2001, http://www.avsands.com/ HowTo/interviewjobsm_uga_av.htm

67. John T. Molloy, *The New Dress for Success* (Warner, 1988).

68. John Stewart and Gary D'Angelo, *Together: Communicating Interpersonally* (McGraw-Hill, 1988), 169.

69. Jack Kornfield, *A Path with Heart* (Bantam, 1993).

70. Mihaly Csikszentmihalyi, *Flow: The Psychology of Optimum Experience* (HarperCollins, 1991).

INDEX

ABOUT THE AUTHOR AND CAREER COACH INSTITUTE

Marcia Bench is known as the "Career Coaching Queen" with a history spanning more than 20 years as a world-renowned expert in the field of career coaching and workplace trends. A Master Certified Career Coach,™ she has been coaching and consulting both individual and corporate clients since 1986. She is Founder/Director of Career Coach Institute, LLC, http://www.careercoachinstitute.com as well as other coaching and career development sites – see http://www.marciabench.com for full list.

A former attorney, Marcia has authored 19 previous books, including *Career Infopreneur's Success Roadmap* (High Flight Press 2007). In addition, she has written *Thriving in Transition* (Simon & Schuster), *When 9 to 5 Isn't Enough* (Hay House), *Retire Your Way!*, and more.

Marcia has been a featured speaker/trainer at over 500 local, regional and national conferences, as well as a guest on numerous television and radio programs. Her mission is to help individuals increase their sense of enjoyment and meaning in their work.

Marcia's coaching experience includes work with managers and executives from Fortune 500 firms in a variety of industries as well as dozens of business owners, professionals, and military officers entering the civilian workforce.

Prior to entering the coach training industry, Marcia was Senior Vice President in a dot-com career management firm for 4 years, and previously spent 10 years as President of New Work Directions, a business and consulting firm she founded. Ms. Bench developed her expertise in business start-up and management in part through her 4 years as a practicing attorney specializing in business and employment issues. She is a current member of the International Coach Federation. Marcia's education includes a Juris Doctorate from Northwestern School of Law of Lewis & Clark College and a Bachelor of Science in Psychology from Western Oregon University. In addition, she is a Certified Career Management Practitioner through the International Board of Career Management Certification, a Certified Business Coach, a Certified Teleader and Master Certified Career Coach.

For further information, or to talk with Ms. Bench, contact:

Career Coach Institute
8269G SW Wilsonville Rd. #188
Wilsonville OR 97070
coach@careercoachinstitute.com
www.careercoachinstitute.com

ORDER FORM

We hope that you are enjoying this product! If you would like more information about our kits, we encourage you to visit http://www.careercoachinstitute.com, or copy and complete this form and fax it to 866-226-2244. Our physical mailing address is Career Coach Institute, 8269G SW Wilsonville Road #188, Wilsonville, OR 97070.

Name: _____

Address: _____

City, State, ZIP: _____

Country: _____

Home Telephone: _____

Work Telephone: _____

Fax: _____ Email: _____

How did you hear about us:

___ Internet search

___ Referred by a friend

___ Heard one of the authors speak

___ Read an article written by the authors

___ Other:

Please send me information about:

___ Your product catalog

___ How to become a Certified Career Coach

___ How to become a Certified Executive Career Coach

___ How to start and expand my own coaching business

___ Speaking to our group or event

___ Customized training for our organization

___ Other: _____

Thank you for your request!

CPSIA information can be obtained at www.ICGtesting.com
Printed in the USA
BVOW050855110412

287268BV00009B/2/P

9 780981 700502